Shakespeare: A Study

DARRELL FIGGIS

SHAKESPEARE

A Study

Coracle

San Rafael, Ca

Second, facsimile edition
Coracle Press, 2007
First edition, Mitchell Kennerley, 1911

For information, address:
Coracle, P.O. Box 151011
San Rafael, California 94915, USA

Library of Congress Cataloging-in-Publication Data

Figgis, Darrell, 1882–1925.
Shakespeare : a study / Darrell Figgis. — Reprint ed.

p. cm.

Originally published: 1st ed. New York : Mitchell Kennerly, 1911.
Includes bibliographical references.
ISBN 978-1-59731-310-0 (pbk. : alk. paper)
ISBN 978-1-59731-335-3 (hardback: alk. paper)
1. Shakespeare, William, 1564–1616. 2. Dramatists,
English—Early modern, 1500–1700—Biography.
3. Stratford-upon-Avon (England)—Biography. I. Title.

PR2894.F47 2007
822.3'3—dc22
[B] 2007027344

TO MY BROTHER

A TOKEN OF GRATITUDE AND AFFECTION

CONTENTS

CHAPTER I
	PAGE
INTRODUCTION	1

CHAPTER II
| HIS LIFE | 27 |

CHAPTER III
| HIS STAGE | 86 |

CHAPTER IV
| HIS CRAFT | 137 |

CHAPTER V
| HIS ART | 182 |

CHAPTER VI
| HIS THOUGHT | 229 |

CHAPTER VII
HIS PERSONALITY	281
NOTES	329
INDEX OF NAMES	339

ILLUSTRATIONS

To face page

THE STAGE OF THE GLOBE 94

PLAN AND SECTION OF STAGE OF THE GLOBE . . 126

SHAKESPEARE: A STUDY

CHAPTER I

INTRODUCTION

THERE is probably no artist whose greatness has more stood in the way of his fit appreciation than has been the case with Shakespeare. On one hand and the other he has cast a mist that obtrudes between the eye of the beholder and his own proper person and achievement. The splendour of his stature, the breadth of his outlook, the strange quality of his vision, partly account for this. For the understanding being a limited instrument, all things that transcend the reason pass the limitations of its function. A chorus of voices, from the company of his contemporaries until this present hour of grace, have acclaimed him as the only utterance of Nature. So quick are men to take up any case that has been raised, that this universality of acclaim may by no means necessarily mean the truth of the thing testified; nevertheless, we feel the truth of it, and in no way is the truth better tokened than by the very similar attitude that is adopted both towards Shakespeare and towards Nature. In both we feel a synthesis, yet cannot think it out. Over both, therefore, we argue in contrary terms, without advancing ourselves much in the matter. We seek to submit both to the utter folly of logical processes, and when they elude us, cry out on them; or, it may be, we fail to see what has eluded us, and acclaim our partial vision for the whole matter. Therefore we fail to appreciate that what has eluded us may have been caught by our neighbour, and that what we have caught is what has fled his thought, and that therefore there is comic laughter in the inevitable quarrel that ensues. It is as though two draughtsmen were to limn different aspects of some cathedral, and each, on the virtue of his own design, deny the truth of the other's vision, forgetting that not only is the cathedral in question more than either design, but considerably more than the joint product of both designs.

In this Shakespeare was indeed like Nature. And he was also like Nature in his use of Waste—a commodity which all philosophers condemn themselves by disregarding. That there should be a thousand seeds cast forth for only one to germinate and fructify, is spoken of as waste; and what is meant by that is that there is no use served by the nine hundred and ninety-nine. In other words, it is assumed that the thousand were cast forth for the chance intention of the one result, overlooking entirely the possibility that the fructification of the one was but the chance bye-product of the nine hundred and ninety-nine. Man is always stumbling

INTRODUCTION 3

over the arch-fallacy of utility. Each system of philosophy demands an economy of procedure; and in that it condemns itself as an effort to discover a purpose in things. For without a purpose in things there could be no philosophy. Exactly what purpose is served by the function of Waste can be best seen in Shakespeare's own work—for Shakespeare, however wide his vision, being less wide than Nature, is more easily, and more frequently, approached than Nature. For example, no Hamlet could ever have been economically created. An Antony, a Lear, demand that the seeds be strewn broadcast. Those who have spoken of a divine largess in his method of work, have struck on a penetrating truth. It is the divine way of work; for it is the only way to produce results that are divine. A classic temple seeks to achieve a perfect poise. Were it possible to carry the process still further, the temple would achieve such an inner adjustment that it would disappear, it would pass into an inner nothingness. In other words, the process is towards annihilation, the reverse of creation. But in a Gothic cathedral, its very waste of design is of the very principle of creation; for by that very waste it becomes more and more a living thing. It might fly into the heavens; but it would defy annihilation.

In somewhat of the same way, Hamlet, Antony, Lear, and their brothers from the same brain, are imperious with life before us. The process that went to make them was wasteful; but without waste they could not have come into being with the urgency they possess. That is to say, in them, as in the works of Nature, we feel that the waste has served a turn that we cannot define, and that, in our cowardly moments, we will not trust. The result in them is of the same kind as the process which produced it. We cannot find a synthesis, that is to say a logical synthesis, for Hamlet; but we know him for a vital personage, and that is to admit a synthesis for him. He is, say we, what he is: indecision may fasten on this or that feature of him, but he is more than this or that feature of him; he is more than all features of him; he is himself. He could only have been artistically, that is to say creatively, expressed; and he can only be artistically apprehended. It is so men are made; and men spin their philosophies to account for themselves; they cut their philosophical garments to cover their nakedness in a vast universe, each man for himself according to his own needs.

This kinship of Shakespeare with Nature, this aptitude to strike the thing he saw and felt at the moment of vision, and leave it to fall into some higher synthesis he could not express, raises him out of the field of understanding. He may be great, or he may be small; but this faculty in him, be he small or great, thwarts an intellectual appreciation of him in a world that gropes blindly with

INTRODUCTION

outstretched hands of reason with the eyes of vision closed. That is why his interest is perennial. A thing understood is a thing dismissed and done with. Such are the shows of Time. The things of Eternity are never understood: they are eternally delighted in.

With this faculty in Shakespeare there has been mixed another thing that is often confused with it, and which further ravels the problem of appreciating him. This is the weakness that came from himself. This weakness will meet its attention in due course; but at the moment its connection with the matter already mentioned cannot but be noticed. His hand was often nerveless; his pen often went on writing after his thought had left it. We all feel this; we can too often point out marked instances of it; but it defies our wit to define the proper scope of it. And for a very obvious reason. For we feel the functional importance of his instinctive use of what we call Waste; but we cannot define it. But we feel also, instinctively, that there is another waste that does not function; and we are not less at a loss to define that. Both are beyond us; and both being beyond us, we are perplexed; we do not know where to tread, for fear we shall tread in error. One man will see the waste that does not function; and, in his indignation, will pluck the darnel, plucking up, too, good full-eared corn with it. Another man will cry out on such sacrilege. Perceiving, blindly perceiving, the waste that serves its end, he will wonder if after all the waste that seems to come from sloth in Shakespeare is not an evidence of blindness in the beholder. The classic example of this latter attitude is, of course, Coleridge. Whatever he had or had not, he had at least an eye to see; such an eye as few have been dowered with. With this eye he saw so much that his instinct was compelled to approve, but which he could not understand, that he began to be distrustful of his whole critical reason; and was led thus to explain for Wisdom much that all things cry out in us to condemn as folly. In so remote and intuitional a matter it is hazardous to be held down to instances. But perhaps, with all the shortcoming of illustrations, two instances may be chosen from a single play. Take Romeo's call to Juliet:

> "look, love, what envious streaks
> Do lace the severing clouds in yonder east:
> Night's candles are burnt out, and jocund day
> Stands tiptoe on the misty mountain-tops."

The triumph of this is the triumph of a careless abandon. No careful worker could have achieved it. A careful worker would have been doubtful of it had it come across his thought. It was, as one has phrased it, just "pulled-off"; it was struck at blindly, haphazardly, and it came. An imaginative spendthrift could only have done it. But take this other by the same spokesman:

… "O brawling love! O loving hate!
O any thing, of nothing first created!
O heavy lightness! serious vanity!
Misshapen chaos of well-seeming forms!
Feather of lead, bright smoke, cold fire, sick health!"

and so on.

The process is the same in both, but how different the result in each! One "pulled-off"; and the other failed to "pull-off." Both struck wildly; but while one came, the other was a complete failure. The two examples have all the fault of illustrations in this, that they widen a difference to express a truth. Yet, surely, there are instances enough that cannot be given even because they hold both ends in poise—such as Othello's "Like to the Pontic sea," etc. In all these there is a kinship. Failure, doubtful success, and sheer splendour, all evidence their maker's wasteful way of work. Coleridge, seeing the kinship, fitly marvelled at the one; and then, in honour to the kinship he saw, opened his mind to receive the other. However much our judgment disapprove him, we cannot but sympathise with him. We feel, too, that if their maker had not generously opened his breast to the possibility of failure, he would never have achieved his splendour of success; and our censure is again withheld. We feel that the pen writing without the thought must needs be, if the thought is swiftly and unexpectedly to sweep down on it for the purpose of a miracle.

We feel it in Nature. We feel it in Shakespeare. It is part of the perplexity of him; but it is also part of his greatness; and we find it hard to appraise and appreciate him. His weakness and his strength are too mixed to dissever.

Thus the world is brought to him: wise and foolish alike. And in this we discover another reason why his very greatness had hindered a fit appreciation of his work. For he has produced idolatry; that is to say, he has given occasion for mental sloth. One of the most curious things to discover is the type of mind that is stuffed replete with all possible Shakespearian learning, but which, nevertheless, looks out from darkened windows, blinking strangely at the day. It would be impossible to name a treatise or a study on Shakespeare that it has not read; it would be impossible to mention any document or manuscript, in any dusty archive or office, that it does not know or that it has not transcribed, however so remote its application be to Shakespeare: but let mention be made of any contemporary poet or dramatist, and dull incomprehension meets the query. Had such a mind existed in the robustious days of *The Theater* and *The Globe* (happily such products do not seem to have been permitted then), it would have spent its efforts seeking to fetch from archival darkness some very properly discarded poem of Chaucer's, or some new fragment of biography concerning him; and it would have met the news

INTRODUCTION

of *Hamlet* and *Othello* with puzzled disinterestedness or mild beneficence.

Such minds are remote from all quickening impulses, and therefore they can but obscure our Shakespeare. Moreover, they are extolled: a new Shakespearian signature is made an occasion for exultation, while a new original poem is turned coldly upon; and thus the obscuration is the more intensified. It is forgotten that if Shakespeare be quick and living, then only quick and living minds can appreciate him. It is forgotten that the meanest poet in the making of the frailest sonnet is more akin to Shakespeare in that act than the most learned Shakespearian scholar. He may, from divers causes, have been brought to forswear all mention of Shakespeare; yet ye cannot forswear his relationship with him; whereas the others are aliens. Poets, however dissimilar, are always nearer one another than any poet can ever be to his most devout disciple.

Thus it has come about that Shakespeare has become a pedestal deity: a fetish on men's mouths. The pity is that Shakespeare has come to be regarded as a man who spoke in the days of Elizabeth, instead of as a man who is speaking to-day; and this, even while the lips repeat the phrase that he is "not for an age, but for all time"! A profounder disservice to Shakespeare could scarcely be imagined. Obloquy and active hate were better. But a deeper trouble has been caused, a trouble harder to disentangle.

For many of the artists whose works have been neglected in favour of archival interest in Shakespeare have risen against their brother. In truth, the issue has been thrust upon them, for they have been called out to meet the competition of the Dead Hand. A strange situation has thus arisen: Shakespeare's own kinsmen, whom, if he were here, he would be the first to seek out, have arisen against him, and he has had to rely for his proper defence on men who are nothing to him. The hewers of wood and drawers of water have had to champion him against those who, like him, have sprung from the loins of aristocracy. From wherever he views our scene, it is not a sight, this, calculated to move a spirit of joy in him.

Wide as is his vision, lofty as is his stature, strange, perplexing, and capricious as are his ways of work, he has provided a sufficient field for disagreement and misunderstanding. The tribute of enmity is a tribute indeed, yet it scarcely makes for understanding; and idolatry assuredly cannot help the matter more. Indeed, there is more aid in antagonism than in idolatry; for criticism, however unjust, is the bone and marrow of antagonism, whereas idolatry can but murmur platitudes. An antagonist does at least measure his height with his opponent; which is a wholly manly thing to do. Idolatry kneels. Thus out of the noise of combat there have emerged a number of questions that deal with the very essentials of Shakespeare's art; the unravelling and examination

INTRODUCTION

of which must expose the whole basis of it, and so elucidate some of the principles that lie at the root of all Art.

For example, one has said, grudgingly, that Shakespeare was certainly great, but that he had severe limitations; that, in the way of instance, *King Lear* was a great drama undoubtedly, but that, so far as construction was concerned, Shakespeare would at least have to doff his cap to Henrik Ibsen. Here, at once, is a question raised that cuts at the very root of drama. For what is construction? And what is construction both in Shakespeare and in Ibsen? Another will say that Shakespeare's greatness was but of a bastard sort, seeing that the basis of it was romantic sentimentality. Again, the further question is raised: What is sentimentality? What is romance? What relation have they to the springs of all action and the root of life? We are at once fronted by the profound problem of discovering what are the elements in life, and consequently in Drama, that should awake our admiration. For replication is not less legitimate than query. Similarly, it is said that Shakespeare indulges in the ruinous glamour of sexual infatuation. But what is infatuation? Not what it appears to be; for there are none so ingenuous as not to know that; but what it actually is. This is a question that lies at the root of Shakespeare's attitude towards sex, which again cannot be rightly approached until the deeper question of sex itself is first approached.

The whole roots of Drama are laid bare in this way.

It will be seen that, for such reasons as these, there has probably been no time so favourable as the present for a study of Shakespeare's Art. As one traces the history of Shakespearian criticism down from Ben Jonson to the present day, the noticeable feature of every stage of it has been that, however differently one or another may regard him, they all unite in this, that they think of him and do not examine the causes that went to the making of his Art. He is accepted as a phenomenon, and appraised as such. Criticism has never yet gone behind him, though on a noteworthy occasion it succeeded in going considerably above him.

Such criticism was scarcely to be expected of Ben Jonson. It is not generally possible in a man's own age to expose the roots of his work. Moreover, the critical records of Ben Jonson are a scanty matter. Whatever high debate echoed at night in the Mermaid Tavern, there remain only his *Timber, or Discoveries*, and such of his conversation as Drummond has recorded, to indicate to us his opinion on Shakespeare and dramatic art. In any case, the opinions of rare Ben approach Shakespeare so nearly that they belong rather to a study of his Art and Craft; and therefore the attention travels on to one who stands out as both expressive of an age ill-fitted to understand Shakespeare, and as a man robust of vigour and sagacity. In a sense it is, of course, true

INTRODUCTION 13

that all the voices of an age in pledge to gentilities were thereby unfitted for an intelligent interest in the maker of *King Lear*. On the other hand, Samuel Johnson possessed an attitude rare among Shakespearian critics. No man was he to bend in duteous service. The man who could write, "He has scenes of undoubted and perpetual excellence, but perhaps not one play, which, if it were now exhibited as the work of a contemporary writer, would be heard to the conclusion," is not only a man singular, among Shakespearian critics, for his independence of thought, but one, too, who strikes past platitudes, so awaking an examination of fundamentals.

In spite of this he does not search into the causes of things. He is fearless enough; as fearless to praise as to dismiss, which is of the essence of courage; but he judges rather than criticises. That is to say, he does not examine the standards of criticism. Rather, he accepts certain standards without demur; and when he has to praise in the teeth of them he does so in a forthright, downright sort of a way, finely characteristic of him, but somewhat destructive of his principles. For example, this is how he sums up the matter: "This therefore is the praise of Shakespeare, that his drama is the mirrour of life; that he who has mazed his imagination in following the phantoms which other writers raise up before him, may here be cured of his delirous extasies by reading human sentiments in human language, by scenes from which a hermit may estimate the transactions of the world, and a confessor predict the progress of the passions." It is a famous passage, and therefore little thought on. But, looking at it anew, how perplexing it is! "Human sentiments in human language," "scenes from which a hermit may estimate the transactions of the world": are these "the praise of Shakespeare," or are they the puzzled pronouncements of a vigorous apostle of common-sense, seeking to find place for something which he cannot quite understand, but which compels his admiration? One thinks of Lear and Hamlet, and one wonders.

Then one discovers with a shock that it is not *Lear* or *Hamlet* he is thinking of at all. "In tragedy," says the learned doctor, "he often writes with great appearance of wit and study, what is written at last with little felicity; but in his comick scenes, he seems to produce without labour what no labour can improve. In tragedy he is always struggling after some occasion to be comick; but in comedy he seems to repose, or to luxuriate, as in a mode of thinking congenial to his nature. In his tragic scenes there is always something wanting, but his comedy often surpasses expectation or desire. His comedy pleases by the thoughts and the language, and his tragedy for the greater part by incident and action. His tragedy seems to be skill, his comedy to be instinct." This pronouncement is astonishing enough, in all conscience. Regarding it from without, it is as though he said that black were white and white black; as though he had suddenly been afflicted with the spirit of opposition for the sake of devilry of a much later day; but regarded from within it is even more full of perplexity. To name four typical comedies, are *Midsummer Night's Dream*, *Merry Wives of Windsor*, *Much Ado About Nothing*, and *Winter's Tale*, then, such plays that a hermit may estimate from them the transactions of the world? Are they? And when he says that Shakespeare's comedy "pleases by the thoughts and the language," whereas his tragedy pleases "for the greater part by incident and action," has he not just inverted the proper application of his attribution?

It is a sufficient tangle, this. Nor can it be properly explained by saying that Shakespeare's age and Johnson's age were diametrically opposed in their conceptions of life. For one thing, Life is one, and therefore no two ages can be diametrically opposed, to the frustration of grounds of sympathy, save in a logician's antithesis. Yet, if this were so, this would even more fail to express the confusion. There is no necessary confusion in opposition. Opposition is often more clearly defined than unity. But that it was not opposition is sufficiently obvious from the fact that Johnson was seeking faithfully to express the "praise of Shakespeare." What alone can account for the confusion, is something much deeper than opposition, much deeper, even, than sympathy. It is nothing less than this: that something had appealed to Johnson compelling his admiration, and that he sought to express this in terms of a different perception. Something came before him that challenged his standards, and which, therefore, his standards challenged no less. The obvious thing should have been to have examined the standards in the light of this new powerful appeal, fearlessly and courageously; instead of which he still endeavoured to express one in the terms of the other, to the injury of both, and to the confusion of clear vision.

But after Johnson there came one with clouds about his brow, stepping through an intricacy of bright glory with rapt eyes and an ecstacy of vision. An angel is a loftier, and, strictly speaking, a more trustworthy, being than a man; but he is more perplexing withal. And for precisely the same reason Coleridge is loftier and more trustworthy, and yet, at the same time, more perplexing, than Johnson. He is more trustworthy because he is able to perceive that quality in Shakespeare that was his special glory, and which Johnson could only acknowledge afar off. His own errors, even those things in him that go to make him so frequently perplexing, spring, not from a lack of perception, but from a perception so swift that it overreaches itself. There is a rugged earthiness about Johnson, even as there is a piercing translunar quality about Coleridge; and it is the everlasting refutation of those who find in Shakespeare very little more than an earthy being intent on mundane success, that it was Coleridge and not Johnson who was the better fitted to understand him.

For instance, Johnson praised his Shakespeare, and in his praise he is perplexed. He settles on the pastured lowlands, and finds the thunder-riven uplands little to his liking. Coleridge scorns the lowlands, and steps from crag to crag among the peaks, hearing in the thunder voices full of meaning to him. The lightnings of King Lear would have scorched Johnson's understanding; but they play harmlessly about Coleridge, and illuminate his brow. Johnson, thinking the seventeenth century the crown of gentility, said: "The English nation, in the time of Shakespeare, was yet struggling to emerge from barbarity." It was left to Coleridge to say, "that the supposed irregularity and extravagancies of Shakespeare were the mere dreams of a pedantry that arraigned the eagle because it had not the dimensions of the swan." Or again: "I have said, and I say it again, that great as was the genius of Shakespeare, his judgment was at least equal to it. Of this anyone will be convinced, who attentively considers those points in which the dramas of Greece and England differ, from the dissimilitude of circumstances by which each was modified and influenced."

He who spoke thus had seen something. That is to say, he must either be rejected as moon-stricken, and the history of the world proves this to be a dangerous expedient at best, or his vision must be accepted and examined. The affirmative voice of a seer may safely, if only perhaps tentatively, be trusted in the teeth of a thousand reasoned negatives, because there is authority in it. Yet it would have been thought, having glimpsed this sight of Shakespeare as a constructive craftsman, that he would have proceeded to analyse what this construction meant. Yet now he fails. In spite of some illuminating and suggestive comparisons between Shakespeare's procedure and the procedure of the old Greek tragedians, he fails, because he does not go on to analyse what dramatic construction is, nor what it purports to achieve. It is true, he could not well do so. There was nothing urgent to prick him into doing so. Having seen, it was but necessary in him to affirm. His vision was at once accepted, and a chorus of praise of Shakespeare rose around him. Those about him and after him thought of nothing so much as to write a typically Elizabethan play. Had his vision been rejected, it would have been necessary for him to press yet further back, and examine the whole basis of the matter. He would probably have withdrawn into his clouds, and wrapt his seer's cloak closer about him; but the necessity would have remained. As it happened, the necessity did not even arise.

Johnson saw the vision of Shakespeare, blindly; and was bewildered at it. Coleridge saw it, clearly, with ecstasy; and went on bended knee to it. Confronted with the passage already quoted, " O brawl-

INTRODUCTION 19

ing love! O loving hate!" he can but say with meek humility, "I dare not pronounce such passages as these to be absolutely unnatural, not merely because I consider the author a much better judge than I can be, but because I can understand and allow for an effort of the mind, when it would describe what it cannot satisfy itself with the description of, to reconcile opposites and qualify contradictions, leaving a middle state of mind more strictly appropriate to the imagination than any other, when it is, as it were, hovering between images." We are strongly reminded in this of Crabb Robinson's laconic comment of some of Coleridge's lectures on Shakespeare, "He surpassed himself in the art of talking in a very interesting way, without talking at all on the subject." Of course, Romeo does not hover between images; he plays with them; and similarly Coleridge does not explain the passage before him, he explains with his extraordinary subtlety something quite different. But this is the very nadir of abnegation. Certainly not from it can a complete exposition of Shakespeare come. It denies itself the very instrument that must undertake such an exposition. It does not go behind Shakespeare; it goes high above him. From that altitude it partly sees behind him; but that is a different thing to examining the causes that brought him into being.

Such an abnegation was not without echoes. In Hazlitt it was attendant on a shrewd sagacity, serving only to sharpen a sharp perception. It was the whet to an eager mind ; with the result that there are few joys so keen as a journey through the Shakespeare realms of wonder with the voice of Hazlitt by one's ear. In Swinburne, however, it awoke the following: "The word Shakespeare connects more than any other man's name that ever was written or spoken upon earth. The bearer of that name was the one supreme creator of men who ever rose among mortals to show them and to leave with them an all but innumerable race of evident and indisputable immortals. No child of man and woman was too high or too low for his perfect apprehension and appreciation. Of good and evil, in all their subtlest and sublimest forms of thought and action and revelation, he knew more than ever it has been given to any other man to know. All this incomparable birthright might conceivably have been bestowed on a man from whom the birthright of song had by equitable compensation been absolutely withheld. But except upon the greatest of lyric and prophetic poets it has never been bestowed in ampler or more entrancing measure."

All this produced the result that might have been foreseen. The diggers and delvers of the earth have come over in their herds to make of Shakespeare a happy venture ground. The fair landscape of his country has been obscured by chimney stacks and factories, by authorship disputations and biographical documents. Like a wronged Deity he has been thrust into buildings and technicalities, and held remote from life with its eager business. He has been surfeited with praise in the stead of understanding. He has been made to encumber the earth, and preclude newer visions, he who was ever quick and sympathetic in work and in life. And so, as has already been said, he has been criticised anew; and his newer critics have worn the cap of revolution and enmity.

Foremost among those critics has been Bernard Shaw. There have not wanted critics of Shakespeare whose works have been luminous and recreative. Among the many the very intensity of whose labours to prove Shakespeare an adherent of this or that faith have disproved their own findings; among the many who have sought to make books on matters that should have served for concordances, taking Shakespeare's reference to this or that matter of passing interest; among the many who have spent years of seemingly inexhaustible labour in Black-letter researches—there have been those whose criticisms, even after all that has gone before, have broken new ground and illuminated their subject anew in newer ways. But the crack of Bernard Shaw's voice has been singular in this, that it has driven us back on fundamentals. The very perversity of his mind has aided to this. Jonson saw a beauty he could not understand, and in his praise evinced his perplexity; Coleridge saw clearly and praised intricately. But they both accepted. Partly because Shakespeare obstructed his own proper recognition, partly because he had a philosophy to propound that assumed the opposite of Shakespeare's vision, and largely by his very love of opposition, his desire to win recognition by the swiftest method of travel, Mr Shaw came into the field and challenged the basis of all judgment.

For example, the whole music of Shakespeare's praise has rung to the dominant of his kinship with Nature. An interesting collection might be made of those who have spoken of Shakespeare's art as being the most immediate voice of Nature, or who use the very word "nature" in some or other application to his work; and it would be found to include all who have written on him, from Ben Jonson onwards. Bernard Shaw steps into the field, however, saying that it is in no way akin to Nature; that it is unnatural, that it is sentimental, fustian, and bombastical. Such an assertion does not examine the roots of the matter. In blandly assuming an antithesis, its begs its question as surely as did Coleridge, but with far less reason. It is opposition that requires to make good its ground, not an earlier affirmation. But in its very assumption it clears the air as only a challenge can.

Again, it has been the praise of Shakespeare that he is supremely and supereminently a dramatist. But of Mr Shaw it is said[1] that when he came to judge the works of Shakespeare and Ibsen " by the tests of intellectual force and dramatic insight, quite apart from beauty of expression, he found that

INTRODUCTION 23

'Ibsen comes out with a double first-class, whereas Shakespeare comes out hardly anywhere'"; and that "if the fellow had not been a great poet, his rubbish would have been forgotten long ago." The clumsy thinking that speaks of "intellectual force and dramatic insight, *quite apart from beauty of expression*," as though beauty of expression were not at one and the same time both intellectual force and dramatic insight, may pass for the nonce. So also the confusion of the latter quotation, as though rubbish were ever great poetry, or great poetry rubbish. The main matter is that certain fundamentals have been attacked; and that it is wholly desirable that they should be attacked, however inadequately or confusedly it be done.

Moreover, the same critic has declared his lack of sympathy with Shakespeare because his "pregnant observations and demonstrations of life are not co-ordinated into any philosophy or religion." To this, of course, there are a considerable number of replies. One is, that it is impossible to give vent to "pregnant observations," or to get at continual "demonstrations of life," without expressing a philosophy; and that philosophies become less and less philosophies the more and more they are co-ordinated. Another is, that Shakespeare does indeed suggest a higher synthesis to his philosophical outlook, whereas Mr Shaw as dramatist is ever and deliberately, eluding any decisive co-ordination to his thinking; but that, while Shakespeare, when he eludes us, does so in healthy humour and a wide sympathy, Mr Shaw does so in cruel and unhealthy cynicism. Also, that the dramatist of his choice and praise, Henrik Ibsen, has no philosophy, since negation and obscuration, on Mr Shaw's own showing, can never form a philosophy. Further, that not only is there an impermissible assumption, but also internecine warfare, in his identity of drama with an articulated scheme of the universe. Yet by this very fact there is at once opened up a discussion of what drama is, in origin and in intention, that must needs be dealt with in any adequate study of Shakespeare.

The same critic touches a deeper matter, however, when he says: "When your Shakespears . . . huddle up the matter at the end by killing somebody and covering your eyes with the undertaker's handkerchief, duly onioned with some pathetic phrase, as The flight of angels sing thee to thy rest, or *Adsum*, or the like, I have no respect for them at all: such maudlin tricks may impose on tea-drunkards, not on me." The whole question of tragedy is opened at once: tragedy in general, and Shakespeare's conception of tragedy in particular. It may happen that by his very framing of tragedy Shakespeare may convey his philosophy of the universe, for it is true, as Coleridge said, that "no man was ever a great poet without being a great philosopher." It is not necessary for a dramatist consciously to formulate a philosophy, or consciously to hold one;

INTRODUCTION 25

in the casting of tragedy it will out; while it is an undeniable and inerradicable instinct in man that tragedy is the loftiest of all works of the creative mind, since it strikes down to the roots of all actions human and divine. If this be so, then it appears that Bernard Shaw's imperious rejection of "such maudlin tricks" does not at all mean that Shakespeare has no philosophy, but that Mr Bernard Shaw does not happen to like Shakespeare's philosophy—quite a different matter. In any case, the philosophical basis of tragedy is opened for investigation, and a new avenue opened for the understanding of Shakespeare.

In all this it is apparent that the time has passed for either mere praise or appraisal of Shakespeare. The acceptation of him as a figure on the stream of years belongs to yesterday; it is the business of to-day to examine the causes that went to the making of him. And when such causes are spoken of, it is not sufficient only to mean his Elizabethan environment; it is not less necessary to investigate the assumptions of his art, the conditions of his craft, his philosophical outlook on life, both in expressed judgments and in tacit attitudes, the life he himself lived, the disappointments he suffered, the struggles he undertook, the successes he achieved, and the opinions his friends held of him. Nor will it only be necessary to envisage the man in his work. The work as the product of the man requires no less an attention. We are past the days when everything that bore his signature was held to be the work of a faultless god. Mistakes enough abound in his work; and, as has already been intimated, some of those very seeming mistakes seem to have a functional importance, and give him a glory that would otherwise never have been his. Yet, whatever be said, should be said fearlessly. He must needs be faced, frankly, openly, as man to man; and perhaps there was never a time so opportune for such a task as the present.

Before such a scheme be set about, however, it is necessary that the life he lived be framed clearly before the eye, that thus the quality of the work he achieved, and the manner of its achievement, might give the fit and adequate structure to the design.

CHAPTER II

HIS LIFE

IT is a frequent saying, that is to say it is the general impression, that we neither have, nor can have, any detailed knowledge of the facts of Shakespeare's life. To aver, therefore, in the face of this, that we not only know as much of his life as we do of most men who have written and lived, but that our very paucity of knowledge leads us to a greater accuracy of judgment, would seem like cracking a paradox for the humour of perversity. Yet a little examination will show this to be strictly just. It is true, for example, that we have very little knowledge of his family intimacies. This might very well be taken to mean that, as a matter of fact, he had little family intimacy; but, leaving this fair inference on one side, it might be asked, what do we know of the family intimacy of other writers? Generally, when a modern celebrity has died, and a sufficient period of time has elapsed, a biographer is carefully chosen, whose chief business it is to tread from dry rock to dry rock, carefully stepping over swirls of passion and eddies of frailty, all intimacy of detail in fact, finally to deposit his hero on the farther Elysian fields of perduring and gracious fame. This injustice, at least, has not been done Shakespeare. In his case, at least, we are sure that no tender myth has been carefully engineered, by craft, innocence, or affection, into the field of literature. What we know of him is as sharp and clear as a desert shadow: what lies in darkness may or may not safely be inferred from what we see in the light, but generally we may know when we step from one to the other.

This fact, in itself, is an immense advantage in more ways than one. Thus only the purposeful acts of his life will rise up into knowledge; what comes to us will come to us from him, and not from the ingenuity of another. That such and such a man should have lived in such and such a place is not knowledge of the man, it is only the satisfaction of an idle curiosity in the reader. But that a man should have chosen an indicated abode for a purposeful and specific motive is knowledge gained of the man. It is more. It is the safe indication to further knowledge. It opens the door to inferential thinking, and a logical inference has all the fine strength of native truth; it is not swayed by any active force of personal influence. Thus, if two facts in a man's life may be declared irrefragable, then it should be evident that the latter fact flowed justly, and with some purpose, from the first, or at least that the first gave rise to some intermediate power that in its turn was sufficient to produce the other. For all that the short-sightedness of scientific specialists has obscured the fact, it is a safety in thinking to know that each effect must have its sufficient cause.

In such a way, and by such methods, it should be possible to construct Shakespeare's life with conviction and clarity. It may not contain all that is true, but all that is contained in it should be true. The rumours that have been handed down concerning him have been many and varied. They may all be true; but it is at least safe to say that some of them are true. And if the sequence of his life demands that some one or other of them be brought to apply at some particular moment, and if it be found that that rumour both can apply and is also of honest repute as to its sources, then it is just to procure its aid. Its selection from among its companions need be no imputation on their fair fame and veracity, but can only mean that it, at least, is buttressed and supported by a collateral requirement. It has its place in an entity that may or may not cast its raiment over its companions.

There are certain facts, truly enough, that admit neither of evasion nor inference: such as the stupendous fact of his birth. They who desire to believe that he was born on the same date of the year as his death, injure none by their conviction. That this was also St George's Day is a very pleasant sop to a patriotic conviction that regards the poet as a national dispensation, a sign of favour with the Most High. But, at any rate, if he was not born on April 23, 1564, he was born thereabouts, for the Stratford parish registers proclaim him as having been baptized on April 26 of that year; and it seemed as though the hazard of birth had seen fit to cast his lines in pleasant places, for both his father and his mother were of influence and property in the neighbourhood.

It is not only the inevitable human ambition to discover the antecedents to any event that leads the biographical instinct to recount a man's parentage. It falls to it to cast the lot of his life. Even after he has assumed stature it awakes crises in his life that decide the whole course of his work. It certainly was so with Shakespeare. That he was on excellent terms with his father appears from the fact that the latter is reported to have said that "Will was a good honest fellow, but he darest have crackt a jest with him at any time."[1] The indication so given of easy and amicable relations finds its place in more than one event of importance in Shakespeare. Not only, however, was John Shakespeare a "merry-cheeked old man," but he was a burgher of good repute and standing in the town of Stratford-on-Avon. His wife, Mary Arden, was a woman of fortune; and, on her marriage, brought to the union the property of Asbies, which comprised a house and fifty acres of land, and which she held in fee-simple. Asbies was situated at Wilmcote, near Stratford, which not only was the home of the Ardens, but is also one of the three places that vie each with the other as having supplied the ale that was responsible for the good slumber that befell Christopher Sly in the *Taming of the Shrew*. John Shakespeare himself, doubtless partly owing to his wife's property, filled a position of importance in Stratford. He was a trader of sorts, handling most things that were apt to be required in the town; and his career was prosperous. In 1556 he purchased two freehold properties in the town—one in Henley Street and the other in Greenhill Street. The following year he was elected to the pleasant task of ale-tasting. In the two years that followed he was twice appointed one of four petty constables. Twice also he exercised the office of affeeror, when it fell to his task to decide what fines should meet such offences as had no penalties apportioned by statute. Three years before the birth of his son Will, in 1561, he rose to be one of the two chamberlains of the borough; on July 4, 1565, he achieved the further dignity of an alderman; and finally, in 1568, he reached the height of civic glory in being elected as the bailiff of the town.

But the summit of achievement was the prelude to disaster. Some further purchase of property in 1575 is proof that he hung at the summit awhile ere he swept to his declension. But on November 14, 1578, a somewhat sharp catastrophe was struck when he mortgaged Asbies to his wife's brother-in-law, Edmund Lambert, of Barton-on-the-Heath—the Burton Heath whence Christopher Sly hailed. There is no doubt that this mortgage rankled in John Shake-

speare's pride; for two years after we find him
offering to pay off the mortgage, to meet the retort
that there were also other debts which must first
be met. Moreover, creditors began a long assault
on him from this time onwards; and to such a pass
had he arrived that in 1586 one of his creditors,
John Brown, having obtained his writ of distraint,
found that there remained no goods to levy on. In
the same year he was stripped of his alderman's
gown because he had so long absented himself from
the meetings of the council.

All this has a close bearing on Will Shakespeare's
affairs. Later, in London, he was to be brought
into close contact with "the law's delay, the in-
solence of office"; but now, here, at the very
threshold of life, he was to have his first taste of
it. But it was also coincident with the second event
in his personal life that leaves its print in public
records. Speculation and conjecture have made
merry over the somewhat curious evidences that
attest and attend his marriage. They not only
yield conflicting inferences, but they are in themselves conflicting. For example, it is recorded that
on November 27, 1582, a William Shakespeare was
granted a licence by the Bishop of Worcester to
marry an Anne Whately of Temple Grafton. But
on the following day Fulk Sandells and John
Richardson, "husbandmen of Stratford," the former
of whom at least being a considerable friend of
a certain Richard Hathwey, entered into a formal

surety of £40 in the Consistory Court of Worcester to free the bishop from any liability, " by reason of any precontract or consanguinity," in the marriage of a William Shakespeare and an " Anne Hathwey " of Shottery, the daughter of Fulk Sandells' friend. To explain this curious juxtaposition there have been several theories put into the field. It has been suggested, the names Whately and Hathwey not being so very dissimilar, that a clerkly error is responsible for the confusion, and that both Annes referred to are one and the same person. It is true that even in this more literate age stranger things have happened in the annals of clerkship; but the fact that the several patronymics hail from different neighbourhoods does not give much countenance to this theory. It has also been suggested that different William Shakespeares were involved in each event; and to this it must be agreed that William Shakespeare does not appear to have been a very rare name in the somewhat extensive diocese of Worcester.

Another theory has been put forward, however, that is supported by several lines of independent evidence. In this it is claimed that Shakespeare desired to wed Anne Whately, but had incurred an earlier responsibility with Anne Hathaway: in view of which situation Sandells and Richardson came vigorously forward and compelled Shakespeare to complete his honourable obligations by marrying their friend's daughter. That this seems the likelier hazard is doubly supported by the birth of a daughter, Susanna, on May 26 of the following year, and by the many references throughout his work that hold out solemn warnings against prenuptial intimacy. Moreover, in *Twelfth Night*, the Duke gives it as his counsel that "woman" should "take an elder than herself": which cannot but remind us that Anne Hathaway was Shakespeare's elder by some years. It has also been said that his marriage brought unhappiness in its train; and that, in consequence of this, he avoided Stratford as much as possible. Whether his marriage was or was not unhappy is another consideration. But it will be seen that he was far from avoiding Stratford in future years; in fact, that up to the end of his days he always spent at Stratford all the time he could well spare from his theatrical duties, and that he ever elected to be known as an inhabitant of Stratford.

That is to anticipate, however. The more immediate fact is, that now, as a youth of nineteen, he found himself burdened with the responsibility of both wife and child. Nor could his father aid him. Indeed, his father was himself in penury and perplexity; and so he was frustrated of such employment as might have aided him from that quarter in an earlier day. It was at best a sufficiently difficult situation. Rowe stated, in 1709, that Shakespeare about this time fell into evil company, and "made a frequent practice of deer-stealing"; and this is supported by the local testimony of Archdeacon Davies, who declared that he "was much given to all unluckiness in stealing venison and rabbits, particularly from Sir Thomas Lucy, who had him oft whipt, and sometimes imprisoned, and at last made him fly his native county to his great advancement." If this was so, it might well have been due as much to penury as roguery.

At any rate, his worldly position, whatever he turned his attention to, whether schoolmastering, as the seventeenth century William Beeston would have us believe, or not, was at least perplexing if not precarious. And if his reported deer-stealing was not the result of penury, it certainly added to his difficulties in the harassing Sir Thomas Lucy gave him. Yet, as though these things were not in themselves sufficient, further difficulties brought their visitation upon him, through his own affairs and through his father. Within two years of the birth of his first child, on February 2, 1585, he had his responsibilities further added to by the birth of twins, Hamnet and Judith. Moreover, John Shakespeare, harassed and perplexed beyond measure, sought at last to sell the fee-simple of his wife's estate, Asbies, to his brother-in-law, Lambert, for another £20, over and above the initial mortgage of £40. But to this it was necessary that William's permission should first be sought, he being his mother's heir. Though this was given without demur, the transaction does not seem to have been completed, for in his later days of prosperity Shakespeare sought to recover the property by an action at law.

Thus the sequence of facts in Shakespeare's life may be set out thus: In 1564 he was born, in 1582 he married, 1583 saw the birth of his first child, early in 1584 twins were born, and in 1587 he agreed to part with his right in his mother's hereditament so as to ease his parents' distress; all of which points to a fairly continuous life in Stratford, culminating in distress in the year 1587. Here the sequence breaks; and Stratford records nothing more of him for another ten years. So the eye looks ahead for the next event that seems to indicate Shakespeare's presence anywhere in the field of action, that thus, thinking backward and forward, it may seek to establish the necessary sequence between the two dates.

Such an event appears in 1592; on March 3 of which year we find a company of players, under the direction of Edward Alleyn, and claiming patronage from the Earl of Derby, producing a play at the Rose in Southwark, which Henslowe, financier of the company, and father-in-law to Alleyn, enters in his diary as "harej the vj." Were there any doubt that this was the play that Shakespeare wrote a large part of, Greene's famous reference to the "absolute Johannes factotum," who "is, in his own conceit, the only Shake-scene in a country," coupled with his perverted quotation from the *Henry VI.* that has come down to us as Shakespeare's own

HIS LIFE

product, should be sufficient to dissipate it. The year 1592, and the events that belong to it, are a matter for subsequent examination. It is only sufficient now to say that, to establish a complete sequence for Shakespeare's life, it will be necessary fitly to bridge the darkness between the years 1587 and 1592.

Happily, this is not difficult of achievement. In the first place, there is this hint cast us, that Shakespeare in 1592 seems little likely to have been a newcomer to Lord Derby's company. It was the custom of the time to entrust the more experienced copyists of a company with the revision of any old play that had been chosen for revival; and *Henry VI.* was such a play. It had been written by Marlowe and Greene (probably Kyd, too, had participated in its collaboration), and had been already staged by a company wholly separate from Alleyn's control. So that, in seeking to discover a fit and apt sequence for the five years thrust between 1587 and 1592, it will be necessary that such a sequence should embrace in its explanation three things: firstly, how Shakespeare came to be connected with the Earl of Derby's company; secondly, how Alleyn, the director of that company, came to choose Shakespeare for the responsible task of revising a play by such admitted masters as Marlowe and Greene, he being, so far as records may guide us, an author yet unacted, if an author at all; and thirdly, how a play that had been written for a wholly different company ever came into Alleyn's possession. In this manner, such a sequence should not only explain Shakespeare's doings in the lapse of time, but should also explain much else of interest in the dramatic history of the day.

Late in 1585, the very year, in fact, in which Anne Shakespeare presented her husband with further responsibilities in the shape of twins, a company gathered itself together under the patronage of the Earl of Leicester for the purposes of continental and provincial travel. This company had probably no connection with the company that two years previously had passed from his care to the Queen's patronage. Assuredly it matters little. The more substantial fact is that they left London in December for a prolonged tour. Early the following year they were in Denmark, having been commended by Leicester to the King; in the autumn they were in Saxony; in the spring of 1587 they came to London, and passed on a provincial tour that carried them to Stratford in the autumn of that year.[2] Or, in other words, in the very year that Shakespeare's affairs had tied themselves into the most tortuous perplexity, a player's company visited his native town with all the glamour of travel on them. If he fled his distresses, fled, too, Sir Thomas Lucy's persecution, by joining such a company, it could be but little wondered at in him.

Assuming, then, that this was veritably the case, the sequence would necessarily be taken up by this company of Leicester's. The Earl of Leicester himself was not long to remain patron of it, for in September of the following year he died, and the company had therefore to seek elsewhere for some patron who would provide them with the necessary licence to play. So Edward Alleyn, who till then had been playing with Worcester's men, left his old company, gathered Leicester's men together, and procured the patronage of Ferdinando Stanley, Lord Strange, who, on September 25, 1592, shortly before his men went to the Rose in Southwark, duly became the Earl of Derby. In other words, the darkness is bridged by an inevitable sequence. Shakespeare must have joined the company at its visit to Stratford in 1587, and have worked his way up from impotence to importance till he emerged to notice in 1592. Rowe, writing in 1709, says that Shakespeare "was received into the company then in being at first in a very mean rank." Malone, in 1780, stated that a tradition existed that his "first office in the theatre was that of prompter's attendant." This seems likely enough, for Shakespeare's position was such in 1587 that he would necessarily have had to make shift as best he could.[3]

The intervening history of the company seems only to confirm the inference. For the company on its return to London played at none of the regular playhouses. Edward Alleyn's father had been a "Citizen and Innholder" of London, and his brother had succeeded his father, the inn itself being situate in Bishopsgate. So that Edward Alleyn's first inclinations would probably lead him to fix his dramatic abode in an innyard. This, in point of fact, he did. In the Cross Keys Tavern in Gracechurch Street some manner of permanent stage, it would appear, was erected,[4] and to this he therefore repaired. Now some two hundred years after this a tradition was passed on by Rowe, and printed by Jordan, to the effect that when the gallants of the time came to see the play, Shakespeare's "business was to take their horses to the inn and order them to be fed until the play was over, and then see that they were returned to their owners"; and to this it has been objected that stables and sheds were scarcely of such vital importance during a two or three hours' performance.[5] But if Shakespeare's company was playing, not at a playhouse, but at an innyard, what more likely than that the gallants coming to witness an afternoon's performance should have their horses housed in the usual way? And what more likely than that an eager, pushful spirit, zealous of greater things, should undertake this task by the novel method, as rumour records it, of organising a brigade of boys under him? Moreover, the remote ends of knowledge that Shakespeare shows through his plays is also largely accounted for. There could be few better places to acquire such knowledge than a tavern in the restless Elizabethan days. The fact that Shakespeare appears at any early period of his life in London to have resided in the parish of St

Helens in Bishopsgate Ward, or, in other words, quite near to Gracechurch Street, wears at once a new interest.[6] An "absolute Johannes factotum" would require to be at near call.

For some four years, thus, Lord Strange's men played irregularly and intermittently at the Cross Keys innyard under Alleyn's direction. Then, in the closing days of 1591, a couple of circumstances arose that both made it advisable for him to move to more ambitious quarters, and also provided the quarter to which a move would be desirable. Fitly to understand the manner of Shakespeare's life, it will be necessary to furnish the anterior history of these circumstances.

When, in the early months of 1587, the Queen decided to become patron of a company of her own, in characteristic manner she swept down upon all that was best in some of the companies then existing. Thus it came about that stout James Burbage, who seven years previously had built a playhouse in Holywell, and entitled it prophetically the Theater, passed, with the best portion of his company, to her care. In this first and most notorious of playhouses he held direct patronage from the Sovereign. Yet these joint distinctions were not without their attendant disadvantages. On the one hand, Giles Allen was, as ground landlords are wont to be, a fastidious and somewhat obstreperous person. Either he was envious of Burbage's profit; or else pulpit rhetoric at, and mayoralty and shrievalty denunciation of, the godless audiences that frequented the Theater fetched a wholesome fear into his soul. Anyway, he was an element sufficiently perturbing on the one hand. On the other hand, Burbage was in a far more intimate complication with his brother-in-law, John Braynes, over the actual management of the playhouse. Seeing that when the lease had first been acquired, and the Theater built, in 1576, the money for the venture had been provided by Braynes, the main direction lying in Burbage's hands ("who," says a Lord Mayor's flunkey, "was a stubborn fellow"), it was little likely that the lion lay down peaceably with the lamb in the years that followed. But when Braynes died, in 1586, a veritable host of legal suits were unloosed. Certain persons to whom he had made over deeds of gifts yielding them some hold on the Theater, together with his widow Margaret, proceeded against Burbage forthwith. He, with characteristic energy, was first in the field against them all. Thus lawsuit followed lawsuit: cross-suit met suit: and pleadings and hearings mingled with each other. It is not in the purse of man to meet many years of this; and so, in the closing days of 1591, the Theater was closed and the Queen's men largely disbanded.

Thus plays and players were unloosed from their sometime moorings. Such players as John Hemings and Richard Burbage were without occupation. Also certain plays seem to have been put into the market, probably to raise capital for the

HIS LIFE 43

Burbage lawsuits; plays by Greene, Marlowe, Kyd, and Lodge, done severally, or in collaboration; not to speak of Tarleton's *Seven Deadly Sins*, the particular worth of which is that in the list of actors serving in its subsequent portrayal the history of events can clearly be traced.

Meanwhile, one Philip Henslowe had since 1586 been building, or contemplating, a playhouse in Southwark.[7] Early in 1592 this was completed, and called the Rose. Exactly what preceded, it is, of course, impossible to say. But the main facts stand thus: Henslowe and Alleyn joined forces, Henslowe as financier, and Alleyn as director, of a company that opened a season at the Rose on February 19 of the year 1592; and, further, probably to cement the partnership, later in the year Alleyn married Henslowe's heiress daughter-in-law, Joan Woodward. The company that they took with them to the Rose still owned the patronage of Lord Strange, now Earl of Derby; but it was more extended than formerly, including, as it did, some of the disbanded Queen's company. Five of the players figuring in this amalgamation, and illustrating the amalgamation as in a microcosm, are to play a very significant part in Shakespeare's subsequent life: Richard Burbage, Will. Kempe, John Hemings, Augustine Phillips, and Thomas Pope.[8] Moreover, a number of plays that had anciently been done by the Queen's company also make appearance: among others a play in which Marlowe and Greene, and probably also Kyd, had participated: *Henry VI.*, to wit. Whether Alleyn, being approached by Henslowe, sought to procure such plays and players as the closing of the Theater had disbanded, or whether having the offer of such plays and players, he approached Henslowe, matters little. The substantial concern is that an important move forward was achieved in which Shakespeare was to play a part.

The situation is an interesting one. Internal literary evidence leads to the almost inevitable conclusion that *Love's Labour's Lost*, in its original form, was written first of all Shakespeare's plays, and prior to the year 1592. With all its lack of form, its precocity, its hard cleverness, it belongs obviously to prentice days. Whether it was acted at all before 1598, when it was revised and republished for a Court performance, it is impossible to say, as no record of it exists. But if one may imagine it being shown to Alleyn in 1590 or 1591, it suggests a curiously interesting position. Alleyn was a generous, big-souled man; yet it would require no call on his greatness of heart to perceive that he had in his company an ambitious and supremely able man, if withal a man whose work wanted discipline. What more likely then, if he were preparing for a strong occupancy of a new playhouse, that he should turn his original-minded copyist on to some of the plays that had come into his hand, that thus they might present some point of distinction to win them to newer attention?

In his later days Shakespeare spoke of the tide in the affairs of men which, taken at the flood, leads on to fortune; and the words ring like the metal struck from experience. Such a tide was setting in for him now. What his earlier years had brought to him of bitterness and frustrated ambition, we cannot know, though there do not lack indications in his plays that their brackish taste had gone to his lips. But the breath of change had come down on the wind to him. In the Christmas festivities at Court for the year 1591, the Queen's men, in witness of their trembling fall, appear only once, giving place to Lord Strange's men. This meant much. It meant that the stream of lordly gallants would follow the bent of royal favour. Since Shakespeare achieved the personal patronage of the Earl of Southampton about this time, it is not too much to assume that this was so, and that it was thus that Shakespeare made the friendship that was to mean so much to him. And it is additionally interesting to note that he seems, from two lines of evidence mutually independent, to have moved from his lodging in St Helens, Bishopsgate, to the liberty of the Clink in Southwark, in the shrievalty of Surrey and Sussex, where Alleyn and Henslowe lived, so as again to be near and ready to his work. Apparently he left some debts behind him in Bishopsgate, which in his later days of prosperity seem to have been duly cleared up.

Henry VI. was a sudden projection into a placid pool. Previously all had been unperturbed; but now eddies ring round about in witness of a new event. When Nash in his "Pierce Pennilesse" speaks of "ten thousand spectators at least" as having witnessed it, we are doubtless on the path of wholesome exaggeration; but when he says, "How it would have joyed brave Talbot (the terror of the French) to thinke that, after he had lyen two hundred yeare in his tomb, he should triumph againe on the stage," we hear him praising those parts of the play that were indubitably Shakespeare's, even though the maturing author of the future *Macbeth* did dip his pen in Marlowe's ink for awhile. Yet Greene's abuse is even better tribute. It is certainly a notable contribution to biographical knowledge; for its wording throws up into relief Shakespeare's earlier occupation with quite menial tasks, and his consequent inferiority of rank beside the dramatists of the day. In his "Groatsworth of Wit bought with a Million of Repentance," he addresses Marlowe, Nash, and Peele, and bids them be warned by him concerning "antics garnished in our colours." And when he proceeds to speak of "an upstart crow beautified with our feathers, that, with his *Tyger's heart wrapt in a Player's hide*, supposes he is as well able to bumbast out a blanke verse as the best of you," we hear his anger at meeting power when he least expected it, and we hear, too, perhaps a far echo of some line that Shakespeare had ruthlessly altered of his, or some line that had awoken debate at the collaborator's table, and in

which he had been bested. But when he further
writes of " an absolute *Johannes factotum* " who " is in
his owne conceit the only Shakescene in a countrie,"
we hear two things: first, that an angry dramatist
is taunting Shakespeare with his late lowly and
varied part in matters dramatical; and second, that
Shakespeare, however "gentle," was probably not
above the mortal frailty of preening his pride a little
in his new glory. The first of these we hear again
when Greene goes on to speak in snorting contempt
of "rude groomes," "buckram gentlemen," "such
peasants": all of which do not fail to depict the man
whose father fell from splendour, and who came up
from the country to tend horses, as tradition has it,
in a player's company.

Yet, however noteworthy this increase was in
worldly position, it neither seems to have been
maintained nor made good. The season at the Rose
opened on February 19, and on March 3 *Henry VI.*
was played. During the days that followed he had
an opportunity of hearing, and participating in, plays
by Marlowe, Lodge, Greene, Kyd, and Peele, but
never, apparently, by himself. Meanwhile, the
plague, the interrupter of most playhouse pro-
grammes at the time, stepped in, and, after June
10, the company had to remove to Newington Butts
at the order of the Archbishop of Canterbury, where
an innyard was probably reopened for stage performances.[9] There was no return to the Rose
till the following year; and even then the plague

and the playhouse waged war, with alternate and intermittent predominance for awhile, and with final victory to the former.

But he had come to know the Earl of Southampton, and this was to mean much to him. He had also come to learn something of his power; and he seemingly determined that in the intermittences of acting (lengthy intermittences, owing to the plague) he would achieve something he could fitly dedicate to the young Earl in the manner of the time. It has sometimes been assumed that when Shakespeare, in the dedication of "Venus and Adonis," spoke of that poem as the "first heire of my invention," he thereby indicated it as first fruits of all his work, dramatic or otherwise. Seeing that as yet, so far as records may guide us, he had undertaken no independent work of his own, apart from revision, and, perhaps, collaboration, this may well have chanced to be the case. But that the poem was written immediately prior to its publication early in 1593 is clearly indicated by the fact that in the selfsame dedication he proceeds to register a "vowe to take advantage of all idle houres, till I have honoured you with some graver labour." And promptly the following year "The Rape of Lucrece" appears. But apart from the fact that "Venus and Adonis" shows as clear an advance on those portions of *Henry VI.* we know for Shakespeare's, as "The Rape of Lucrece" does upon "Venus and Adonis," thus pointing a clear progression in writing, there stands out this fact:

that, having come to know Southampton, he was desirous of winning that young nobleman's favour. If his Court reputation belies him not, few things could have been better calculated to that end than the subjects of the two poems in question.

The year in which he published "Venus and Adonis" is one worthy of note. It was in this year that Edward Alleyn's company, being forbidden to play " within seven miles of London or of the Court," that is to say, either at the Rose or at Newington Butts, took its way on travel. They proceeded to Bristol and other places: but, though several of the old Queen's company formed part of the tour, Shakespeare remained in London. Moreover, Richard Burbage was also in London. The former had business on hand in the publication of his book, whereas the latter must needs have been occupied with the litigation concerning the Theater. Knowing the affection that later arose between these two, not to speak of their intimate relations in matters dramatical, this is a matter that cannot but arouse interest. It means that whereas Shakespeare, who only the year before had arisen from obscurity, was laying the basis of a wealthy patronage, the Burbages were in fierce litigation over the playhouse that had brought them fame, and that therefore their exchequer was in depletion.

A review of Shakespeare's position at this moment is interesting. Marlowe's death on June 1, 1593, meant that the three dramatic giants of the previous era, the era of glory for the Theater—Marlowe, Greene, and Kyd—were no longer able to compete against any rising dramatist. Moreover, to such a state of distress had the Burbages arrived that the final remnants of the old Queen's company were now finally disbanded. And Shakespeare stood in the newly-won friendship of a singularly wealthy patron in the Earl of Southampton. A juncture such as this needs only some stirring event to awaken its potentiality into activity; and, in view of Shakespeare's subsequent financial success, it is at least remarkable that such an event was to arrive in the following year.

Yet as a dramatic author, Shakespeare had won no fame as yet. The following year, on the return of Edward Alleyn to the Rose, *Titus Andronicus* was played at that playhouse. *Titus Andronicus* is at best but slender argument for Shakespeare's dramatic fame, for while it is certain that he had some part in it, seeing it was mentioned later by Meres and included in the First Folio, it is also as certain that his part was no very large one. That his part, however great or little, had nothing to do with the structure and plot of the play is seen partly by the fact that it is so unlike his usual method of work, and partly by the fact that, however gory it be, in structural skill at least it shows a far more masterly experience than do his other plays of the period. Such plays were *Love's Labour's Lost* and *Two Gentlemen of Verona*, must have been written at this time; which is to say that they must have been written before other plays that appear immediately after this time. That there is no trace of their having been acted seems to drive one to the conclusion that at the opening of the year 1594 he had revised two plays by other hands—*Henry VI.* and *Titus Andronicus*—and possessed one or two other plays for which he had not found an outlet. They may have been produced in the old days at the Cross Keys; but, in that case, had they been successful, Alleyn would scarcely have neglected them in his present larger scope of management.

Thus in the early months of 1594 all things stood in perplexed poise, awaiting some stroke that should resolve the issue. The stroke came on the 16th of April; for on that day Lord Strange, the Earl of Derby, died, and a new patronage had to be devised. It is usually said that the patronage of his company passed on to Henry Carey, first Lord Hunsdon, and Lord Chamberlain; but this is a somewhat careless statement of the position of affairs. For Edward Alleyn had been the leader of the Earl of Derby's company. But he had also been, in his proper person, the "Lord Admiral's servant"; and we find him, consequently, opening a season at the Rose on May 14 with a company that is called the Lord Admiral's company, but which, in directorship, financial control, and largely in personnel, is the same as that which had served him two years previously, and which he had taken on tour with him. A company under the patronage of the Lord Chamberlain does indeed come into existence at this time; but we find it owing leadership to Burbage and Shakespeare, if not others. In the early days of this company, from June 3 to 13, we find it sharing a season with the Lord Admiral's men at Newington Butts: which at least is an evidence of equable goodwill ruling between them. But later in the year we find the Lord Chamberlain petitioning the Lord Mayor to permit his men to play at the Cross Keys, guaranteeing that they shall study a more orderly behaviour, and observe more convenient hours, than seem to have been the rule with players' companies at the time. They do not seem to have received the necessary permission, for they promptly, in the same month of October, reopened the old Theater—a move that was to bring back in splendour the great days of that first of playhouses. What had happened to account for all this? It had required money, as it had required influence.

The procuring of the patronage of Lord Hunsdon we can readily understand. That that came from old James Burbage there can be no doubt. An old document exists declaring that, some ten years prior to this, when the Lord Mayor had commanded James Burbage to attend before him, to account for the disorders prevailing at and about the Theater, the stout old man had sent back word that he would not, and that he was "the Lord of Hunsdon's man." This could only have been in personal capacity, for at that time he was in control of the Queen's company. So it would seem that on the death of the Earl of Derby, whereas Alleyn turned to his proper patron, the Burbages also turned to their proper patron. But to what end could they have done so? How came it that the Burbages so suddenly recovered from the financial embarrassments that beset them so short a time before? Moreover, how came it that Shakespeare should so suddenly and unaccountably rise to this position of trust and power? His fame as a dramatist was not high; yet he seems to have been the only dramatist at first in the new company. Only a few years before he had been in penury, tending horses and giving prompter's calls; yet now he is called in to take part in the control of the most famous of the playhouses. Such things, in an earth of cause and effect, do not spring up by chance.

There is one, and, it would seem, only one, possible cause to account for so noteworthy an effect. It might be put thus: it, of course, is evident that when the Burbages reopened the Theater, it meant that money from somewhere had been called on to achieve that desirable end; but if it so happened that Shakespeare could have procured that money, it is obvious that he could have claimed his subsequent position of power as a natural and proper return for that service. Did he procure that money? If he did so, he could only have procured it from his patron, the Earl of Southampton.

Now it is in this connection an interesting, though late, tradition comes to light. Sir William D'Avenant, who took great pride in the rumour that he was Shakespeare's proper son, and who was reputed as being "very well acquainted with Shakespeare's affairs," informed Rowe, "that my Lord Southampton at one time gave him a thousand pounds to enable him to go through with a purchase which he heard he had a mind to." He adds that this is "a bounty very great and very rare at any time"; and, seeing that a thousand pounds of Elizabethan money may be taken as worth between eight and ten thousand pounds of modern, he may be judged as being pretty accurate in his remark. It has been suggested that Shakespeare's purchase of New Place was being referred to thus. But if it was this gift that Shakespeare had in mind when, in the dedication to "The Rape of Lucrece," in this very year of 1594, he spoke of "the warrant I have of your honourable disposition," this may at once be set aside. He did not purchase New Place till 1597, and he was little likely to have let the money lie idle in the meantime. If the tale of the gift be true, however tradition may or may not have puffed out the amount, then his sudden rise to power becomes intelligible and reasonable. Certainly the tradition has excellent antecedents; certainly Shakespeare's increase of temporal power demands some apt explanation; and certainly Shakespeare's dedication to "The Rape of Lucrece" in this important year of 1594 implies that he had received some or other welcome and noteworthy assistance from a very wealthy patron. It is very difficult to avoid the pure, clear inference that the events themselves supply. The matter itself is wrapt in a great darkness; but other and lesser facts stand out in the light and point where it lies.

The very wording of the D'Avenant story is significant. It states that the thousand pounds was to enable Shakespeare "to go through with a purchase which he had a mind to." Now, since we know that at a further remove of years the Globe was held by five others besides the Burbages, of which five Shakespeare was one; and since we know, too, that all these five were with Edward Alleyn in the season he opened at the Rose early in 1592: it is no very wide conjecture to assume that the opening of the Theater in 1594 was the result of a general rally, and that Shakespeare was anxious, if possible, to purchase some share in the new management. If such a rally prevailed, it would not only have a very fair inducement to urge it by attraction before; it would have had a very powerful discomfort to prick it from behind. Alleyn, it would seem, was a man of a great and generous soul. But not so his father-in-law Henslowe. His diary reveals him as one who had brought to a fine art the system of employing methods of usury so as to hold his actors in his power; and he had his skill in this deftly blent with sanctimony withal. Whereas a man of intelligence finds it a quite sufficient indignity to work for any man on hire without having that obligation hasped in shackles on his wrists.

If it be true that Shakespeare had some such sum given him, and if it be true, moreover, that he employed it to purchase a holding in a reconstituted company, it would be interesting to discover what a thousand pounds (to take the figure at its full statement) would mean as against what the Burbages had to offer from their side. We know, for example, that when James Burbage first built the Theater, he did so chiefly on moneys borrowed from his brother-in-law Braynes. What portion he himself contributed is not known; yet it is known that he borrowed about £600 from Braynes. This was all capital outlay; yet, even so, it was only part of the capital outlay, for actors had to be engaged and equipped, advertising by bill and procession had to be organised, and the ordinary business of the playhouse had to be proceeded with. Probably in all this Braynes bore the lion's share of expenditure, even as Burbage bore the lion's share of initiative and work. Nevertheless, on Braynes' death, if not during the whole course of business, the substantial benefit of the continuous expenditure would fall due to Burbage, even as if Burbage had died first the substantial benefit of his initiative would have fallen due to Braynes and not to Cuthbert and Richard Burbage. The man in possession would have benefited. In truth, this formed the whole basis of the litigation that arose out of Braynes' death. Not to go into details of what such continuous expenditure would have meant (which could approximately be arrived at from the details supplied in Henslowe's diary concerning the business of another company), we know that the Burbages up to this time had made about two thousand pounds, from their own declaration. In other words, the Burbage interest would be: two thousand pounds (whether sunk in litigation, as seems likely, or still standing, is not material); a playhouse that originally cost some £700, and on which a further £200 had since been expended; stage properties of a highly expensive character, and actors' gear even yet more expensive (how expensive let Henslowe testify!); and a goodwill, or what was of the same benefit, an evil-will, that was of considerable value, since the Theater was notorious all over London, having had the free and excellent advertisement of several sermons preached against it at St Paul's Cross. Thus, if Shakespeare had indeed come forward with a full thousand pounds in the year 1594, that sum would only be able to purchase him some or other fractional holding. This being so, it is interesting to find that subsequently, in later years, his share in the Globe was a tenth, and his share in the Blackfriars a seventh. And, in support of the fact that something of this kind must needs have happened at this time, it is even more interesting to note old James Burbage, to judge from a statement made by his ground landlord, Giles Allen, made over his property to his sons.[10] This he was likely enough to do, so as to simplify matters, if other interests had entered on the scene.

However that be, most surely Shakespeare's position at the Theater was a matter of pivotal function in his life. Up till now he had moved in darkness, shrouded with obscurity. Henceforward he is to step in the light of public importance and the fame of his increasing achievement. In the Court performances of this year, 1594, he figures for the first time, and his companions are Richard Burbage and Will. Kempe, the successor in broad comedy and general clownage to the celebrated Tarleton. For this they were well paid, though it was not till March 15 of the following year that they received their moneys. Probably one of the plays acted on this occasion was the *Comedy of Errors*, since it was also acted earlier the same day at Gray's Inn. Moreover, as it is indubitable that he must have followed *Henry VI.* at once with its meet continuation in *Richard III.*, this was probably also done at the same time. Thus Shakespeare's acknowledged achievement at thirty years of age would be, his two poems, "Venus and Adonis" and "The Rape of Lucrece," and his acted plays *Henry VI., Titus Andronicus, Richard III.*, and the *Comedy of Errors*, in the first two of which he was not so much an author as a refurbisher. To these must be added *Love's Labour's Lost* and *Two Gentlemen of Verona*, which cannot but have preceded the others, but concerning the staging of which there is no possible trace.

He must have been very busy writing, however. There is no record of any other dramatist with his company at this time, and thus a considerable body of work would devolve on him. It is here a very interesting question arises. For the company owned a good number of plays; most of which had belonged originally to the Burbages, and which seem to have returned naturally to them when some of the old Lord Derby's company, with Shakespeare, broke from the Alleyn control and established the new Lord Chamberlain's company. In his earlier work, when he had not the structure of a previous play, he had not been very strong in the technique of dramatic invention. But as the reviser of the work of others he had won sudden fame, bestowing power and beauty on scenes that had hitherto altogether lacked in ability, and giving such slight turns and twists to the plan of a play as gave quick life to dead tissues. It now became his function to continue in this task: to overhaul the company's stock, and to refurbish it for new presentation. For he would scarcely have the time to provide them with a series of new plays, despite the fact that the Chamberlain's company never appear to have averaged more than four plays annually. Since it it well known to have been Shakespeare's habit as a playwright to derive his plots from well-known sources, this may well have been the origin of the practice. Indeed, it is an interesting enough study to note how frequently he derives even from himself, continually repeating stock scenes and accustomed devices. He worked largely on stock themes; and in revising the stock plays of the Lord Chamberlain's company he came finally to writing out all in them that did not derive from his own pen. In some his work is confined to specific portions, as, for example, *The Taming of the Shrew*; in most his work is complete; yet, even to the end, even in plays like *Macbeth* and *King Lear*, there are passages embedded in his work that we scarcely recognise as his. This treatment of old plays and old themes became habitual, except for some striking defections from his practice. Therefore it becomes of more than ordinary interest when we discover that the old play on *Hamlet*, perhaps by Kyd, was acted at the Theater shortly before 1596.[11]

Yet, however busy he was as a playwright, he cannot have been so busy acting. The fact that in the two years following his presence at the Court, that is to say in 1595 and 1596, his company played again before the Queen, but this time without him, would seem to argue his absence from London. And this is supported in several ways. For example, Ben Jonson's reference to Falstaff in *Every Man Out of His Humour* proves that *Henry IV.* was written at any rate before 1599; whereas the textual argument places it early in 1596 or 1597. But it is

HIS LIFE

full of references to Stratford and its neighbourhood; not only topographically, but in speaking of definitely traceable families, such as "William Visor of Woncot," and "Clement Perkes of the Hill." Other plays, too, of this time, such as *The Taming of the Shrew*, are not less redolent of home memories. Not to speak of the fact that Bardolph and Fluellen in the following play of *Henry V.*, are both names familiar in the Warwickshire of his day.[12] Thus the attention turns to Stratford-on-Avon, and at once the full significance of his new importance at the Theater shines out with full meaning.

For affairs with Shakespeare's father had become increasingly parlous. Creditors ringed him with their importunity; and from this lamentable position he had only learnt one relief, this being the eager adoption of a creditor attitude towards some one solitary man who chanced to be in debt to him. Indeed, his son William had scarcely established himself at the Theater than, on March 9, 1595, creditors assailed him again. Here he was joined as defendant with two others, a chandler Phillip Green, and a butcher Henry Rogers, in a suit for the recovery of five pounds. But in this a curious fact arises. For during the course of the action his name is dropped out of the defence altogether, the suit proceeding only against his late colleagues in unhappiness. Moreover, as though this were not enough, to it must be added the still stranger fact that in the following year we find him actually seeking a coat-of-arms for himself, and claiming that his "parentes and late antecessors were for theire valeant and faithfull service advanced and rewarded by the most prudent prince, King Henry the Seventh, of famous memory, sythence which tyme they have continued at those partes (in Warwickshire, that is) in good reputation and credit." Seeing that the previous year he had to dispose of even the little land attached to his dwelling-house in Henley Street, to a George Badger, and that his wife had had occasion lately to borrow forty shillings from Thomas Whittington, lately her father's shepherd, this latter claim reads strangely —humorously even. A change so sudden and so marked demands the intervention of some external aid; and it needs no excess of wit or wisdom to seek for that intervention in the dramatist son that had lately established himself at the Theater. Anyway, William Shakespeare must have been at Stratford the following year, for on August 11, 1596, his son Hamnet was buried at the parish church.

Whether his father's appearance at the court, or whether his hour of prosperity waking memories of home in him, coupled with the desire to establish his worldly position, brought him to Stratford, does not greatly matter. Certain it is that he utilised his visits to the latter end. It is to the son's ambition that his father's application to the College of Heralds for a coat-of-arms must be ascribed, since it would be necessary for him to

HIS LIFE 63

apply through his father, his father being living. The fact that the reply to his application was suspended for awhile did not deter him, however, from setting his house in order in other and various ways. The application itself was actually granted in 1599: indeed, it was not granted then; but it was taken by the College of Heralds as having duly been assigned to John Shakespeare when he was bailiff of Stratford, which may be read as a heraldic device for saying both yea and nay in the same breath. Having received it thus, the Shakespeares asked further that the father should impale, and the son, with his brothers, should quarter, the Arden coat-of-arms with their own. Since in this case it was rather more difficult to devise a means of blowing both hot and cold at once, the application does not seem to have been persisted in, and the noble efforts of the heralds went consequently for nought.

In the meantime, Shakespeare proceeded with other matters. On May 4, 1597, he purchased New Place, which was the largest house in Stratford, and possessed two barns and two gardens. He paid £60 for it in money of that time; and later on added to it steadily, at annual average of £70.[13] Noting this fact, and observing its year, it is curious to think how much had happened in ten years. In 1587 he had been compelled to flee the town ignominiously, and had engaged himself to a player's company as "Johannes Factotum." Five years after, in 1592, he emerged from obscurity as the popular emendator of an historical play. Again, five years later, he rescues his father from his parlous affairs, and becomes one of the chief inhabitants of Stratford. What his importance was can best be judged from the way in which his fellow-inhabitants regard him. For example, early the following year a famine ravaged Stratford, and only two of its inhabitants were credited with a large holding of corn. One of these was Shakespeare, who is stated as the possessor of ten quarters. In this year, moreover, we find him rebuilding New Place, and establishing an orchard to it. A certain Stratfordian, Richard Quiney, appeals to him by letter as a "loving countryman" for the loan of £30; though he might, had he been blest with prophetic sight, have appealed as the father of a son who should later marry one of Shakespeare's daughters. Another Stratfordian, Abraham Sturley, writing to his brother, says that "it seemeth," by his father's motion, "that our countryman, William Shakespere, is willing to disburse some money upon some odd yardland or other at Shottery, or near about us: he thinketh it a very fit pattern to move him to deal in the matter of our tithes. By the instructions you can give him thereof, and by the friends he can make therefor, we think it a fair mark for him to shoot at, and would do us much good." Writing to Richard Quiney, the same writer says later that since the town could not meet a certain subsidy demanded of it (that Quiney was in London to seek remission of), owing to the corn famine, he hoped "that our countryman, Wm. Shak., would procure us money, which I will like of, as I shall hear when, and where, and how." That Shakespeare himself esteemed these Stratford connections, and wished himself to be regarded as primarily an inhabitant of that town, is evident in other ways; for hereafter he is always designated as "William Shakespeare of Stratford, Gentleman."

All this points to prosperity with Shakespeare; and so permits us to see how important was the position he had lately acquired at the Theater. For he certainly could not have achieved so much when with Edward Alleyn. Yet it points to more than mere prosperity. It indicates with sure digit Shakespeare's determination absolutely to sever all links with his earlier years of stress. They who see in these things signs of mundane proclivities can never have had to undertake the keen bitter struggle, such as was his prior to 1592. A man need not necessarily be mundane to raise bulwarks betwixt himself and a proved bitter experience.

Yet it was not only in Stratford that he sought to establish himself. The manner of procedure with Elizabethan players' companies helps to account largely for his movements between London and Stratford. The playhouses being circular and roofless enclosures, even a substantial portion of the stage being without cover, it was impossible for a performance to take place in very inclement weather. Each playhouse had a flagstaff, up to which a pennon was run to advertise the fact that a play was to proceed. Thus winters would not be the best of occasions for playhouse performances, although winters, as Henslowe's diary is itself sufficient to show, were by no means precluded. In this way a number of opportunities presented themselves to Shakespeare for a journey to Stratford; and it is curious to note some of his appearances in his native town at such months and during such times as inclement weather may be presumed.

After his purchase of New Place, however, his return to London would be imperious; and, human nature being what it is, a perplexity consistent in its inconsistencies, it would perhaps be not altogether likely that a man coming from the new glory of his position in Stratford would return to his sometime lodging in the liberty of the Clink. Now, according to the Mountjoy documents,[14] it would appear from Shakespeare's own depositions that he lodged at the house of one Christopher Mountjoy, at the corner of Mugwell Street and Silver Street, in Cripplegate, onwards from about the year 1597. A certain Stephen Bellott had been apprenticed to Mountjoy, in the fashionable task of making head-dresses and wigs, in the year 1598, having been persuaded to this by Bellott's step-father, Humphrey Fludd, whose wife, like Mountjoy, was a French citizen. It is worthy of note that at the time Bellott had already been resident with Mountjoy a year. Subsequently Bellott married Mountjoy's daughter, being promised certain advantages with the contract in the shape of a dower, useful household properties, and the promise of a legacy. In 1612 Bellott brought a suit against Mountjoy, alleging that those fair promises had not properly been ratified. He cited several to testify their relation of the events in question, among them a certain " William Shakespeare, gent." Thus Shakespeare is brought into the field of action; and thus it is not only assured that he did indeed reside at Mountjoy's house, but it is possible to discover when he first began to do so.

At first flush the quest is discouraging; for, deposing in 1612, he declares he has known the parties "tenne yeres or thereabouts." Yet, under a further head, he proceeds to declare that "he did know the complainant when he was servant with the deffandant, and that duringe the tyme of his the complainantes service wth the said deffandant he the said Complainante to this deponentes knowledge did well and honestly behave himselfe." In other words, this carries back the date of his knowledge of Bellot and Mountjoy, and therefore presumably the matter of his indubitable residence with the latter, to 1598, or, if Bellott did any manner of service in the year prior to his actual articles of apprenticeship, to 1597; which is the very date, on the grounds of the plausibility and consonancy of human action, that it was suggested Shakespeare, on his return from the purchase of New Place, would desire to move from his lodging at Southwark, seeking more spacious and appropriate quarters. But, apart from such sentimental promptings as urge the overwhelming majority of human actions, there are not wanting other, and more empirical, motives for such a move. For Silver Street would be at near call to the Theater, even as the Clink was near the Rose, and St Helens was near the Cross Keys Tavern. In addition to this, in coming to Cripplegate he was entering the neighbourhood where several writers and dramatists clustered. Ben Jonson, either now or later, lived here; so also Thomas Dekker and Nathaniel Field; to say nothing of John Heminges and Henry Condell, fellow-members of his company, and subsequently the editors of the First Folio. The neighbourhood preserved something of this character right down to the days when the strident Samuel Johnson declared that Grub Street was "much inhabited by writers of small histories, dictionaries, and temporary poems." Moreover, Silver Street was near the Mermaid Tavern; being, indeed, situate betwixt the Theater and the Mermaid. Not to speak of its being, as Ben has it in his *Staple of News*, "the region of money," a commodity that Shakespeare was now becoming more happily familiar with.

Having moved his lodging near the Theater, it was perhaps only a fitting irony that the tenure of the Burbages at that famous playhouse should fall into insecurity. Giles Allen, the ground landlord, had ever been a thorn in its side. Now he swelled to something more than a thorny inconvenience. He rose to active importance. In the spring of this very year, 1597, the lease had fallen due; and, try as the Burbages would, they could wake no favourable renewal out of him. What to do became a very earnest matter. To proceed, in the teeth of a lapsed agreement, was not only unwise, but was to play into Allen's hands. As a preliminary move, therefore, and probably as a hint to Allen that they were in no way dependent on him, it was decided to close the Theater. This was done accordingly on July 28; and the whole company moved to the Curtain, near by, also within the precinct of the sometime Priory of Holywell. Being settled here, they opened their season with *Romeo and Juliet*. The inner evidence of the play leads to the conclusion that this was a revision; yet this is the first record of it. It was hither Ben Jonson (not less dissatisfied than others with Henslowe's usurious soul, of which this year he had thrice been a victim) brought his play, *Every Man in His Humour*. The story runs, in proof of Shakespeare's authoritative importance, that it had already been refused, when Shakespeare, hearing its dismissal, took it, read it, and duly accepted it.

All this year this unsatisfactory position continued: and all the next. In the meantime, in the midst of all these perplexed negotiations, old James Burbage died. He bequeathed the Theater to his son Cuthbert, and the Blackfriars, an indoor playhouse he had just built within the liberties, to Richard. The fact that these separate distinctions of ownership were never rigidly observed is a hint that there were other interests observed. For example, the Theater, as already said, was Cuthbert's property; yet Cuthbert was not the only one concerned in the present responsibility. Firstly, his brother Richard was also interested; but, in addition to his concern, there were also Shakespeare, Will. Kempe, John Heminges, Augustine Phillips, and Thomas Pope; all of whom had been with Alleyn in 1592, and who had joined the Lord Chamberlain's company on its formation. Their interest in the present situation transpires in what follows.

In the later legal suits that succeeded the immediate perplexity, Giles Allen declared that it had been his intention, "seeing the greate and greevous abuses that grewe by the Theater, to pull downe the same and to converte the wood and timber thereof to some better use." But in the original lease granted to James Burbage it had been stipulated that if he or his successors or assigns were to expend £200 in building on the property at any time subsequent to their initial tenure, they would then be entitled to pull down the Theater and remove it elsewhere. What "better use" Allen had in mind for the "wood and timber thereof" can never be known, for the step he meditated was put into execution by the other side. First of all, however, now that it was intended to move out of the field of leases held by the Burbages, it was dedicated to formulate a legal position accurately. The question of any earlier arrangement can only be a matter for inferential reasoning; inductions from certain patent facts that carry their own necessary implications: the subsequent arrangement comes into the clearer atmosphere of legal definition. Yet the fact that this legal definition should first be drawn up, that it should be distinctly articulated before any move should be effected, is its own hint of an earlier understanding.

As the matter was finally drawn out, it was decided that all subsequent responsibilities and profits should be defined into two clear halves: one half being taken by the two Burbages, and divided equally between them; the other half being taken by Shakespeare and his four companions, and divided equally between them. The latter half-holding was created into a legal *tenancy-in-common* by the whole five granting their half to two outsiders, Thomas Savage and William Levison, and receiving it back from them in fifth shares. It was intended by this that each man should hold his right as distinct and individual, in fair hereditament: a matter that was to mean trouble to them subsequently.[15]

Three days after they had legalised this arrangement, on the 28th December 1598, they hired a builder and carpenter named Peter Street, and, with a goodly company, forthwith proceeded to pull down the Theater, so as to erect its materials on a site they jointly leased from Sir Nicholas Brend between Maiden Lane and Bankside in Southwark. From the subsequent action that arose out of this arbitrary act, it appears that these "divers persons, to the number of twelve," were not permitted to proceed unmolested with their task. They had to arm "themselves with dyvers and manye unlawfull and offensive weapons, as namlye, swordes, daggers, bills, axes, and such like." They had to proceed "in verye ryotous, outragious, and forcyble manner" apparently. At any rate, they did manage to "take and carrye awaye from thence all the wood and timber thereof unto the Banksyde in the parishe of St Marye Overyes, and there erect a newe playhouse with the sayd timber and wood." This "newe playhouse" they called the Globe, of great memory.

If the unprofitable method of dividing Shakespeare's life into sections be adopted, the first section would be occupied by his life in Stratford, continuing to the visit of the Earl of Leicester's company in 1587. The next period would embrace the years of his obscurity, until his emergence early in 1592 as a reviser of plays at the Rose in Southwark, and extend beyond to cover the subsequent two years, completing the term of his connection with Edward Alleyn's directorship. His work for this period has been seen already. The next section would discover his sudden rise to power and opportunity at the Theater (or, more strictly, perhaps, a little earlier, at the establishment of the Lord Chamberlain's company), and would extend to the razing of that famous playhouse for the erection of the Globe, covering the intercalatory season at the Curtain. His production for this period of time is readily discoverable. For the previous year a divine schoolmaster, by the name of Francis Meres, had published a general collection of apophthegms under the title of "Palladis Tamia." In this he speaks of Shakespeare as a noteworthy person indeed. Says he: "The Muses would speak Shakespeare's fine filed phrase if they could speak English"; and goes on to speak of his excellency " in both kinds for the stage," instancing them thus: *Gentlemen of Verona, Errors, Love's Labour's Lost, Love's Labour's Won, Midsummer Night's Dream,* and *Merchant of Venice,* for the comedies; and *Richard II., Richard III., Henry IV., John, Titus Andronicus,* and *Romeo and Juliet,* for the tragedies. To these he adds mention of the poems, "Venus and Adonis" and "Lucrece"; speaking also of his "sugred sonnets among his private friends." If from these we abstract the plays that Shakespeare would appear to have written prior to his establishment at the Theater, his labour for what has roughly been termed the third period of his life would be: *Love's Labour's Won, Midsummer Night's Dream, Merchant of Venice, Richard II., Henry IV., John,* and *Romeo and Juliet. Love's Labour's Won* is hard to decide on, since it was largely rewritten later even than this, and called *All's Well that Ends Well*—even as *Love's Labour's Lost* was rewritten, to a lesser extent, for the Christmas festivities at the Court for 1597, and printed (for the company's use, if the Cutbert Burby of the title-page be taken as Cuthbert Burbage) the following year. Yet, apart from this, the growth of power in this later text is very marked and distinct.

The erection of the Globe opened the next period in Shakespeare's life, and rang the dominant to which he could not fail to respond. For he was now, for the first time as far as we may judge, a legal partner of a playhouse;—with the settlement of which event he duly received his coat-of-arms. Power was on him; and responsibility. Yet, more than this, a newer opportunity lay to his hand. The playing fields of Finsbury, near which the Theater had lain, were notoriously the resort of the hurly-burly apprentices. The Bankside, however, on which the Globe was built, housed the tennis-courts, to which a gentler congregation was wont to resort. On the first, the higher subtleties of drama would be lost; with the second, they would have a more obvious appeal. In tragedy, the first would demand the trial-scene in *The Merchant of Venice*, with its somewhat obvious stagecraft and its rather fustian appeal; whereas the latter would best appreciate the nunnery-scene in *Hamlet*, with its terrible exposure of ruined faith and sexual abhorrence. In comedy, it would be difficult to imagine *As You*

Like It, which he was just about to write, being produced, as we have it, before the apprentice of Finsbury playing fields. It cannot but be owned that his newer opportunity came fortunately to hand with his growth of power.

His prosperity at this time is evidenced from without and from within. Stratford that had seen creditor after creditor assail the father, now saw debtor on debtor assailed by the son. It is not possible to define his annual earnings at a date so early as this, but his annual profit from his share in the Globe, apart from his similar subsequent share in the Blackfriars, apart, also, from what would be excellent remunerations as actor and playwright, has lately been estimated at the outside figure of £300 in money of the present day.[16] Several reasons weigh against this estimate; yet, even so, it would probably have meant more in Stratford than in London, a matter that is apt to be forgotten. Nevertheless, it is in happy opposition to the conception of Shakespeare as a man whose god was mammon. Yet, with all that, his outward prosperity at this time is not without its proof. The land he had purchased at Stratford was yielding its due of harvest; and we find him, therefore, in July of 1604, suing Phillip Rogers, a fellow-inhabitant of Stratford, who had failed to make payment for malt purchased of him. Other similar litigation between 1600 and 1610, in London and Stratford, stands in witness of his fair worldly estate: a worldly estate that had been added to by the death of his father in 1601, and the passing of the houses in Henley Street to the son.

The inward evidence is not less authentic, yet was soon to be clouded. He had no sooner been settled at the Globe than *Much Ado about Nothing*, *As You Like It*, and *Twelfth Night*, flowed from his pen. Yet these flowed on into the bitter revision of *Love's Labour's Won* to *All's Well that Ends Well* (for which possible development Jaques in Arden and Malvolio in the mad cell gave more than hints), the cynic *Troilus and Cressida*, the tragic *Julius Cæsar*, and *Hamlet*, and the angry *Measure for Measure*. It is curious to note that all the three comedies of this period appear to have been revisions of earlier work of his. It is as though, finding a mordaunt and tragic mood eruptive in him, a mood that seems to touch with a dark abhorrence full of shudders the whole thought of sex, he would not trust himself to structure comedy; and, when he sought to refurbish some earlier work of his in that manner, the darkness swept through him, and, snatching his pen, wrote what it would, and not what he would. Yet this, and what may have caused it, belongs, not to his biography, but to a later framing of the manner of man he was; and may be dismissed for the nonce.

Two matters, however, were to throw a temporary shade over Shakespeare and the affairs at the Globe. The first was the famous " War of the

Theatres." The rare, yet choleric and furious, Ben Jonson was the chief origin of this. Since Shakespeare had accepted his play, *Every Man in His Humour*, in the summer of 1598, he had continued with the company. But in the meantime a fellow-playwright, John Marston, lampooned him on the stage; and won a whipping reply in *Every Man Out of His Humour*. This led to Ben leaving the Globe for the Blackfriars, and the adoption of a cross fusillade of plays.

Yet this was not all. Indeed, it but gave sting to a deeper trouble. For the Blackfriars had been built in 1596 by James Burbage, and leased to a Henry Evans. He installed a company of children's players there, that began straightway to win new favour from the Queen. Thus the Blackfriars was not only the centre from which Ben Jonson waged a war of bitter personalities (in all of which his tenderness for Shakespeare peeps out, even if the latter had indeed caused him to choose some base for his campaign other than the Globe); but the Queen's patronage of that more private playhouse threw the Globe into disfavour. In truth, the Globe had to be closed, and its company had to proceed on travel.

So far as posterity is concerned there is no great cause of complaint in this. For the company proposed to visit the universities; and thus Shakespeare took up the old play on the question of Hamlet's revenge, recasting and rewriting it for that purpose. Hamlet was imbued with profound philosophic thought, being tragic withal, and he and his friend Horatio are seen as students of the University at Wittenberg. In fact the play bears within itself the causes of its origin. For when the players in it arrive at Elsinore, Hamlet at once enquires: "How chances it they travel?" Rosencrantz replies: "I think their inhibition comes by the means of the late innovation," adding, "There is, sir, an eyrie of children, little eyases, that cry out on the top of question, and are most tyrannically clapped for't: these are now the fashion, and so berattle the common stages—as they call them—that many wearing rapiers are afraid of goosequills, and dare scarce come thither."

There is probably a deeper cause for this than appears at first flush: deeper than any mere change of fashion in Court or Queen. For the Essex conspiracy had lately been afoot, and Shakespeare and the Lord Chamberlain's Company had permitted themselves to take an aloof part in it. His play, *King Richard II.*, had been acted prior to 1597, having had two editions published in that year. Yet on none of these occasions had there been pourtrayed the scene in which Richard is deposed. But now, on the testimony of the Queen herself, "This tragedy was played forty times in open streets and houses"; and the deposition scene was played in full. The reason for it was very obvious; for Shakespeare's benefactor, the Earl of Southampton, was involved in the plot; and some such deed by

Shakespeare would be in some manner of exchange for the earlier kindness done him by the Earl. The Queen, however, had not been slow to see the reference; nor had she failed to flash out her anger. "I am Richard II.; know ye not that?" she is reported to have said. Her patronage of children's companies in preference to men's companies, after this, is a very intelligible progression of mind in the irate old Queen, with all that it meant to Shakespeare.

But with the ascension of James in 1603, all this was changed. It now fell to the men's companies to receive the good things of the earth. Back in the year 1599 a party of English players had visited Scotland; and the four Sessions of the Kirk in Edinburgh had met in solemn conclave and "enacted their flocks to forbear and not to come to or haunt profane games, sports, or plays." Whereupon James had promptly summoned the Sessions before him in Council, compelling them, however recalcitrant withal, to withdraw their enactions. Now, as King of England, he had a wider opportunity in which to display his dramatic interest; and he was not slow to take advantage of it. Indeed, he threw his cloak of patronage over as wide a field as it well could cover. The company acting at the Fortune playhouse came under the Prince's patronage; those at the Red Bull passed to the Queen's care; while Shakespeare's company at the Globe became known as the King's men. Nor was this an idle honour. It carried with it for each player a representation as a member of the King's household. It meant that they held official position as Grooms of the Chamberlain, with official fees attached to that honour. It involved attendance at Court, and it led, in 1604, to the whole company being summoned to attend the Spanish Embassador Extraordinary at Somerset House on the occasion of his peace mission. For this Augustine Phillips and John Hemynges, as treasurer and manager of the company, received the official fees in the name of their fellows. These honours, such as they were, were probably the reflex of Shakespeare's earlier disfavour, in more senses than one. For, with the ascension of the King, Southampton was released, and received into high favour.[17]

Yet it meant, not alone a swift ascension for men players, but no less a sharp declension for the children players. So poignant was the case with the latter that Evans was compelled to forego his lease. Thereupon Richard Burbage stepped in. He and the "householders" of the Globe (changed now somewhat from its original holding; for Kempe, clutching at too much, missed all, returning to Henslowe's company at the Globe, whereupon a reconstitution took place) took over the control of the Blackfriars in shares of an equal seventh apiece. Thus again Shakespeare's power was extended, with attendant increase of remuneration.

This was not, however, till 1608. In the meantime the influence of the King had been extended

HIS LIFE

for the fullest advantage of the drama. Faults enough he had; yet his interest in playhouses was not the interested pursuit of personal pleasure it had been with Elizabeth. He was concerned seriously with Dramatic Art. Dramatists were encouraged now to touch loftier and supremer heights, irrespective of puzzled and unappreciative audiences. Jonson, for one, turned now from his Comedies of Manners and his Satires to his *Volpone*, his *Alchemist*, his *Epicœne*. Chapman, too, turned from his comedies to his ponderous, gloomy tragedies. The trend was everywhere. Seeing it, and noting it, it throws a strange illumination over the fact that Shakespeare no longer, now, sought to write comedies, with disastrous effect, as in *Troilus and Cressida* and *Measure for Measure*; no longer held his tragedy in relief, as in *Julius Cæsar*, or endeavoured to mingle it with sardonic humour, as in *Hamlet*: but gave himself over to the full fury and darkness of *Othello*, *Lear*, *Macbeth*, *Timon*. These coincidences of Shakespeare's ripeness of mind with external promptings are curiously interesting.

It has generally been assumed, chiefly on the authority of Nicholas Rowe, that, in the closing years of his life, Shakespeare retired to Stratford, weary and prematurely aged. There is no reason, however, to think this. As has been seen, ever since 1595 he had spent a varying portion of most years at Stratford; and this he continued to do to the end. He had a considerable amount of property there, which would necessarily argue an increasing attention. The sleek unction of Rowe's own words should suggest that his sense of fitness, he being the originator of the idea, stood in function of paternity to the thought. Yet there do not want indications that Shakespeare seemed to feel towards the end that he had filled his round of speech, and wished to make conclusion. His mighty tragedies flowed into a richness of gentle fantasy, mature with wisdom and untroubled in blood, such as bespeak the topmost stones in an arch. Having in mind the whole output of his brain, it is difficult to imagine any further work as succeeding to such plays as *Winter's Tale*, *Cymbeline*, and *The Tempest*. It is no fantasy to see in Prospero, in this last of plays, Shakespeare's whimsical suggestion of himself. For Prospero had to be done with enchantments, or tell his tale twice over. So it was with Shakespeare. He had said his say. More would be a superfluity—which he was too good an artist to desire.

Also, there are inner indications of this. *Cymbeline* could only have been written by a man of power who no longer found any inducement to be powerful. Prospero's account of his earlier life to Miranda flows not so much from a weary pen, as from a pen too slothful for care and craft. All this latter work bears on its face the appearance of having passed through a mind that was full of vitality, whose vitality burst forth ever and anon in sweeping effortless power to lapse again into contented indolence, like some strong-winged gull on a summer's noon.

It was such a mood that probably led him to take up his residence in New Place, which he did at some date prior to 1611. In 1608 his mother had died, the year after his eldest daughter Susanna's marriage with a physician of the name of John Hall. In 1613, during the festivities for the marriage of Princess Elizabeth, seven of his plays were given at Court, *Much Ado about Nothing*, *Tempest*, *Winter's Tale*, *Sir John Falstaff* (probably *Merry Wives of Windsor*), *Othello*, *Julius Cæsar*, and *Hotspur* (probably *Henry IV.*). During the same year, in proof of his buxom interest in this earth, he bought some property, in the form of a house and yard, within a short distance of the Blackfriars playhouse.

All this argues, indeed, an increase of leisure with him. Something of the reason was doubtless, as has been suggested, that he felt he had reaped his harvest of thought. Such moments may be traced in the maturer years of many artists and thinkers. Then there remain but three alternatives: repetition, which the many do; cessation, which the few adopt, among them Shakespeare; and a new fierce burst of exhausting thought, and a reconstruction of all things—a high, but a heroic, thing. Shakespeare left the hero's task to others, and turned to easier ways. It may be, had he lived, he would have re-arisen and wrought anew, for he died in the height of mental power.

Yet the reason for this was not wholly inward. Once again there came the strange outward inducement to synchronise with his mental mood. For the ravages of the plague were heavy in the latter years of his work. Playhouses had continually to be closed for lengthy periods. On one occasion, indeed, they had to be closed for no less a length of time than seventeen months continuously. Moreover, in June of 1613, the Globe was burnt down, and its re-erection caused delay. Very naturally, these things made a considerably lighter call on his pen. It would be unlike human experience if this lengthy taste of ease, coming at the time it did, did not awake in him a sudden desire to continue its peaceful succession. Harness once laid by is not easily taken up again. Moreover, he was prosperous, too, though perhaps not so prosperous as he once was thought to have been: and prosperity and high ideals do not usually cleave fast together. Besides which, the inhabitants of Stratford, finding in him an ease of purse and an indulgent disposition, were not slow, as there wants not evidence to show, to demand local function of him, implying local expenditure.

On April 23, 1616, he died: suddenly. Not altogether unexpectedly, however, for earlier in the year he had drawn up his will, and married his daughter Judith to Thomas Quiney. Tradition has it that Ben Jonson and Michael Drayton were visiting him at the time, and that they "had a merry meeting," whereat "itt seemes" they "drank too hard, for Shakespeare died of a feavour there contracted." On the 25th he was buried in Stratford Church. So the clay of him passed to dust, leaving the fervour of the spirit of him beating quickly in works, that he wrote for his age truly, but which other and all ages have thought to be of vital and perpetual moment—with what cause is the present question. Yet before the permanent matter of his achievement can be touched, it will be necessary to note the temporal conditions to which he had to conform, and the stage which made and marked him.

CHAPTER III

HIS STAGE

Dr Johnson declared of Shakespeare that "he has scenes of undoubted and perpetual excellence, but perhaps not one play, which, if it were now exhibited as the work of a contemporary writer, would be heard to the conclusion." A statement such as that throws one back on thought. What does it mean? There is a certain thing that is Drama. It is a thing apart by itself: apart from the telling of a tale, apart from the depicture of characters, apart from the discoveries, or recoveries, of Poetry, apart from the striking of Wisdom, apart from any enunciation of Truth; however much it may include any and all of these, it is not so much a thing above all these as it is a thing apart from all these. It is a thing in itself. Therefore, if a man should once have created this thing in itself, and if his creation be recognised as indisputably genuine, how comes it, then, that the age that gives the recognition should declare in the same breath that a similar creation in its own day would not be tolerated? Is it false, then, to say that Drama is a thing in itself? Or does Dr Johnson mean that Drama is indeed a thing in itself, but that Shakespeare did not achieve it, but wrought something else? If so, is he to be interpreted as implying that his own age has the monopoly of such creation; or, at least, a monopoly as opposed to the Elizabethan age? Because, if that be the case, it is obvious that the Elizabethans have a precisely similar retort on Johnson, or on any other age that would wish to employ the same argument.

The stout doctor, however, goes on to say: "I am indeed far from thinking, that his works were wrought to his own ideas of perfection; when they were such as would satisfy the audience, they satisfied the writer. It is seldom that authors, though more studious of fame than Shakespeare, rise much above the standard of their own age." Despite the fact that it would be quite possible for the Elizabethans to speak with similar condescension with regard to the eighteenth century, and with a great deal more reason, it is in this, nevertheless, that the thought strikes something, which, if faithfully followed out, would solve the perplexity. For it seems that whatever Drama be in itself, the manner of its appearance depends upon the age which seeks to render it in its own language. When Johnson, that is to say, declared that "perhaps not one play, . . . exhibited as the work of a contemporary writer, would be heard to the conclusion," he meant that his age lacked something that the Elizabethans possessed, a something that won Shakespeare's plays to their whole-hearted attention. Whether that something were good or foolish can very easily be discovered from a comparison of the respective ages.

Yet it means more than merely this. Shakespeare spoke not only a certain emotional language. He had to translate Drama in certain terms of the stage. Even as ancient Æschylus had of need to employ certain mechanisms to render the thing called Drama, for it to have intelligible approach to his audience, so, too, Shakespeare had other mechanisms that he was compelled to use, under pain of silence. It was, indeed, a greater compulsion on Shakespeare than on a dramatist in most other ages; for in his day the appeal of the printed page for dramatic matter was somewhat lightly esteemed. It is not to be imagined that this did not lay its restrictions on him. It harassed him in many ways; but it conveyed a challenge to him. It demanded of him that he should not merely, and grudgingly, employ such conditions as an Elizabethan playhouse and an Elizabethan audience, but that he should so use these things that they should be turned from restrictions to beauties. It asked of him such craftsmanship, that Drama should not be weakened in its translation through conditions, but that it should be strengthened, even as some uncouth word may be turned to music by a richened modulation of voice.

Thus, before any approach can be made to an understanding of Shakespeare, it will be necessary to perceive the stage for which he wrote and the audience he addressed. He must be heard, that is, in the terms of his own speech; and, if possible, it would be well could we discover how some one or other of his plays was organised throughout on his actual stage.

Fortunately it is not impossible for us to recreate in general effect the structure of an average playhouse of the time. For when Shakespeare and his companions erected the Globe, his one-time leader, Edward Alleyn, removed from the Rose near by, and built another playhouse north of the river, in Golden Lane, west of the Curtain, which he called the Fortune. The building contract of this we possess. Moreover, besides providing us with the plans for the building of the Fortune, we have hints in it as to the scheme of the Globe; for it is stipulated continuously that several items are to be structured in the same manner as they are "made and contryved in and to the late-erected Play-house on the Bancke in the said parish of Saint Saviours, called the Globe." Also, there are odd sketches and illustrations in divers places; most of which, to be true, appear to be of doubtful value when tested by internal and external evidence. And there are plays innumerable, some of which do not lack for full and specific stage instructions.[1]

Reconstructed in this way, an Elizabethan playhouse appears as a wooden frame-structure surrounding a yard that lay open to the sky. Seeing that playhouses derived largely from the innyards that preceded them for dramatic display, the origin of this can easily be understood. Thus, too, even as the rooms of the inn surrounded its yard, so here other "rooms" surrounded the yard. The enclosing woodwork, whether circular, as in the Globe, or square, as in the Fortune, was fitted up with chambers, to which access could only be made from the yard. Right on into modern conditions have these rooms prevailed, leaving their last evidence in the "boxes" of the present day; only, with the Elizabethans, the "rooms" ran completely round the frame in three tiers.

So far, so good. In this general scheme of the building there can be no difficulty, so united is all authority. It is when the attention approaches the stage itself, with all the appurtenances thereof, that difficulties begin to arise; and with difficulties, oppositions. There being no obtrusion in the external structure of the building, the actual stage itself lay in the yard, obtruding from the actors' tiring house, and thrust forward like a snout towards the public entrance. Initially, perhaps, it was a mere platform, similar to, though not so lofty as, the platforms that were drawn about the countryside in the old Moralities and Mysteries. Indeed, if one could imagine such a platform set down at one end of an innyard surrounded by the rooms of the inn, one could well discover the birth of the idea for a playhouse. Only, unlike an open platform such as that would have been, the stage in a playhouse was boarded to the ground, and stood scarcely so high as a man's shoulder. Thus, thrust out as it was, it would be surrounded on three sides by those standing in the yard; and actors in the delivery of their lines would often enough be standing right amid their audience —within easy striking distance, be it noted, of a disapproving apple-core.

To the very joints of the stage with the rondure of the house ran the surrounding "rooms"; and behind the stage lay the actors' apartments, with the doors leading from one to the other. If one were to imagine a circular structure (since the Globe certainly was such), an important matter would reveal itself here. For just where the stage joined the building the last room finished. So that if the suggestion of the inner curve of the building was continued on to the stage for a while, and doors cut in it on each side, the result would be that the doors would half face each other and half face outward. This is worthy of notice and attention. For, on general grounds of visual satisfaction, if these doors were now to be used as doors to a building, as often they were, it would be necessary for them to be in sight of the audience. That is to say, they could not face each other. But, on the other hand, Shakespeare, and other dramatists, often cause bodies of soldiers to enter at one door, pass across the stage, and out through the other; as in the first scene of the fourth act of *Hamlet*, and in many other places. Now, if the doors faced foursquare to the audience, this would be at best but a cumbersome proceeding.

Therefore it would be necessary for such doors to lie diagonally, which, it is seen, the very inner curve of the building itself would demand.

How far the curve was continued beyond the doors is immaterial. Probably a space sufficient to attain a general symmetry of design was given before a curtain was hung across from side to side covering a small inner stage. To this inner stage there were also doors; but how many there were cannot be said. If there were three, one at each side, out of sight of the audience, and one in front, then with the curtains drawn the whole stage would have five entrances; whereas with the curtains closed there would be three, the curtain itself being one. It was on this inner stage that Hamlet set his play "wherein to catch the conscience of the king." Above the broken curve provided by the outer entrances and the closed curtains ran a gallery; so that standing on the extreme ends of such a gallery, over the doors, that is to say, it would be possible to see within the inner stage once the curtains were drawn. Within this gallery lay casements: such casements as Romeo leaned out of to view the "jocund day stand tiptoe on the misty mountain-tops." The gallery itself served divers and many purposes. To Romeo it was a window balcony. In *Timon of Athens* it was the top of the wall on which the senators of Athens appeared on the summons of Alcibiades, the closed curtains beneath them being the gates of the city.

HIS STAGE

Over these casements went a shade, spoken of in the Fortune contract as a "shadow," and frequently referred to as the "heavens." It stretched out over, and probably covered about half of, the outer stage, serving the double purpose of a shelter in inclement weather, and, as one of its names implies, a representation of the dome of heaven. This "shadow" was supported at its extreme ends by carved pillars, topped with satyrs' heads, that rested not on the stage, but continued through the stage to the ground. How high this "shadow" was cannot be said; but over it, and extending above the surrounding frame-structure so as to form a turret, the crown of the building lifted its head. This turret, too, served a double purpose. On it was mounted the flag that proclaimed to all and sundry that a play was in progress, or about to begin. Moreover, it would seem that some portion of it extended out over the "shadow." For through the "shadow," or "heavens," heavenly beings were wont to descend on the mortals on the stage below; such as when, in *Cymbeline*, "Jupiter descends in thunder and lightning, sitting upon an eagle." Now, if the turret did not extend out over the "shadow," those standing at the back of the yard, and most of those in the rooms, would be able to see the scene-shifters leaning out of the turret working the pulley apparatus through a hole in the "heavens"! They would even be able to see Jupiter getting on to his eagle, and arranging a flaming appearance! Surely this is scarcely likely to have been the case, since a slight structural device could so easily have obviated it.

Somewhere on the stage, doubtless below the "shadow," a trap-door was cut, leading to the space beneath. Up through this infernal beings rose to the earth above, in contrast to the descent of the heavenly creatures already mentioned. It was thus the various apparitions rose before the conscience-riven Macbeth in his dark consultation with the witches. And in the space beneath walked Hamlet's unhappy forbear, pricking him to resolution. It is worthy of passing note that not all the supernatural beings spurned the five possible entrances available to ordinary mortals; yet there were occasions enough, then as now, on which it was necessary for their manner of appearance to give dramatic pungency to their origin.

In this way it is possible to discover the stage conditions for which Shakespeare wrote. The advantages are obvious. Instead of his characters having to group themselves artificially as in a framed picture, as now, they were enabled to mingle freely as the clash of emotions demanded. Moreover, instead of having to shout out to the audience from an encompassed box, they could speak their lines, as Hamlet demanded they should, "trippingly on the tongue," in something of the swift, earnest speech of daily life, right amid the audience. The test was more natural; and, being more natural, healthier.

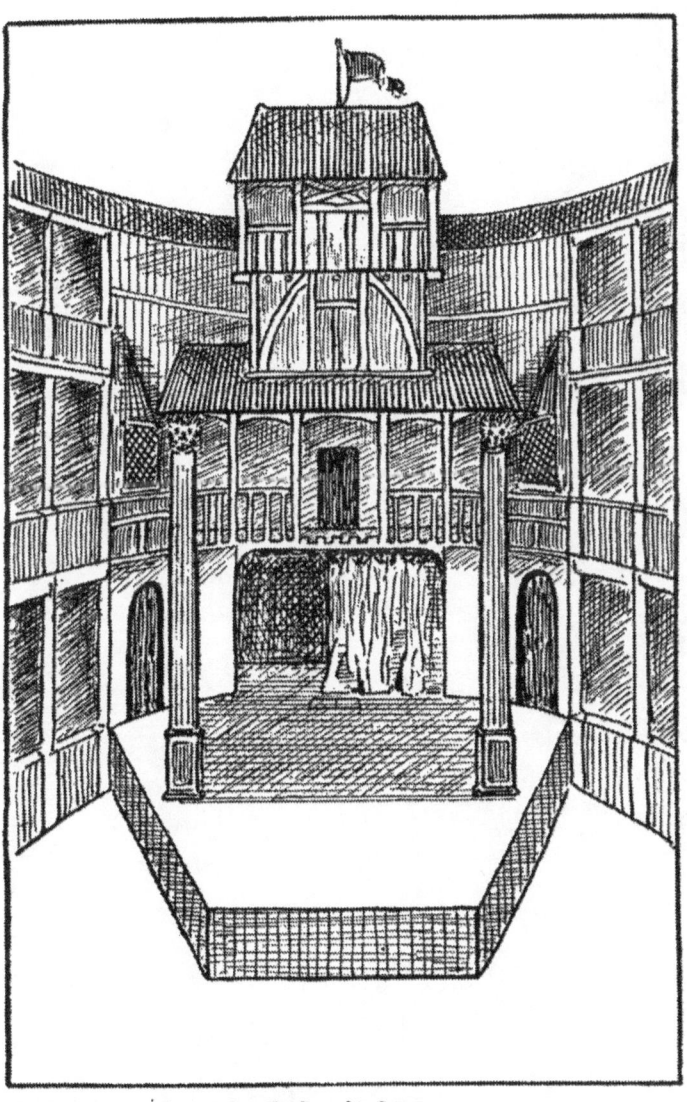

THE · STAGE · OF · THE · GLOBE
Conceived by Darrell Figgis
Executed by H Crespin Scarfe

One of the results was, what has been called, and much miscalled, Rhetoric.² Othello, for instance, expresses himself freely and fully, and with a certain energy that demands a fullness of emotion. Those who say that this energy and fullness are unlike life (which is the only meaning of Rhetoric, Rhetoric being artificiality of speech) can have little knowledge of life. Men under violent stress of emotion do not express themselves in the brevity of the modern dramatist: they express themselves fully, or not at all. If they express themselves fully, they express themselves violently; if they do not speak, they think the more. And to the dramatist the silence means not less than the energy; for, speech being the only agency of drama, it is the business of the dramatist to make the silence voiceful, and fitly voiceful. Not to forestall the deeper discussion that this demands, it is obvious that whereas such energy of speech would necessarily sound pompous spoken from a shut-in box through a picture-frame at the audience, it need not at all be so when spoken on a stage surrounded on three sides by the audience. The very choice of poetic speech is rendered intelligible. For poetry is the most intimate of all things. Nothing evidences this more than the instinctive diffidence of men to utter or recite poetry each to the other. Poetry is the confidence of soul to soul. And when confidences are given they are not hailed out from a distance. They are spoken earnestly at close quarters. It would be difficult to speak such intimacies out through a frame, across an orchestra; but it would be very possible to deliver them at near call. Indeed, the intimacy of distance would demand the intimacy of emotion. For it must ever be remembered that, whereas characters in drama speak to each other, or to themselves, and not to the audience, they speak for an audience to overhear. Moreover, the very spaciousness of the conditions gave its own spaciousness to the drama framed for them, even as the modern confinement of the stage has confined the structure of a modern play.

All this, truly enough, spelt its bondage as well as its liberty, as will be seen. It held the playwright more at the whim of his audience, seeing it was so nigh at hand. Yet it is the present matter, having discovered the structure of Shakespeare's stage, to learn both its manner of manipulation and the use to which he put it. For it has been seen that such a stage consisted of two portions, an outer stage, some portion of which was covered by the "shadow," and an inner stage; between which two a curtain intervened, hanging from the balcony above, and running between the diagonal doorways. At once, then, these interesting questions arise: What distinct purposes did outer and inner stages serve? What was the precise function of the curtain? And what did its drawing or closing imply?

Some confusion has been imported into the question of Shakespeare's stage by the matter of his gentle mockery of the stage conditions of Bottom and his histrionic confederates in *Midsummer Night's Dream*. By some extraordinary mental confusion it has been assumed that the conditions he spun his gentle laughter around were the conditions that prevailed on his own stage; forgetting that in mocking them he implied his height above them. In point of fact there is no reason to suppose that his stage was other than a highly finished and thought-out product. For instance, we know from Henslowe's diary that certain sceneries were employed. We read of his expending money on cloths on which were painted various representations. Yet it is obvious that, on a stage three sides of which were unenclosed, it would be impossible to hang such cloths anywhere save at the back. Properties, even expensive properties, might be placed, and were placed, on the stage, but painted scenery could only be hung at the back. Moreover, since a curtain already hung there in full sight of the audience, such scenery could only be hung behind the curtain, at the back of the inner stage. And thus an important principle appears.

It is clear that if a painted scene hung across the back of the inner stage, and the curtains were drawn, inner and outer stages would not only fall into one, but that the whole would take its character from the scene represented at its far end. It would at once become localised. Whereas, if the curtains were closed, it would simply lose its localisation, and become whatever the dramatist chose to imagine. Obviously localised scenes would more probably be interiors, even as scenes that were not localised would probably be exteriors; but this need by no means have always been the case. In fact, it was not always the case. Yet in the main it was so. When in *The Merchant of Venice* the court of justice was represented, the scenery and properties would be placed on the inner stage, being discovered by the drawing of the curtains; whereupon the whole stage would promptly become the court of justice, and wherever the characters stood, even at its utmost edge, they would yet be in the court. This would not mean that the characters, at the close of the scene, would necessarily have to leave the scene by means of the inner stage doors. For, on a principle that has been excellently stated,[3] it is clearly one matter for a number of characters to emerge naturally from the confined space of the inner stage to fill the whole stage, outer and inner, but quite another matter for them to crowd back together again. In truth, it would not be necessary; for on the drawing of the curtain the two outer doors would become a natural function of the one scene; and characters could issue thereby, one way and another, in as well as out.

This threw another challenge to Shakespeare. It was not possible for him, save on the rarest occasions, to evade half the apt difficulties of a scene by ringing down the curtain at its crucial moment. It was not possible for him to shut off the audience with the hated rivals in a deadly grip, and the agonised maiden gazing on in silent sorrow. Possessing no such cowardly subterfuge, he had to make the rivals make an end of the business; for the fortunate victor to face the agonised maiden with a death on his hands; and for dead and living to be disposed of so as to leave a clean stage. No slight task! Thus it is that we find Fortinbras closing the play of *Hamlet* with the instruction to his soldiers to " Take up the bodies "; with many enough other such instructions in other plays. On the rare occasions, however, on which it was possible for his characters to die on the inner stage, a simpler matter met him. Desdemona's bed, for instance, was an interior property on the inner stage, though most of the characters that later entered the scene, entered by the outer doors, and stood and spoke outside the limits of the curtain. But it was on her bed that she was smothered; and it was across her bed that Othello fell after he had stabbed himself; and thus it is that Lodovico, pointing to the sight, should bid Iago " Look on the tragic loading of this bed "; adding, "Let it be hid," meaning thereby that the curtains should be closed across it.

This principle of localised and unlocalised scenes, or interiors and exteriors, is very important to a right intelligence with regard to Shakespeare. It is not generally remembered that in the plays, as we have them from Shakespeare's hands, there are no scene specifications at all. These are all additions by later officious editors, of whom not a few have hung between Shakespeare and his readers their numerous misunderstandings. In some cases in the First Folio there are not even any indications of scenes where modern editing has interpolated them. For example, one instance will serve; and that an instance where modern editing is enabled to justify itself from the text. In the second act of *Julius Cæsar* the whole act is given on the stage as one continuous scene. The words, Scene I., Scene II., Scene III., and Scene IV., to say nothing of the specifications that follow these instructions, have nothing to do with the text. All four scenes appear as a continuous text under the common heading "Actus Secundus."

The reason for this is obvious. Shakespeare was not concerned with events in Rome. His concern was with the stage of the Globe; on which there could appear no such mimicry of ancient Rome as would enable him to lean on it instead of on powerful writing and forceful acting. All we are permitted to know is that as the act opens we are to be transported to Brutus' orchard, for here we have the more than usually explicit stage instruction, "Enter Brutus in his Orchard." The curtain would be closed across, and Brutus would enter the outer stage from one of the diagonal doorways. Some properties would be distributed about the stage in the shape of chairs and tables; but little else. This must be remembered, not only for a complete understanding of the conditions that beset Shakespeare, but for a right understanding of the very text of the scene in question. The audience would see Brutus enter on to the stage; but they would know nothing further. They would neither know where he was supposed to be, nor whether it was supposed to be day or night. They would only know that an actor had appeared on an open platform stage, around three parts of which they themselves surged; and that the afternoon sun shone about him and them in an open theatre. At one time nuncupation signs were used. It is unlikely that they were ever at any time used regularly; but it is fairly certain that they were seldom, if ever, employed in the maturer days of splendour at the Globe. Thus it lay with Shakespeare so to saturate his dialogue with the necessary environment that the audience would, subconsciously, follow the action in the terms of the imagined scene.

It is interesting to notice with what promptness Shakespeare does this; and how naturally. First, and directly he enters, Brutus calls Lucius. "What, Lucius, ho!" Then he puckers his brow and gazes upward, saying puzzledly:

> I cannot by the progress of the stars,
> Give guess how near to day.

Immediately, with the intentness of minds that did

not think, but perceived only, the audience was aware that the scene was night, and towards dawn. Breaking off impatiently, having, be it noted, conveyed the information quite tersely and naturally, Brutus calls Lucius again:

> Lucius, I say!
> I would it were my fault to sleep so soundly.
> When, Lucius, when? Awake, I say! What, Lucius!

Then Lucius enters through the closed curtains, rubbing his eyes; and if the previous hint had failed, the emotion of night is now unavoidable. It surges about the imagination, and the whole scene is steeped in darkness and mystery and stealthiness.

Nor is the conjured mood permitted to slip back into daylight. Brutus immediately orders Lucius to get him a taper in his study against his coming (a quiet insistence of darkness); and when Lucius returns to tell him it is ready Brutus bids him get back to bed again, because "it is not day." Then when the conspirators knock, and Lucius returns to inform Brutus that Cassius and some others are at the door, but that who the others are he cannot say since "their hats are pulled about their ears, and half their faces buried in their cloaks," Brutus immediately exclaims:

> O conspiracy,
> Sham'st thou to show thy dangerous brow by night,
> When evils are most free? O then, by day
> Where wilt thou find a cavern dark enough
> To mask thy monstrous visage?

How appropriate to the occasion it all is! Yet how telling! It progresses the matter in hand, yet conveys the atmosphere. Similarly, later, when it is desirous that Brutus and Cassius should consult privately together, that thus Cassius should convey a swift information to him concerning the plot in hand, while the two retire to the back of the stage, the others come forward and consult together thus:

Decius. Here lies the east: doth not the day break here?
Casca. No.
Cin. O, pardon, sir, it doth; and yon grey lines
 That fret the clouds are messengers of day.
Casca. You shall confess that you are both deceived.
 Here, as I point my sword, the sun arises;
 Which is a great way growing on the south,
 Weighing the youthful season of the year.
 Some two months hence, up higher toward the north
 He first presents his fire, and the high east
 Stands, as the Capitol, directly here.

Here is exemplified one of the things that pricked Shakespeare into his many vivid nature touches. Where, in those parts of all drama that demand more or less of crafty filling-out, the modern dramatist is so often engaged in would-be small talk, Shakespeare was busy conveying his atmosphere. It had its disadvantages. There is more than a hint often of artifice; but there is no dramatist in which this is not the case. And with Shakespeare it is far less so than with others, since Nature is more natural than small talk: happily so. But what gold ore it has given us! For to this selfsame need of atmosphere conveyed by the lips of the characters are due the many inimitable dawn scenes: such as Romeo's exquisite and " envious streaks that laced the severing clouds in yonder east "; or, when Hamlet, standing on the bare platform of an Elizabethan stage, suddenly exclaimed:

> But see, the morn in russet mantle clad
> Walks o'er the dew on yon high eastern hill,

and so whipped the minds of his listeners to the requisite excitement. All drama is illusion; and illusion of such a nature as this is infinitely more potent than the child's illusion of paints and tinsel, because it operates even there where the conflict itself is occasioned—in the minds of the audience. Not only was this necessity pressed upon Shakespeare by the needs of his stage conditions; there is no doubt it even led him to more intimacy with, and desire for, a knowledge of Nature, so enriching his work in innumerable ways.

To cleave fast, however, to the more immediate matter: When, after Portia has visited Brutus, Lucius and Ligarius enter to him, he bids them go with him that thus, as they go together, he may make them aware of the plot in hand to slay Cæsar. They go; and the stage is left empty. There is no indication in the original text that there is any change of scene; because, in fact, there is indeed no change of scene. The stage is even as it was before. Brutus went off by the left or right door; and, even as he went off, or, more probably, soon after, Cæsar entered by the opposing door or through the centre curtain to the same stage. It lay obviously to Shakespeare's responsibility by some sudden means to convey to the mind of his audience that Cæsar does not enter to Brutus' orchard. And he does it. He does it with such boldness as to startle and arrest. The stage-instruction reads: "Enter Julius Cæsar in his nightgown"! The imaginative readjustment is inevitable; and far more successful than elaborate scenery could have effected. Even as Cæsar started to speak, the privacy of his own house is at once accepted by his hearers. And it is not less swiftly confirmed, for in the tenth line Calphurnia says, "You shall not stir out of your house to-day"; to meet the reply, "Cæsar shall forth."

Similarly when Publius and the conspirators have come to fetch Cæsar to the Capitol, and they all leave the scene for the purpose, Shakespeare has to convey the sense of a different location to the audience by other means than artificial scenery. Again he achieves his end consummately. Previously he had employed the agency of a nightgown. Now he avoids so direct a system: he employs an agency subtler far; but not less successful. Artemidorus enters the scene reading a note of warning he had just penned for Cæsar; and when he has read it, he folds it, saying:

> Here will I stand till Cæsar pass along,
> And as a suitor will I give him this.

So he passes off, while Portia and Lucius enter to the same location.

In this way a complete act, which modern editions have subdivided into four scenes, passed off without let or hindrance in the way of curtain interruptions. The action took place, not on the boards of an Elizabethan stage, but in the minds of the spectators; and when a change of location had to be wrought there, it was struck swiftly, or conveyed subtly, but always achieved successfully. "All Art is a collaboration," a great mind has said; and in this case the collaborators were Shakespeare and his audience. Moreover, dramatic Art is an illusion: and therefore is it the stronger for not being buttressed with mimic reality; it is the nobler for striking to the centre of illusion in the mind of the audience.

It will be noticed, however, that in all this the inner stage had never occasion to be employed. That is to say, no furniture or tapestries were used to localise the scene. How came they to be employed? Moreover, it would be well to discover, if one may, in what manner Shakespeare conveyed an entire play through its course. By such a method it would be possible to search the possibilities of his stage, and also to discover how Shakespeare turned them to service. Yet it is sufficiently difficult to come to a decision. The folly and ineptitude of much editing, in seeking to visualise the imaginary sites instead of seeking to visualise Shakespeare's own stage conditions, has left so broad a scar over all his works that play after play rises insurgent for attention. There are, however, two plays that suggest peculiar complication, because in each of them Shakespeare had thought fit to intertwist a double plot. These are *The Merchant of Venice* and *King Lear*. If the first of these be examined in detail, therefore, Shakespeare will be discovered, not alone in the presentation of one of his dramas, but in one of the most complicated of them.

Nevertheless, before this be done, an instance may be chosen from *Romeo and Juliet* to point the moral and to indicate the procedure. If the fourth scene of the first act in all modern editions be turned to, it will be discovered that "Romeo, Mercutio, Benvolio, with five or six Masquers, Torchbearers, and others," enter on what is declared to be "A Street." Having concluded their dialogue, and having heard Romeo's "On, lusty gentlemen!" we learn that they make their *Exeunt*. The next scene in its turn is declared to be "A Hall in Capulet's House"; and in the midst of it we learn that there "Enter Capulet, Lady Capulet, Juliet, Tybalt, and others of the house, with the Guests and Masquers." There is no hint of Romeo, be it noted. He, being a Montague, obviously could not enter with the Capulets' private company. Since he made his departure from the previous "scene" we have not heard of him. Nevertheless, in line thirty-nine of this present "scene," suddenly we discover him asking one of the servants, "What lady's that, which doth enrich the hand of yonder knight?" How he made his entrance we are not informed; and it is not customary in such matters to think him dropped by an angel there. It is strange. It is perplexing. Turning, however, to the First Folio, to the text uncontaminated by modern editing, the whole perplexity resolves itself into a matter of ease and simplicity. We learn there, that in the middle of the first act, the stage being empty, there "Enter Romeo, Mercutio, Benvolio, with five or six other Maskers, Torchbearers." And when Romeo calls his "On, lusty gentlemen," they do not pass from the stage at all. The word *Exeunt* is lacking. Instead, we read (what modern editing has thought fit altogether to delete): "They march about the stage, and servingmen come forth with their napkins." In other words, while Romeo and his comrades retain possession of the outer stage, the curtains are drawn aside, revealing the equipment for a feast. The scene thus is swiftly converted into an interior; and out from the inner stage issue the servingmen. When they in their turn have accomplished their task of moving the trenchers, joint-stools, court-cupboard, plate, and provender from the inner stage to the outer, as their chatter together indicates, they pass off the stage by one of the doors. Directly they have done this, we read, "Enter all the Guests and

Gentlewomen to the Maskers "—a stage instruction that makes ironical comparison with the emendation of modern editors. Thus it is simplicity itself to account for Romeo's appearance. He was all the time on the stage! It is all so simple that one can but marvel at the ineptitude displayed in modern texts. But the height of very humour is reached when one remembers that the text has to be mutilated to achieve it. Yet now an important consideration asserts itself. For the whole stage, both inner and outer portions of it, is full. Tables, and the general equipment of a feast, bestrew it. However much the players may leave the stage, it is obvious that there can be no further acting on it till there has been a general clearance. Then we discover that the act closes here, so that an opportunity might be afforded to this end before another act should occupy the stage. And since the next act is opened by a chorus, in function of Prologue, it is easy to see that this is to cover the operations of the removers, for there very likely was no cessation in the acting from beginning to end of a play.

In similar manner, in the next act, there is neither orchard nor wall, nor climbing of walls, nor leaping down from them. These are all the fanciful exploits of middle-aged gentlemen in search of excitement as editors. The simple stage instruction is, "Enter Romeo, alone." He enters by one doorway, or from the balcony, and, as he speaks the two lines apportioned to him, he steps to the back of the stage. When he has made his way there, and spoken his two lines, Benvolio and Mercutio enter by the opposite doorway (it is well to remember that these doors were probably always open, unless certain effects were to be achieved) and proceed at once to the front of the stage calling for Romeo; who, they declare, had "run this way and leapt this orchard wall." The wall was imagined as off the stage. If they both came down from the balcony above, that might truly have been imagined as the wall; but this is unlikely for several reasons, the chief of which being that the balcony in question is forthwith to figure as the balcony of Juliet's room. Yet, wherever the orchard wall was, it is at least certain that they are all on the same side of it: that is to say, they are all on the one common stage, Romeo at the rear, and Benvolio and Mercutio in front calling for him. Nor were the audience called upon to imagine anything save such as the stage itself suggested. For example, Romeo being to the rear of them, they might well not see him—the more so as he would obviously desire them to miss him, and would therefore not obtrude his presence. He could see them, however. And he could hear them. For Mercutio jests shrewdly to Benvolio on love's wound; and when they both have gone, Romeo comes forward, saying: "He jests at scars that never felt a wound." In truth, and indeed, it is actually suggested that Romeo deliberately avoided them. For Benvolio, as they go, says:

"Go, then, for 'tis in vain to seek him here, that means not to be found." There was never any attempt on Shakespeare's part to mar likelihood. It was all clean and straightforward, in the full view of his audience; a continuous, complete, plausible, united scene; till after Juliet's appearance at her casement. Then when she has retired, and he has passed out the way he came, the curtains of the inner stage are drawn aside to discover the Friar's apartment, and the Friar alone there with a basket before him.

Thus, the *Merchant of Venice*, with its continuous employment of inner and outer scenes, is arrived at. With all its complexity of plot, with all its ramification in detail, it is nevertheless doubtful if there need have been any halting or abeyance in the continuous acting of this play. The words would be spoken "trippingly on the tongue": swiftly, that is, eagerly, and with zest, such as the intimacy with the audience would permit. Never would the interest be permitted to flag. Never would the quickening plot abate from its gathering intensity. Never would the moment of momentum be lost by the need for scenic alteration. Once the interest is struck in the minds of the audience, it is continued swiftly to the end of all.

As the first act opens, the curtains are closed across, and the two outer doors are open. To the outer stage, then, there enter Antonio, Salarino, and Salanio, speaking together. With Antonio's gentle melancholy the mind is made ready for a tenderness in him for friendship; and with the entrance of Bassanio, with his declared wish to court the fair Portia, and Antonio's offer to him to pledge his credit to the utmost to find the money withal, the whole business of the play is set afloat. Then they leave the stage together; and as they do so, the curtains of the inner stage are withdrawn, and Portia is either found, or enters, within, speaking with her maid Nerissa. In fine, by the drawing of the curtains the whole stage is forthwith converted into an interior, in keeping with whatever scenery and furniture chances to be found on the inner stage. As Portia and Nerissa speak together the general question of her courtship, the formidable obstacle of the casket is broached, and we are given to learn that Bassanio's courtship will be no trite affair. Yet they passed off; and as they do so, the curtains are closed across at once, and the stage is again unlocalised. No sooner has this been done, however, than Shylock walks through one of the outer doorways, followed by the supplicating Bassanio, and, later, the gentle Antonio. In three swift scenes, so, with neither stay nor hesitation, the act closes, and the whole business of the play is before us, with its possible perplexities and complexities hinted in the ear.

Yet it is extremely doubtful if there were any halt at the conclusion of the act. Certainly there need not have been. As Antonio and Bassanio follow Shylock to the Notary's, and proceed off the outer stage, the curtains could be drawn aside at once, making the stage once more an interior, with the memory in the mind of the audience that it had last been identified with Portia's room. As the curtains are drawn, there is a flourish of cornets, and Portia and Morocco appear, followed by their several trains. She leads him to the Caskets, across the inner stage, where the dialogue takes place. In fact, the scene is as though it were a sudden arrest of their progress to the Caskets, in order that the audience may learn that the judgment of the stipulated formula is already proceeding. The curtains are closed again, and Launcelot Gobbo enters the outer stage. After his soliloquy his antique father enters to him. Indeed, Bassanio, Leonardo, Gratiano, and the two Gobbos pass off and on throughout the scene; but the chief matter is, and the most important, that the audience is clearly informed (or as clearly, that is to say, as the two Gobbos have power to render their interesting suit) that Launcelot is to leave Shylock's service in order to enter Bassanio's so soon as he can take leave of his old master. This may seem a simple matter. It is. Yet it is subtle withal. For, apart from the fact that the interchange of service is to bring him more before the attention of the audience in his capacity as Clown, the hint thrown out is to obviate any possibility of confusion in the next scene. When Bassanio and Gratiano pass off, the curtains again are drawn aside. When last this happened the interior suggested was Portia's, and the audience might well think, in the continuity of imagination, that this again was so. But they cannot. There is Launcelot; and the scene is fixed forthwith, and surely, as an interior in the Jew's house. There is no deliberation demanded of the audience; the thing is wrought imaginatively for them with no possibility of failure. The subconsciousness has been smitten. Furthermore, by the same means the young girl who enters with him, and who has not previously been seen, is also fixed forthwith, and surely, as Shylock's daughter. And as she tells of her love for Lorenzo, who, she declares, is Bassanio's guest, another knot is tied in the plot, and the perplexity still further ravelled.

Nor is it permitted to remain at that. She passes off, and, the curtains being closed, the scene is again an exterior. To this there enter four men, three of whom have already been seen, Gratiano, Salarino and Salanio, and one who is a stranger. Then there enters Launcelot with the letter Jessica has lately entrusted to him. This he hands to the stranger; who therefore is known for Lorenzo. Never once, thus, is the attention of the audience permitted to slip from the criss-cross texture of the plot. No stitch is dropped. All is gathered up, and presented as a complete whole, however involved. And there are those who say that Shakespeare had no skilled craftsmanship!

Yet they, too, go their way; and as they go, Lorenzo informs Gratiano that Jessica is to flee with him, with what of the Jew's money she may be able to bring with her. Two things are wrought thereby. The first is that Shylock, through his daughter, Lorenzo, Gratiano, and Bassanio, in link on link, is now joined up in unity with Portia and the casket. The second is that in the scene to follow the whole interest is made poignant and vivid. For there we learn that it is Shylock's intention to be away from home that evening; and that so an opportunity is hung out for Jessica's escape.

Be it noted that as Gratiano and Lorenzo issue off by one doorway the other door might well be closed. Or the door they pass through may be closed after them. Either of which doors, as Shylock, with Launcelot, enters the outer stage after them, might serve as the door for his house. Yet it is more likely that both doors are left as before, and that the closed curtain is made to serve that purpose. Through this, as he hails her, she issues to him, to receive the keys of the house, with his charge to guard it zealously: she who is pledged to Lorenzo. Says he:

> Lock up my doors, and when you hear the drum
> And the vile squeaking of the wry-neckt fife,
> Clamber not you up to the casements then,
> Nor thrust your head into the public street
> To gaze on Christian fools with varnished faces:
> But stop my house's ears, I mean my casements,

> Let not the sound of shallow fopperie enter
> My sober house.

Even as he speaks Lorenzo's last words are up-called: "Fair Jessica shall be my torch-bearer." So he passes off, and she enters the house, while after them both enter the various maskers. Among them comes Lorenzo, who at once hails her. She appears to him at the casement above. Throwing down to him the casket containing the ducats and jewels of much subsequent lament, she disappears; to appear again below, finally to pass off with the maskers as Lorenzo's torch-bearer.

The next scene demands attention. The stage instruction reads: "Enter Portia with Morocco, and both their trains." The first words of the excellent Portia are: "Go, draw aside the curtains, and discover the several caskets to this noble Prince." The suggestion is clear, though it calls for understanding. When Lorenzo and Jessica, with the others, have passed on one side, Portia and Morocco enter on the other. At her first words the curtains are flung aside. The casket on a table, with the other requisite furniture, are discovered within, and the scene becomes an interior. It will be noticed that for one brief moment the scene is neither exterior nor interior. Yet this would be little likely to win notice. It would assuredly not swing the attention aside. And at worst, it would not intrude artificiality more than can often enough be noticed on a modern stage.

Yet, be that as it may, the caskets are discovered to Morocco, and he makes his fatal choice and passes to oblivion. "A gentle riddance," says Portia: "draw the curtains, go: let all of his complexion choose me so." With the word the curtains are drawn to a flourish of cornets, and the stage appears again as an exterior. To this Salarino and Salanio enter to tell of Shylock's mingled grief for his stones, his ducats, and his daughter, with the hint of a possible failure of Antonio to the Jew's bond. Their business done, the curtains are again drawn, this time at Nerissa's desire:

> Quick, quick I pray thee, draw the curtain strait,
> The Prince of Arragon hath ta'en his oath,
> And comes to his election presently.

The servitor she has with her draws the curtains, and Portia is now discovered entering the inner stage, with the Prince of Arragon for his ill-fated choice. When he has gone, she says, "Come, draw the curtain, Nerissa," and passes on to the outer stage to learn that Bassanio has arrived.

So closed the second act. Then to the open stage left by the passage of Portia and Nerissa came Salanio and Salarino, with Shylock following them, in order that the Jew's claim for the redemption of his bond may now loom as a possibility. Again the alteration of scenes is adopted, and the inner stage reveals the casket-scene again, with Bassanio to make his happy decision and choice.

When he has made his choice through the front doorways, there enter Lorenzo, Jessica, and Salerio, bearing a letter that informs Bassanio that Shylock has now indeed claimed his bond. Away speeds Bassanio to attend to it; the curtains are drawn; and to the outer stage enters the Jew, with a following and supplicating Antonio: the pathos following hard on the heels of the hint of it.

The next scene again, in its turn, employs the inner stage, when Portia determines to proceed to Antonio's assistance. Then the curtains are drawn, while Launcelot and Jessica, with subsequently Lorenzo, enter to an outer and unlocalised scene. While this is taking place the inner stage is rapidly being altered; so that, on its conclusion, the curtains may be withdrawn again to display the Duke and the Magnificoes entering to a scene that has been set out as a Court of Justice. Now in this scene Shakespeare's deft manipulation of his stage conditions is somewhat finely exemplified. In the earlier interior scenes it is doubtful whether or not the characters flowed out from the exact properties of the inner stage to the outer stage. There certainly was no need for them to have done so; yet, had they done so, it would not have been very difficult for them to return thither whence they came. The very lack of necessity for such an overflowing would have made its rectification easy. The few characters deployed would have obviated difficulty in both cases — though it should always be borne in memory that, with the curtains withdrawn, the doors of the outer stage became doors leading to and fro from an interior scene, so that the scene could always have been emptied with ease. But in the present instance there are many manifest difficulties. Be it noticed how they are overcome. The curtains being drawn, the Duke and the Magnificoes enter by the doors of the inner stage and take their seats. This being done, Shylock enters by one of the doors of the outer stage; from which doors enter Nerissa and Portia in their turn. Both stages are now fairly full, though it must needs be emphasised that the court properties are placed behind the curtain opening on the inner stage. It would, therefore, not be possible for him to adopt the modern subterfuge of dropping a curtain on a stage full of characters standing in the artificial proportions of an effective picture. Had the curtains been closed over, the stage properties and fittings, the Duke and the Magnificoes, and probably Portia and Nerissa, as the Doctor of Laws and his attendant, with perhaps also Antonio, would have been shut off, and the rest would have been left, sans occupation and sans justification, on a scene unqualified. Manifestly, this would never do. Note how the difficulty is overcome.

First, Shylock is dismissed. The subsequent company to be left must be one of mutual gratulation; and so he certainly cannot be permitted to remain. Therefore he must go before the Duke and his company. This is a matter of absolute necessity; yet, therewithal, with what splendid psychology and with what aptness his dismissal is effected. He being gone, however, there remains the inner stage to clear. So the Duke and his train pass through the doors of the inner stage. After them go Portia and Nerissa. Persistently thus, and unobtrusively, the number of characters are reduced to manageable proportions. Then Gratiano is sent after them; and when he is gone, Antonio, Bassanio, and their friends pass out through one of the outer doorways, while with their going the curtains are drawn, and the whole stage is again clear. For the sake of argument it may be imagined the Duke and his train, followed by Portia and Nerissa, after whom speeds Gratiano, have all issued out by the left door of the inner stage, while Antonio and Bassanio take their ways by means of the right door of the outer stage. When the curtain is drawn, then, what better and more natural sequence could be imagined than Portia and Nerissa, followed by Gratiano, should enter the now empty stage by the left door of the outer stage? The very fact would suggest a continuity of action between their exit in the previous scene and their entrance in this: such a continuity of action as it is obvious Shakespeare had in mind. The subtlety of Elizabethan stage management will never be understood unless such swift ellipses be received into the imagination. Surely they had their counterpart in the mind of the audience. An ellipsis is always the product of imaginative excitement: and to such an excitement an audience was inevitably wrought. For example: if the curtains were drawn, and a man were thus discovered sitting in a furnished room; and if then he were to rise and pass to the outer stage, while the curtains were closed behind him—obviously, and without any lack of propriety, even without thinking of it—any receptive audience would construe him as having passed out of the house into the street. And the Elizabethans were full of this.

To conclude, however! There is but one scene in the fifth act. While Gratiano was engaged in delivering his own and Bassanio's rings to Portia and Nerissa, behind the curtains the scene is being rapidly altered. The court properties are removed. Then, when Portia, Nerissa, and Gratiano have passed off, the curtains are drawn, and the whole scene becomes a garden, since garden properties, including a grassy bank, are discovered on the inner stage. Thus passes the whole play in one unruffled movement, with neither catch, hitch, nor halt.

Such an achievement for such a play is not only noteworthy, but was possible only on such a stage as Shakespeare wrote for. Doubtless the stage was largely framed for the conditions of such plays. Yet, even so, it demanded a skilled craftmanship. Other playwrights there were, writing for the same conditions; and an attentive examination of their plays seems to indicate that so smooth and complete a movement would call for not a little ingenuity in presentation, if indeed it were possible at all. Others, too, such as Ben Jonson, who in their infinite love for classic conditions framed the action of their plays in such a way that they offered little variety of position. It was left to Shakespeare to open wide the range of his play and yet pass it off in one complete movement, like some wave of the sea swelling, rising, and passing away in easy grace of action. In truth, the very variety was wrung from him by an imperious necessity. It is obvious that an audience put to the task of attending so long a performance, unbroken withal, would discover an intolerable strain in too fierce an insistence on the dominant. This Shakespeare speedily perceived. So he passed from anxiety to humour; returning to anxiety anon, knowing that his audience would follow him now with quick memories and refreshed thews. Had an audience dispersed to regather at the conclusion of each act or scene, it would have dissipated the sequence of their memory. Had he compelled their attendance, and not have given them relief, the tense and continued strain of emotion would have wearied and exhausted them. But his stage permitted him to do both; and he seized on the proffered advantage eagerly, using it to the full. This, in its turn, held out to him another possibility which he was not slow to see.

It has ever been the desire of dramatists to achieve the fine irony of simultaneous actions working in unknown opposition to each other. In ancient Greek drama the remote action, whether of gods or mortals, was hinted obscurely in the chants of the chorus. In the artificial conditions of modern drama this end is sought by passing deadly enemies alternately across a common room; for changes of location being infrequent, owing to cumbrous scenery, either the irony must be lost or the conflicting agencies must be brought to a common centre at all cost of probability. But Shakespeare had only deftly to use the inner and outer stages, arresting one action for the due display of the other; and if he chose, or created, suitable moments for each action to give place to the other, so that they might almost seem to pass each into the other, the effect of mutually interdependent action suggested in this way would be tremendous. Such a thing may be discovered in the famous third act of *King Lear*. At the conclusion of the second act the tempest-driven King has virtually been expelled from the castle that contains the daughters who have flaunted him. We would follow them both, the daughters and the father. If we followed the father to the end of his urgent grief, then our thoughts would seek to learn what should befall the daughters at the consummation of their desires, not to speak of old Gloster left in their untender care. Similarly, had we continued in Gloster's castle, our thoughts must inevitably have hungered after the King in his sorrow. But we are doomed to neither; we go with them both. The inner stage becomes the castle's interior; the outer stage is the storm-tost heath, with one of its doorways serving for the entrance to the requisite hovel. And when at last the King, in Scene VI., is brought out of the storm, in his opening words Gloster is careful to indicate that the outer stage is no longer the furious heath, saying : " Here is better than the open air." Moreover, it is worthy of note that this is one of the rare places in the plays as they came from Shakespeare's hands that the scenes are definitely indicated as Scene Prima, Scene Secunda, and so forth.

Many things fall into orderly understanding once such fundamental principles of stage organisation are clearly perceived. Asides, for example, the derision of many a critic, can very properly be understood. When in the third scene of the first act of *Macbeth*, that aspiring chieftain declared that "this supernatural soliciting cannot be ill; cannot be good," there was nothing in it that could not have been dramatically probable. Ross and Angus had entered to the stage by the door opposite to that by which Macbeth and Banquo had entered, soon after the witches disappeared down the opening in the stage. Such an opening would probably have been within the line leading from entrance to entrance. The four of them—Macbeth, Banquo, Ross, and Angus—had spoken awhile together ; and then Banquo took the latter two aside a moment for a word, saying,

"Cousins, a word, I pray you." Musingly there, Macbeth, left alone, ejaculates his wonder at the coincidence he was after having revealed to him. Then, with a courteous bow, and "I thank you, gentlemen," he walks to the front of the stage, a matter of some fifteen to twenty feet, to struggle with the thoughts that arise in him. Nor need he thus have spoken so loudly that his three friends behind him could have heard more than a mere murmur of his speech.

The far more dramatic matter of soliloquies is expounded too. And here an important reference asserts itself for more adequate interpretation. The visit of Shakespeare and his company to Oxford with *Hamlet*, and other plays, moved some unknown but worthy person there to display the chief of these actors in cavalierly derision of university methods in drama. Whether he wished to display the amazing ignorance of such heroes as these travelling actors, or to scoff at his magisterial colleagues, is immaterial; but the following passage is famous:

> *Kempe.*—The slaves are somewhat proud, and besides it is a good sport in a part to see them never speake in their walke, but at the end of the stage, just as though in walking with a fellow we should never speake but at a stile, a gate, or a ditch, where a man can go no farther.
>
> *Burbage.*—A little teaching will mend these faults, and it may bee besides they will be able to pen a part.
>
> *Kempe.*—Few of the University plaies well, they smell too much of that writer *Ovid*, and that writer *Metamorphosis*, and talke too much of *Proserpine* and *Juppiter*. Why heres our

> fellow Shakespeare put them all downe, I and Ben Jonson too. O that Ben Jonson is a pestilent fellow, he brought up Horace, giving the poets a pill, but our fellow Shakespeare hath given him a purge that made him bewray his credit.

Kempe's later speech has formed the base of many an edifice that struck at the stars. It has, indeed, withdrawn attention from his earlier comment; which is not less important. There he says that ambitious university actors never deliver their speech save "at the end of the stage," the implication being, obviously, that actors at the Globe spoke all the way. What he is concerned with, it seems, is that a speechless walk of this description (the distance from curtain to stage front being, at the Fortune, for example, nearly thirty feet) could not help but be an awkward and stilted proceeding. In other words, an earnest conversation would cover and give grace to such a walk across a bare stage. Now this would be admirable if two or more were to enter together. But how if occasion required that one should enter alone, and hold the dramatic situation in reception of others? He too would need to cover the walk across the stage, from the entrance to the audience, with the grace of speech. And so soliloquy would be thrust upon the dramatist, to grow in his hands to richer subtlety of usefulness.

Far more so than with the stage of a later day the audience held the mastery of the situation.

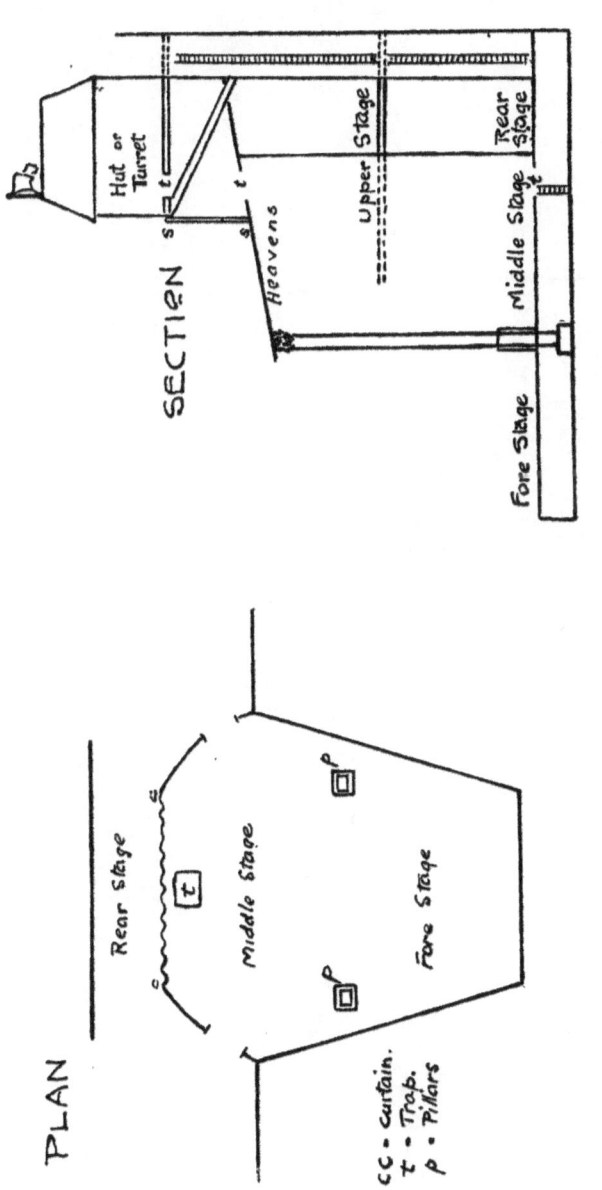

And this had its vices with its virtues. It has already been indicated that, however Shakespeare's genius was riper for greater things than his wont had been, he was yet held back until either a different audience, or a loftier authority, flung loose the reigns upon him. Whatever strength he achieved, he achieved not by escaping difficulties but by solving them. He could not withdraw himself into the remoter security of an aloof stage. He could not write a choice and select drama for a few sympathetic souls. If he rose to heights, he had to carry the groundlings with him. If he chose to wing the blue, he had to make this course in the empyrean very clear to the general. It was the Titan's task that was given him. That is to say, he had to lift as well as to mount: he had to strike an apprentice's imagination aflame with his own ere he could proceed. His Joy was indeed in widest commonalty spread: and his Terror also.

How he turned their demands into dramatic beauty, and how he failed therein, is itself a study. For example, near to the Globe was a Bear Garden, where sturdy wrestling was to be beheld. So to win an audience to view his drama he gave them the further addition of wrestling (and manful wrestling be very sure it was) in *As You Like It*. Fencing, too, they could see: and so plot and counterplot in *Hamlet* culminate in the foils. It has also been said that the continual use of music throughout all the plays, and the continual firing of ordnance, as twice in *Hamlet*, and repeatedly in the historical and other plays, were to the same end. But this is surely to misunderstand. Not that the audience failed to appreciate them. In truth it may be said that they would be urgent for them were they baulked of them. But the primary purpose was surely a far more insidious matter. For the playhouses were open structures; and thus the effect of music and ordnance would be to advertise the playhouse in question, with its postered play, far and wide. And this was a thing a dramatist, who also happened to be householder in a playhouse, could not afford to neglect.

Topical allusions, too, could not fail to find ready acceptance at the attention of such an audience. With what deftness they are thrown about the plays the textual critic can speedily tell: for by means of them has he often been enabled to date the writing of a play. For example, the nurse says of Juliet, " 'Tis since the earthquake now eleven years, and she was weaned." By such a clue we may discover when Shakespeare first drew out the play he subsequently largely rewrote. But as the lines were spoken there would not fail to be reminders from the wiseacres in the yard of a remembered earthquake in 1580; and such a hint would give not less assistance to a play than a turn of humour in passing. Such an allusion, it is true, would be remote. Yet a more direct illusion is furnished in *The Tempest*, and was actually the origin of one of Shakespeare's strangest creations. In 1600 certain sailors returned to England with an extraordinary account of a shipwreck on one of the islands in the Bermudas—" the still-vexed Bermoothes." They spoke of " the fairies of the rocks" being like "flocks of birds," and " the devils that haunted the woods" like " herds of swine." While this was fresh and still wonderful in the minds of the people, Shakespeare gave them Ariel and Caliban.

Yet, with whatever skill Shakespeare could turn to beauty the cravings of his audience they irked him not the less. We know, for instance, that soon after the Globe was built Kempe, who had continued with Shakespeare since the old days at the Rose in Southwark, and who was now a "householder" in the Globe, disassociated himself from his company and returned to Edward Alleyn, relinquishing his shares jointly to Shakespeare, Heminges, and Phillips. No doubt this was because in the opinion of his copartners he was ambitious for too much power. But that it was traceable to Shakespeare's distaste to subserving the groundlings is evident in several ways. For Kempe's fame as a comedian was not wholly dramatic. His famous dance from London to Norwich in 1600, with a large and unwieldy audience following him, is itself sufficient to prove that, were there not other indications also. This we know. And we know, too, that Hamlet spoke to the players that had come to Elsinore in this wise: " And let those that play your clowns speak no more than is set down for them: for there be of them that will themselves laugh, to set on some quantity of barren spectators to laugh too; though, in the meantime, some necessary question of the play be then to be considered: that's villainous, and shows a most pitiful ambition in the fool that uses it." It demands but little perception to see the connection between this and the dissatisfaction of so famous an extempore wit as Kempe; and so, too, one sees how grudgingly Shakespeare regarded these fools that the people demanded of him in his plays. The whole thing irked him; and in his hour of profounder gloom, it disgusted him. In Touchstone, and the fool in *King Lear*, he might turn this craving on the part of his audience to triumphant account; but how grudgingly he regarded the necessity may be known by the fact that it is with surprise and mystification one learns that there is a clown in *Othello*. It was peculiarly characteristic of Shakespeare that, even while he despised the demand, he should grant it. Ben Jonson would have none of it. He despised fools; and he dismissed fools. But Shakespeare, if he could find a function for them, made splendour out of them; and if he could wake no splendour from them, thrust them into *Othello* to fare as they might, gave them over to disgust and bitterness with Thersites in *Troilus and Cressida*, made them supererogatory in *Twelfth Night*, and even threw a sop to the audience by making the fool in *King Lear* recite doggerel at the conclusion of some of the scenes, when his own interest had concluded, and while his characters were withdrawing from the stage.

Moreover, his audience demanded of him a thing that his stage peculiarly fitted him to give; which, indeed his temperament was by no means averse to. The passage already referred to, in which Hamlet advises the chief of the players as to how his subordinates should comport themselves on the stage, has a many-hued importance. His ideas of dramatic practice are there clearly communicated; and thus his ideas of dramatic creation may also be discovered. We hear Hamlet say, for instance, " In the very torrent, tempest, and, as I may say, the whirlwind of passion, you must acquire and beget a temperance that may give it smoothness. O," he adds, " it offends me to the soul to hear a robustious perriwig-pated fellow tear a passion to tatters, to very rags, to split the ears of the groundlings; who, for the most part, are capable of nothing but inexplicable dumb-shows and noise." Now such a passage demands grave attention. For it is obvious that, however much it wounded his own soul, it very well suited the groundlings. Apart from his own testimony to that effect, the groundlings of the present and every age arise in proof of that. This being so, it being undeniable that they did demand a passion that loosed itself to the full in free declamation, and it being as undeniable that Shakespeare was himself, in his plays, not less fond of a fury of passionate utterance, it is an easy deduction that the first, if not the cause of the latter's being, was at least the vice that tempted the latter to exert and exercise itself.

We think of Marlowe's *Tambourlaine*, of the *Spanish Tragedy* and so through Shakespeare's own histories, through *Juliet*, on to *Othello, Lear, Macbeth*, and *Timon*, and we discover how the free declamation that an intimate stage permitted, could be demanded by an audience that was but crude, and turned finally to terror and beauty. This Shakespeare seems very well aware of. It was the very freedom of declamation that called up a passion of speech. But now he turns about and demands that declamation should be dismissed since the passion of speech was in itself sufficient: though he is careful to add, "Be not too tame neither, but let your own discretion be your tutor."

This freedom of emotional stress in speech merits its subsequent examination; but at the moment it is necessary only to point out the temptations to tumid language that his stage gave him, and to discover with what ruthlessness his audiences could demand it of him. The ill portion of an apple was probably one of the most gentle methods of enforcement. Bombast they asked, and bombast they would have: so, in the manner of him, he gave it them, and reviled at them for their evil taste. One goes far from understanding Shakespeare until one realises that probably he would be the first himself to condemn much of his own work. In his full tragic strength his speech rarely, if ever, loses touch with a full flow of passionate emotion, however much it would seem to toss at the stars. That is to say, even as when the audience demanded them a fool, and he could give them the fool in *Lear*, so when they demanded bombast he could give them Othello's farewell to all that till then had made life for him. But, on the other hand, and particularly in his earlier days, in gratifying the demand on the part of his audience, he filled his plays only too often with some most intolerable fustian.

There was the fustian of conceit: such as the passage already quoted from Romeo's love-lorn discipline. Indeed, so much of *Romeo and Juliet* as seems clearly to belong to the first draft of that play, is full of it. So, also, is the inflated *Love's Labour's Lost*, and all the early plays; for it was the first folly Shakespeare had to rid himself of. Also there was the fustian of fury. Perhaps the prime example of this is King Henry's

>Once more unto the breach, dear friends, once more;
>Or close the wall up with our English dead!
>In peace there's nothing so becomes a man
>As modest stillness and humility:
>But, when the blast of war blows in our ears,
>Then imitate the action of the tiger;
>Stiffen the sinews, summon up the blood,
>Disguise fair nature with hard-favoured rage:
>Then lend the eye a terrible aspect;
>Let it pry through the portage of the head
>Like the brass cannon;

and so forth; in the midst of a battle; while the soldiers arrange themselves round to hear him. Of this the whole play reeks; as do the histories. A subtler manifestation is the fustian of sentiment. For man very properly recognises that sentimentality is a saving grace in him against brutality. He recognises sentiment as emotion gone astray, or strangled by convention; and he knows emotion to be the divine in him. So he holds sentimentality in tender regard; and is moved by its display in drama. More of this anon. Let it now only be seen that sentiment, while good in default of better, is yet not the most excellent. For example, the whole trial-scene of *The Merchant of Venice* merits examination. It is full of the fustian of sentiment. Very little springs from the reality that constitutes the base of drama. The whole figure of Portia as a doctor of laws is an appeal merely to the picturesque. We know all the time that the whole thing is make-believe; and that neither the Duke nor the Magnificoes, nor any of them, would have accepted her in her proffered capacity, or have relegated to her the whole conduct and business of the trial. And when she gives vent to the most famous

> The quality of mercy is not strained;
> It droppeth as the gentle rain from heaven
> Upon the place beneath: it is twice blessed;
> It blesseth him that gives, and him that takes,

with all that follows—why, then we smile, for we

cannot but perceive that the words are directed, not to Shylock, but to the susceptibilities of the audience; that, in fact, the whole play is stayed in its course, while a little gentle and admirable preachment goes forward. It was in his later days of power that Shakespeare developed his extraordinary faculty of making his characters search all moral depths in some weighty apophthegm that lay in, and progressed, the strict dramatic sequence that was toward.

Shakespeare has expressed himself with no little vehemence with regard to these groundlings that made such urgent demands of him. Their desires, that sped hither and thither in the craving for change, and their offensive breath, seemed to have been the chief things that stirred disgust in him. This latter attribute is suggestive. It bespeaks the fact that he, probably as an actor, came sufficiently near them in their collective capacity for it to make itself urgent upon his olfactory senses. This means, too, that he had to come into closer contact with their desires than he would have done merely as a playwright. And thus they were even more able to enforce their wishes and requirements upon him. It was for them he wrote; and though we shall see later that he was not a man void of the ambitions that wing for loftier aims than merely monetary gain, we shall also see that there was a somewhat in his philosophical aspect of life that caused him to discover that no pedant was a wise man, but that wisdom, rather, was a synthesis and not a thesis. And if synthesis be a god with his brow in the heavens, then compromise are the feet thereof.

Even while he wrote for a stage of a certain structure, it was this element that ever entered into the emotions that influenced him. And this element must ever be borne in mind by us. Yet his concession to the demands of his audience did not preclude his making the deftest use of them for the mightiest ends; any more than his adoption of the Elizabethan stage precluded his demonstration of its utmost possibilities. It was in this he displayed his craftsmanship, since an artist is conditioned by his craft. And so it must needs be that the craft of him shall next engage attention in the sequence of this study.

CHAPTER IV

HIS CRAFT

IT has been contended, or assumed, that, whatever Shakespeare had or had not, at least he was no skilled craftsman. Detractors and eulogists alike have proceeded on this assumption. And, to be sure, play after play arises to the memory in explanation of the fact that such an assumption should have been made. Nevertheless, it seems incredible that all should have agreed to such an assumption, and yet that none should have arisen to argue out the basis of its contexture. There was only Coleridge who flung out his challenge to the contrary, stating that the judgment of Shakespeare was at least equal to his genius. And it is at least singular that it should have been given to him to make one of the most penetrating remarks on the subject. Said he: "No work of genius dares want its appropriate form, neither indeed is there any danger of this. As it must not, so genius cannot, be lawless; for it is even this that constitutes its genius—the power of acting creatively under laws of its own origination." A remark such as that is worth whole libraries of eulogy or denunciation, for it does indeed definitely advance the matter. Yet it is somewhat too paradoxically stated to be of eventual value. It is suggestive and indicative rather than radical, for all that the suggestion proclaims him as one who had an eye to see withal.

Partly, the assumption, right or wrong, has arisen from impatience. There has been no attempt to visualise one of Shakespeare's own plays on to the stage for which he made them. Craftsmanship is the adaptation of Beauty to certain formal conditions, without which it could not be expressed, and in which it must be contained. A sculptor has his clay, his marble, his mouldings; a painter his pigments and his canvas. A poet has the use of words around which memories cling, in history or euphony; words which seek to find their linear and paragraphic structure according to their theme and the tone in which they are uttered. A dramatist has not only words, but a stage. His words are not expressive only of Beauty, but also of emotions that in their total effect are the framing of eternal personages; but his stage is what he may please to make it. Thus dramatic rules may differ widely. Aristotle, for example, framed his famous rules having the conditions of the Athenian stage before his mind; and, if he be the wise man his works would declare him to be, he would decry their enforcement, or their attempted and impossible enforcement, on the conditions of a stage widely different in fashion. It is obvious that in a theatre holding some twenty thousand spectators, if the action of a play were not hedged by as many unities as possible, it would be quite impossible for its spectators to receive any impression at all from it. There is only one unity in a play; there is, indeed, only one unity in all Art: and that is the unity of effect. But under conditions so diffuse as provided by an open amphitheatre holding twenty thousand spectators, from which, at best, it would be but difficult to follow the significance of words and actions of players at a far remove, the achievement of that unity would require the collateral support of several subservient and wholly artificial unities, such as the unities of space and time. In an Elizabethan playhouse, however, where the audience surged round three sides of the stage, and had the stage and themselves enclosed together, the theatrical conditions being no longer diffuse, the play itself could be diffuse, and yet the same unity of effect be attained.

Now, if Shakespeare had, conceivably, being enamoured of the formal conditions of the Athenian stage, chosen to write for those remoter conditions, his *King Lear* obviously would have worn a fashion wholly different from that which it now wears. He might well have done so, and yet, being the genius he was, have won a wider audience in the end than some more topical penman of the day to whose plays the rabble flocked. In such a case, Gloster, Edmund, Edgar, Albany, Cornwall, Burgundy, France, Oswald, and the Fool would all have gone. The story of the division of the property would have been taken up as a retrospect by the chorus;

whose song would have been steeped in all the satire, and bitterness, and pity that the Fool provides, in that and in their recital of the further woes that befell the King. Lear, Regan, Goneril, Cordelia, and Kent, with perhaps Cornwall as male antagonist, would alone have been presented; and the action would have commenced at the moment when Cordelia is expecting Lear to awake, and hoping for his sanity. Such would have been the play had Shakespeare elected to display the action of his drama in the formal conditions of an ancient day. But he did not so elect. In truth, he had no election at all in the matter. Penury may not elect; it may only select, with but a limited selection at best. The formal conditions of the Elizabethan stage offered themselves to him; and into these he bent his Art. Those who desire to say that the formal conditions of the Elizabethan playhouse were not so apt to enshrine the living Beauty of Drama as the formal conditions of an Attic amphitheatre or a modern theatre, have their own argument before them, and a difficult argument it will be found to be. That is one thing. But if Shakespeare's craftsmanship is rightly to be apprehended the conditions that presented themselves to him must first be understood, on the principle that, however much more Beauty be than its continent, we may yet not advance to that "Furthermore" except only by means of and through the continent.

Even the very extent of his knowledge of conditions other than his own has been ignored. It is forgotten that the conditions of classic drama lacked not their lusty protagonists in Shakespeare's own circle. In his later conversations with William Drummond, Ben Jonson declared that "Shakspeer wanted arte," meaning thereby his inability or refusal to express his matter in certain formulated conditions, or what, in contradistinction to that matter which itself is Art, is best called Craft. Fuller, among his "Worthies," gave an account of the wit-contests betwixt Shakespeare and Ben Jonson, "which two," says he, "I behold like a Spanish great galleon and an English man-of-war; Master Jonson (like the former) was built far lighter in learning, solid but slow in his performances. Shakespeare, with the English man-of-war, lesser in bulk, but lighter in sailing, could turn with all tides, tack about, and take advantage of all winds by the quickness of his wit and invention." There would not want subject-matter of a various order for such combats; for there were interests quick and throbbing on all hands. Yet assuredly Shakespeare's own plays did not fail to provide their meet and due occasion. Armed with his classical lore Ben would not fail to bear mightily down upon Shakespeare on those nights when players and playwrights gathered at the Globe after a performance of the latter's plays. In fact, there remains one definite trace of such an occasion, when Shakespeare, having heard his blunt friend's searching criticism, admitted its justice, and altered his play accordingly.

The whole of the note, *De Shakespeare Nostrati*, from his *Timber* or *Discoveries*, in which this trace may be found, demands inclusion; for what of it may not bear on the immediate matter nevertheless has its fit application to the larger interest here. "I remember," says Ben, "the players have often mentioned it as an honour to Shakespeare, that in his writing (whatsoever he penned) he never blotted a line. My answer hath been, 'Would he had blotted a thousand,' which they thought a malevolent speech. I had not told posterity this but for their ignorance who chose that circumstance to commend their friend by wherein he most faulted; and to justify mine own candour, for I loved the man, and do honour his memory on this side idolatry as much as any. He was, indeed, honest, and of an open and free nature; had an excellent fantasy, brave notions, and gentle expressions, wherein he flowed with that facility that sometimes it was necessary he should be stopped. '*Sufflaminandus erat*,' as Augustus said of Haterius. His wit was in his own power; would the rule of it had been so, too! Many times he fell into those things, could not escape laughter, as when he said in the person of Cæsar, one speaking to him, 'Cæsar, thou dost me wrong.' He replied, 'Cæsar did never wrong but with just cause'; and such like, which were ridiculous. But he redeemed his vices with his virtues. There was ever more in him to be praised than to be pardoned."

Now, two observations rise up here. One is, that a man wont to speak of his candour is also infallibly a man wont to exercise it. The second is, that when such a man speaks of another's honesty, and open and free nature, he is probably not only praising the other's general attributes, but specifically referring to his reception of the aforesaid candour. In other words, there lurks proof even here that Jonson had borne home on Shakespeare his armoury of criticism. But it is in his closing sentences the proof is found. For the line that he quotes from *Julius Cæsar* is not to be found. Instead of it the passage reads thus:

> Know, Cæsar doth not wrong, nor without cause
> Will he be satisfied.

Cæsar's speech concludes here; and Metellus begins his speech with a new line. That is to say, there is half a line wanted to complete the space: and, be it noted, to complete the sense and cadence moreover. Whereas if the first line were as Jonson gives it, all this would at once be remedied, and the passage would read:

> Know, Cæsar doth not wrong but with just cause,
> Nor without cause will he be satisfied.

What Jonson, in fact, couched his lance at, was not the apparent folly it seems, but a somewhat awkward ellipsis; seeing which, Shakespeare, rather than phrase it anew, struck it out altogether. But the essence of the matter is this, that at the Mermaid Tavern of a merry evening the robustious periwig of the classicists made no small assault on the major portion of Shakespeare's plays for this lack of form and craftsmanship, even to the minute criticism of abrupt ellipses; and that consequently whatever Shakespeare did, he did deliberately, willingly, and, if not on a reasoned scheme, at least with a sufficient intuition of what he was about.

In this regard there are two fundamental considerations that range themselves opposite one another, each of them finding their embodiment in the two personalities engaged. On the one hand there is the fact that most of the criticisms that later days have levelled at Shakespeare were ably, forcibly, and cogently put by Ben Jonson himself; and since they can be discovered in his writings, verse and prose, it is not too much to suppose that they were stated by him in proper person with forceful amplification of detail. On the other hand lies a matter so obvious that it should not need statement, for all that it is so calmly and frequently overlooked. It is, that the author of *King Lear*, *Hamlet*, *Othello*, and *Macbeth* was not a man deficient in perception. Therefore, if Ben Jonson flaunted some or other classic saw before his eyes with regard to the logic of construction in drama, or the importance of the unity of Time, and if he, having this before him, deliberately departed from it, then, by the very greatness of his achievement, he is entitled to more than equal consideration; he is entitled to the demand that his very achievement has annulled the antique rule for his instance. His is the right of the Creator. He has enriched the experience of Drama.

For example, in Jonson's Prologue to the revision in English characters of *Every Man in His Humour*, when he speaks in shrewd contempt of the

> Three rusty swords
> And help of some few foot and half-foot words,
> Fight over York and Lancaster's long jars,
> And in the tyring-house bring wounds to scars—

his reference to Shakespeare is obvious. But he also speaks of "a child new swaddled to proceed Man, and then shoot up, in one beard and weed"; and this very evil Shakespeare exemplified later in the *Winter's Tale*. There is also contempt for the "creaking throne comes down the boys to please"; and Shakespeare not only did this in *Cymbeline*, but even went on to make the throne an eagle. Similarly there is mention of "the rolling bullet heard to say, it thunders," and "the tempestuous drum" that "rumbles to tell you when the storm doth come"; all of which expedients were later employed in *King Lear*. On the one hand, thus, Shakespeare is discovered openly disregarding the contempt of the learned; and on the other hand, as already seen, he is discovered speaking himself in considerable contempt of the many-headed multitude: which can only indicate that he had some or other definite idea of the illusion which it was the business of his craft to convey, as opposed to the crystal and strictly defined principles of Jonson's conception of a dramatist's ideal of workmanship.

Yet, for all that this Benjamin would not have his dramatic coat woven of many colours, he was not blind to the fact that the rules of an ancient day could not, by the very nature of them, express all the possibilities of drama. He was convinced, truly enough, that the main outlines laid down were perdurable; yet he could say: "I know nothing can conduce more to letters than to examine the writings of the ancients, and not to rest in their sole authority, or take all upon trust from them. . . . For to all the observations of the ancients we have our own experience: which, if we will use and apply, we have better means to pronounce. It is true they opened the gates and made the way, that went before us, but as guides, not commanders: *Non domini nostri, sed duces fuere.* Truth lies open to all; it is no man's several."[1] Manly words such as these were finely characteristic of Ben; and to Shakespeare such an attitude cannot but have added greatly to the general strength of his dramatic criticism. When it is remembered that, in addition to all this, Jonson was demonstrably on terms of

HIS CRAFT

more than ordinary friendship with Shakespeare, the whole force of the opposition between them as to dramatic conception is made apparent.

Nothing could better instance the sharp cleavage between them than their very methods of work. If there were not the testimony already adduced from the players of Shakespeare's company that he rarely if ever blotted a line, it would yet not need a diligent study of Shakespeare's work to discover that there hung no intermediate effort between its final product and the heat it awoke in his imagination. He probably travelled to and fro over the ground of a projected play before he committed it to ink. As has already been seen, with a large number of his plays, he probably had a previous play on the subject before him, that had fallen to his lot to revise and refurbish for newer presentation. Or his imagination has been smitten by an old poem, as in *Romeo and Juliet*, or by an Italian novel, as in *Othello*, or by a stirring biography by the garrulous Plutarch, as in the Roman plays, or by some succulent legend in the rich pages of Holinshed, as in *Cymbeline* or *Macbeth*, not to speak of the Histories. In one or two instances, in *Midsummer Night's Dream* and *The Tempest*, for example, neither plot nor theme can be found in the way of imaginative prompter to him. But, even when he was most derivative as to idea, the deeper the examination and comparison of his final product with that which preceded it, the more evident it becomes that Shakespeare imaginatively mastered the whole field before he committed any portion of it to writing. That is to say, he would pass the various scenes, always with his stage before his mind's eye, pictorially before him, adjusting the opening of the narrative, its swell to its apex of interest, its pause awhile, and its concluding climax and gradual close, seeing his characters in all this not so much voiceful as brimmed with those emotions that it was his business to render into speech. Then when he came to write, these characters of his at once spoke into swiftly rushing verse—unless, that is, they were conceived as prose characters. They were conceived as being urgent with verse: indeed, it may well be that in the days of their conception they actually broke into verse in his mind, for there are many lines in his work that convey the idea that they preceded, and gave rise to, the rest of the speech in which they are to be found. His was the true way of the poet and artist: he conceived his work in its final form, whatever might have been his difficulty in realising his conception.

With Jonson, however, the matter was wholly different. He declared, near the end of his days, to Drummond that he wrote all his verses "first in prose." That fact, indeed, might almost have been guessed. Even the best of his lines wear the semblance of having been passed through some foreign medium: they read rather as translations than as creations, having none of the heat of new and urgent matter. He has even declared it as a principle of style that "ready writing makes not good writing, but good writing brings on ready waiting"; and, as though the latter admission seemed too great a concession to the pen of the ready writer, he was quick to add to it, "yet, when we think we have got the faculty, it is even then good to resist it."[2] Nothing more remote from Shakespeare's own manner of procedure than this could very well be imagined. Shakespeare can certainly not be thought of as resisting his faculty for ready writing; though he must have heard this precept of Jonson's laid down many a time and oft, in some such similar terms, over pipes and canary at the Mermaid Tavern, if not in fact in his own lodgings with good Master Mountjoy.

The matter comes closer home when we remember that Jonson declared himself against "the obstinate contemners of all helps and arts; such as presuming on their own naturals (which, perhaps, are excellent), dare deride all diligence, and seem to mock at the terms when they understand not the things."[3] There is a passage in Shakespeare that links up so inevitably with this that it is hard to resist the thought that each in its turn sprang out of some discussion on the subject. It is when Polixenes and Camillo enter to Perdita and Florizel, and Perdita declares she will not have anything to do with "streaked gillyvors," they being but "nature's bastards." The scene then continues thus:

Polix.   Wherefore, gentle maiden,
    Do you neglect them?
Per.   For I have it said,
    There is an art which, in their piedness, shares
    With great creating Nature.
Polix.   Say there be;
    Yet Nature is made better by no mean,
    But Nature makes that mean: so, even that art
    Which you say adds to Nature, is an art
    That Nature makes. You see, sweet maid, we marry
    A gentler scion to the wildest stock;
    And make conceive a bark of baser kind
    By bud of nobler race: this is an art
    Which does mend Nature—change it rather; but
    The art itself is Nature.
Per.   So it is.
Polix.   Then make your garden rich in gillyvors,
    And do not call them bastards.
Per.   I'll not put
    The dibble in earth to set one slip of them.

So she says; and forthwith proceeds to distribute lavender, mint, savory, marjoram, and the marigold, even as her creator himself would not set his dibble in earth to bring forth one of those disciplined products that his friend Ben extolled, preferring the abandon and the miscalled waste of Nature's own way. It would not be unlike Shakespeare gently to laugh at Jonson in this way; and, in any case, Jonson's remark seems to be levelled very obviously at Shakespeare. It may be nothing, though it seems to be much, that it immediately follows the paragraph *De Shakespeare Nostrati*; but when he scoffs at those who, by "a cunning protestation against all reading, and false venditation of their own naturals, think to divert the sagacity of their readers from themselves, and cool the scent of their own fox-like thefts; when they are so rank, as a man may find whole pages together usurped from one another,"—whoever be or be not meant, it is impossible not to think of Shakespeare and his wholesale importations from Plutarch, with, on occasion, the slightest of metrical adjustment.

In all this it is very obvious that Shakespeare had the virtues of discipline in conception and construction emphasised with some pungency at a very near call; and that in turning from it he did so with some kind of a definite ideal before him, consciously held or subconsciously perceived. It need not be said that he failed often enough to fulfil his own ideal. Failure is mortal. And it came even more aptly to Shakespeare to fail betimes, since the loftiest is never achieved save at the risk of the most abysmal. It is only mediocrity, in ambition and in talent, that is infallible within its limited scope. As we shall see later Shakespeare was not a man unacquainted with the pangs of the loftiest ambition in his art. It is sufficient at the moment to quote him when he speaks earnestly of himself as "desiring this man's art, and that man's scope." This being so, he was but little likely to withhold himself from every attempt to apply Jonson's classic lore without a very clear idea as to what he was about.

It was, indeed, to his considerable credit that this was so. He had his own task to achieve; and he set about it, scoffing gently at the other by putting into his senile old statesman's lips the praise of "tragedy, comedy, history, pastoral, pastoral-comical, historical-pastoral, tragical-historical, tragical-comical-historical-pastoral, scene individable, or poem unlimited." Depression fell on him awhile, as it falls on all artists who set out, not to fulfil the precepts of others, but to discover themselves. He could say of his own work in the hour when the strain of other things wrought havoc with his nerves, "With what I most enjoy, contented least." Yet he continued with the work that fell to him; and from his earliest achievements till near the end of his days this work grew comelier and shapelier in his hands.

The peculiar difficulty that fronted him, and which he alone of all the dramatists of his day truly solved, is not generally recognised. For the heritage that passed to him in the tradition of dramatic practice was that of five-act drama—or what would probably be more accurate a statement, regarded from the standpoint of Elizabethan empiric, five main movements in a play, each of which averaged a half hour, that thus the mass of them should fitly fill out the space of time generally required by an afternoon's entertainment. How this came to be the acknowledged practice would make a sufficiently interesting study. The more material question at the moment, however, is to note the difficulties that this involved. For the natural movements of drama would seem to be not five but three. In general terms these are, the

Introduction, the Action, and the Climax: the first of which is occupied, with as swift a procedure as possible, with the task of setting out and rendering intelligible the Action, which in its turn, through plot and counterplot, takes forward the interest to the concluding crisis, this being the Climax; at the moment of which the play may cease, with its interest suspended in mid-air, or it may perhaps continue to a gentler adjustment of the matter. This does not at all necessarily imply that the logical construction is in three acts, each act being occupied severally with each movement. In point of fact, it is far otherwise. For, by the very nature of the case, the first movement, the Introduction, were best done briefly, and the last movement, the Climax, demands incision of treatment under penalty of losing its title. Thus there would be an exceedingly brief first act, a ponderous second act, and a succinct third act, and the play would go forward hunched ungainly like a camel. Indeed, there is not even the obligation to treat the three movements in their logical sequence. Henrik Ibsen, for example, in *Rosmersholm*, after an opening which is no introduction, plunges straightway in an action that opens up its own introduction pace by pace with itself in the way of retrospective dialogue, until, in fact, the most vital piece of information, that which alone makes Rebecca West's whole action intelligible, is not revealed till the very eve of the climax. The more general practice of this dramatist in his most noteworthy achievements, however, was to start the action, holding it in poise awhile as he engaged on his retrospective introduction: then when he was more or less quit of the incubus of this, to let the action proceed simply to a climax, short and sharp, or gentle and prolonged.

Yet to say that these three general movements were otherwise negotiated is to admit their real existence. And to Shakespeare they constituted a very urgent difficulty, for it fell to him not to negotiate them as he might himself best devise, but to negotiate them in an accepted structure. His first plays, to our knowledge, being Histories, constituted no difficulty; for the Histories being but pageants, with neither co-ordination nor scheme in them save such a robustious display of energy and pomp as the chronicles vouchsafed, permitted them to be cut into whatever sized portions a dramatist might fasten his whim on. It is, in fact, an interesting speculation to imagine that he would not have held so resolutely to his heritage had not his first discipline in drama accustomed his imagination to its exactions. It is, of course, only a speculation; but it becomes luminous with interest when we discover that, at a time when he had wellnigh perfected his instrument, in the high-day of his great tragedies, he departed from the principle that underlay his achievement, in *Othello*. But apart from the Histories, which, with some possible exceptions to be mentioned later, flowed from start to finish with no pretence of structure, Shakespeare in his early plays was not a little perplexed at the difficulty thus presented to him. When he could, he leant on the work of earlier playwrights. The *Comedy of Errors*, for instance, was a play that probably demanded no very great skill on his part, seeing that the comedy by Plautus, from which it is derived, the *Manæchmi*, was undoubtedly before him in some form or other. He added new features to it, noteworthily in giving the twin brothers accessories in mystification in the shape of twin servants; but it did not fall to him so to cast the story in such a way that a five-act construction came inevitably to it. The very nature of it obviated that; for a farce needs but one swift flow from its outset to its conclusion.

It was in such plays, therefore, as *Love's Labour's Lost*, *Two Gentlemen of Verona*, *Midsummer Night's Dream*, and *Romeo and Juliet*, that we should expect to discover him in grapple with this perplexity that had been presented him, in the effort to evolve from it that construction, that craftsmanship, which should best express himself, and enable him to add to the achievements of drama instead of being compelled to echo an elder achievement. And we do discover him so. It is a grapple, in truth and in deed. But in order to see exactly what the grapple implied, and what its significance was, it will be well to view it in the light of the answer he finally evolved from it, and which he exhibited in fullest power when he shed himself of the artifice of Comedy, and stood in the exacting franchise of Tragedy.

His perplexity was a perplexity indeed: for while to express five movements in three need be no great exploit, demanding only an economy of procedure, to express three movements in five, and that adequately, is a task indeed. Yet Shakespeare achieved it; and not only achieved it, but added considerably to the strength of Drama in the achievement. For whereas in the ordinary course of Drama the Action mounts to its Crisis in a final Climax, he altered the movement from a logic of three to a logic of five by dividing and distributing the Crisis and the Climax, leading to the concluding Climax through a Crisis that was in the nature of an antithesis to it. By this means, as is obvious, he not only answered his riddle successfully, but he increased the dramatic interest that he was engaged in by a suspense that brought the whole imagination of his audience fiercely into play. The method offered its difficulties. For instance, the Crisis having occurred three-fifths through the play, that is to say in or about the Third Act, the interest would have to pall for awhile, since the contrary action that is to take it to its Climax would require to be set in motion. But this was not necessarily a vital difficulty (particularly when, as on Shakespeare's stage, the play continued through without halt or cessation); for the excitement engendered by the Crisis might safely be relied on to project the interest past the inevitable slackening of tension in the Fourth Act; and by the time such an excitement might in the ordinary course of events have subsided, the concluding interest would be well afoot. Before examining the procedure in Shakespeare's own practice, it would be well to raise the caution that the action of a play takes place strictly not on the boards of a stage, nor in some imaginary scene, but in the mind of its spectator. Therefore, when the word Crisis is used it does not mean that all such Crises were of the same nature. They were not. In one case *Macbeth* might be at the very zenith of success, in another *Hamlet* or *Lear* might be at the very nadir of ill-fortune. That mattered little. The matter of more moment was that in each case a Crisis was achieved that was the culminating effect of the previous action, and which suggested a further Climax that was to be achieved anew by means of a Counter-action.[4]

In all this Shakespeare worked on his own independent lines, even as he was occupied with his own independent problem. It is all the more fascinating, then, to find that in solving his own difficulty he did indeed strike in this way on the very principle of construction that the ancients themselves discovered while occupied with wholly different conditions. They, even as he, mounted to a Crisis some three-fifths of the way through a play; but while they declined the action with some steadiness to the conclusion, with a renewed yet not over-abrupt tightening of interest prior to the final subsidence, he had to

mount again to a higher height than they in his
Climax, and therefore it was incumbent on him, for the
attainment of an adequate balance, to drop the action
somewhat suddenly on the attainment of the Crisis
by turning its course aside and engaging himself with
a remoter interest. Similarly, too, Ibsen, a latter-day
dramatist, when writing a five-act play had to adopt
the same construction, for all that his usual method
was to mount rapidly to a Crisis that was both Crisis
and Climax, being the end of all things. In *The
Lady from the Sea*, the Stranger enters only twice:
firstly in the Third Act to make the Crisis, and lastly
in the Fifth Act to make the Climax. With Ibsen
this was probably less of a discovery than an imitation: yet, even so, it is all the more a tribute to
Shakespeare's independent discovery—or recovery,
since Life is but one, and all its discoveries are after
all only recoveries. With Ibsen, however, the
division between the Crisis and the Climax was a clear
and unequivocal division. With Sophocles, that is
to say, what we have termed the Climax was a gentler
reflection of the Crisis, being a remoter echo of it.
With Shakespeare it was in a sense antithetical to it.
In both, therefore, there was a definite connection
between Crisis and Climax: they were both logical
and apt parts of an orderly structure. But in Ibsen
they are two definite, distinct, and constructionally
unrelated emotional blows repeated in precisely the
same manner. Or it may be put this way. In
Œdipus the same action that carried the emotion to

the height of the Crisis carries it over and downward to a lower and less strenuous Climax; in *Hamlet* the action that achieved the Crisis culminated there, while a newer action, that had hitherto lain embedded in the Introduction, woke to a contrast of power in order to mount to the Climax; in *The Lady from the Sea* the action that carried the emotion to the Crisis, hung there awhile, till the selfsame blow was repeated long after in the Climax. In the first the Climax was a reverberation of the Crisis, and therefore the fourth movement was necessarily merged in with the fifth; in the second it came with contrasted power, and therefore the fourth movement was in the nature of a contrast with the second; in the last it was but repetition, with, if anything, an increase of tension, and therefore the fourth movement was but a halt between two emotions. And this raises the question of Shakespeare's use of the fourth movement—or, to speak in terms of his own drama, his Fourth Act.

With Shakespeare there were obvious difficulties with his Fourth Act: constructionally, for the reasons already intimated, and actually, as reference to any of his tragedies will at once demonstrate. But these difficulties belong so vitally to his whole method of dramatic procedure that it will be necessary to turn to this in order to see the Fourth Act in its proper relation. For, as has already been seen, the stage of Shakespeare being what it was, it was necessary to relieve the attention of the audience by a calculated variety of interest. Tragedy had to be varied by comedy; and bitterness had to make way for mirth, lest the very capacity for bitterness should be ruined. But it was also necessary that the variations should progress the action. In his earlier plays it is easy to see that he met considerable difficulty in this; in fact, it is too often evident that he even dismissed all attempts in that direction, as, for example, in *Henry IV.*, where the variations imply no progress. As he grew in power, however, this became more and more possible to him; until he came finally to achieve this same end by means of the very conflict that his drama was engaged with. In *Hamlet*, for instance, once his Introduction was completed (and among all dramatists Shakespeare stands supreme in the subtle faculty of conveying requisite information in apt and natural dialogue), the King and Hamlet are seen in a covert but none the less strenuous conflict. Hamlet was ever suspicious of his uncle; but now, since the revelations of the Ghost, despite his persistent incredulity with regard to that phantasmal apparition, he is alert to seek confirmation of his suspicion. But suspicion is a thing swiftly communicable. Moreover, Hamlet's manner is strange; nor will the plea of insanity wholly cover the many evidences of a shrewd and penetrating sagacity that the King cannot but notice. Polonius was right in saying that if this was madness there was truly method in it; and the King, in his turn, was suspicious of that method.

Before the First Act is over this conflict is well afoot. The antagonists are obviously watching each other shrewdly, with no advantage as yet to either. It is the King that takes the first move in the conflict; and he does so by sending Guildenstern and Rosencrantz to Hamlet, that they might discover for him precisely what it is that ails his moody nephew. That very fact puts him upmost in the conflict. And when Hamlet sees through the emissaries to the probing mind that sent them, he not only sets himself equal again, but gains a very emphatic advantage, for now he knows what his adversary is after. Furthermore, Rosencrantz and Guildenstern, and, later, Polonius, tell him of the coming of the players; and forthwith a plan for making the King prove his own guilt seizes fast hold of his mind. The King has struck at him; and though he has foiled the lunge, he has not yet had an opportunity of lunging back. This, it is, will give it him. And thus the ascendance now lies emphatically with Hamlet. No sooner has this advantage been won by him than it is quickly lost again. The King, overhearing his conversation with Ophelia in the famous nunnery scene, sees at once that "there's something in his soul, o'er which his melancholy sits on brood," and that that something is striking at himself. He decrees that Hamlet shall be sent to England. Yet since he decides that the decree shall not come of effect till after the play, the situation is once more held as near poise as is possible.

Each adversary has a fell blow pending; and though Hamlet's is bound to fall first, in the face of the King's resolve it is very doubtful what advantage he will be able to gather from it.

After the stupendous success of the play, Hamlet's advantage is unquestionable. But, again, he has no sooner won it than he is to lose it again. That he should abstain from executing his revenge while the King is at prayer is nothing; with the power that lies now in his hands it is not necessary to pluck at such specious advantages. Indeed, his very neglect of the opportunity is as much a tribute to his power as an evidence of his introspective thought. But when he slays Polonius his advantage is at once gone, and the King is both upmost in the conflict again, and provided with a suitable excuse for putting his resolve to banish Hamlet into effect. With the achievement of this resolve the Crisis is complete. The whole play has been wrought to as acute a pass of perplexity as it well could have been; for, while the King is in complete ascendance, it is yet manifest that there is more to follow.

Now, in all this Shakespeare has achieved two things. Firstly, he has achieved, in the very alternation and see-saw of the conflict that was the very essence of the action, the deft variation of theme that the attention of his audience demanded. Also, he achieved his required Crisis by taking his initial action up to its utmost limit of progress along that line. Therefore, with his Climax in view, yet to be attained, he must now, on the consummation of his Crisis and the conclusion of his Third Act, take up some or other wholly new action to begin his Fourth Act.[5] But he had prepared for this far back in the Introduction of the play. There Laertes had been seen with both his father and his sister. Now, therefore, he enters the scene as their joint avenger; and we are carefully permitted to learn that Hamlet has two enemies instead of one, and they in league together, before Horatio is permitted to read a letter informing us that Hamlet is back again in Denmark, to take up the issue against them. In this it is patent that the eager flow of the main action has been suspended awhile for a new matter to be rolled forward. But this is even as it should be. The very balance and symmetry of the play demands it. For a new height to be reached a new ascent must be made; and while it is being begun, the impetus given by the perplexity of the Crisis is more than sufficient to project an intensity of interest well into the gathering movement of the counter-action. To say nothing of the fact that such counter-actions almost inevitably are actions that themselves lay suspended in the Introduction, growing out of thence even as did the action that led to the Crisis, with the mind fully prepared to seize up the interest at once.

One of the advantages that this principle of construction offers can very readily be seen. In *Hamlet*, for instance, the tragedy being one of thought, the whole movement of the play had necessarily to be somewhat lethargic and laboured. In *Macbeth*, the tragedy being one of action, the whole movement had to wear something rapid and cataclysmic in its appearance. Now, it is true that *Hamlet* is, in point of fact, lengthy, whereas *Macbeth* is, in point of fact, considerably briefer; but this does not affect the real difference in appearance between the two plays, which is, that, whatever be their respective lengths, *Hamlet* is slow in its actual movement, whereas *Macbeth* is swift and rapid. A little thought is sufficient to show the simple yet subtly effective cause of this. For if Shakespeare had to convey the effect of rapidity, as in *Macbeth*, it was but necessary for him to draw the Crisis nearer towards the Introduction, to shorten the Action, and to lengthen the Counter-action; whereas, had he to suggest the slow poise of irresolution, as in *Hamlet*, he had only to thrust the Crisis further towards the Climax, to lengthen the Action, and to abbreviate the Counter-action: which is precisely what he happens to have done in each of the examples chosen.

A man's characteristics may be best discovered in his best work; and it is therefore to the mighty series of his tragedies that one naturally turns to discover Shakespeare's method or principles of dramatic procedure. In the light of that discovery, looking before and after, one can see Shakespeare finding his way with some difficulty to the elucidation of the problem set him, and then triumphantly ringing the changes on the principle he had achieved, in Comedy and Tragedy, with what skill he might employ, never owning fealty to any bondage that might harass his freedom. In his first of plays, *Love's Labour's Lost*, for example, we find him frankly puzzled by these five acts required of him. Having started his play swiftly and promptly by letting us know, in Act I., the resolve of the King and his nobles, and illustrating that resolve in the situation as regards Costard, Jaquenetta, and Armado, and having shown us, in Act II., the dissipation of that resolve, he is now confronted by the main difficulty of the play. In a later hour he would have led up to some or other critical juncture in the Third Act (as, for instance, a witnessing, and repudiation, by the Count of the love-making of Armado, they being already half-entrapped themselves), with a Counter-action in the Fourth Act that should lead to the inevitable general discovery in the Fifth Act. Instead of which, he is all the while seeking to fend off the concatenation that would itself conclude the play. All through the Third Act he does this, and successfully withal, though at the cost of interest. Yet he cannot fend it off any longer; and so in the Fourth Act it compels its arrival. The Climax at the end of this Act is so obvious, it rings the note of general conclusion so clearly that it is difficult to think of another Act to succeed. Yet another Act is required of this pupil at the feet of Drama; so a part of the matter proper to the Climax is held over and expanded, while the wholly extraneous additions of Holofernes and the acting of the "Nine Worthies" is brought in to puff out its proportions. Thus, in this first of plays, despite the fact that it was re-written so late as 1598, the playwright confesses in his shifts of perplexity that he has yet to learn his craft.

As has been said, the Histories, by the very nature of them, are negligible from the standpoint of Shakespeare as a playwright in search of a vital principle of construction. Even where, in *Richard II.* and *King John*, the chronicular form is turned away from in favour of a more definite plot, he is yet frustrated of the skill his hand is growing to by the ruthless nature of his historical sequence. Nevertheless, even here the principle that we have seen indicative of his method can distinctly be perceived raising its brow through the intractable matter with which he is beset. Even in a play like *Midsummer Night's Dream*, demanding as it does an unruffled progression of simplicity wrought to intricacy and resolved again into simplicity, the antithetical principle is asserting itself on his instinct. It cannot be forgotten that the Third Act concludes with all the harassed lovers asleep on the dew-wet soil, and that with the Fourth Act Theseus and Hippolyta re-emerge on the scene, having been wrapt from us since the Introduction.

But in *Two Gentlemen of Verona, Romeo and Juliet*,

and *The Merchant of Venice*, the principle has both emerged and developed into full recognition and power. The very suggestion of artificiality it wears in the first is more than a hint that, in coming thus to the growing craftsman, it came not unknown nor unrecked of. But *Two Gentlemen of Verona* was, in more senses than one, a practice ground for *Romeo and Juliet*; and in *Romeo and Juliet* the clear division of the five Acts is an indication not less clear of a craftsman glorying in his newly-won craft. Each Act is occupied with its own movement, Introduction, Action, Crisis, Counter-action, and Climax; and the closing scene of each Act rings the dominant of the Act to follow; save in the sole instance of the Crisis, which, to be a Crisis, demands isolation and surprise. Moreover, it is clear to see that he has also begun to master many of the difficulties presented by the very nature of the Fourth Act. The sudden strokes of alternation introduced by the wooing of County Paris, or the Trial Scene in the *Merchant of Venice*, are not so subtle as the various devices he employed to grip attention in his later tragedies, such as the madness of Ophelia, the tremendous pity engendered by the meeting of Edgar and blind Gloster, or the murder of Macduff's young son—in which last the cause of its being accomplished on the stage, which so stumbled Coleridge, is seen. Yet what they lose in subtlety they gain in vigour: and a growth from vigour to subtlety is the very legitimate growth of Wisdom.

For a more emphatic antithesis to the Second Act of the *Merchant of Venice* than the Trial Scene could not well be imagined. In the Second Act it was Antonio's power that was decadent and Shylock's ascendant; in the Fourth it was Shylock's that was decadent and Antonio's ascendant.

A somewhat quaint fact emerges here. Comedy is the crown on the head of artifice; and therefore in the period that followed the *Merchant of Venice*, in *Much Ado, As You Like It, Twelfth Night, All's Well*, though his principle of procedure is clear in each, it seems as though ofttimes the tendency was to obscure its more resolute lines of development. So when he turned to the more authentic fashion of drama, to Tragedy, that is, in *Julius Cæsar*, it is almost as if he broke out into a sudden shout of joy —and a most unfortunate shout, it must be admitted, it was. For in wishing to emphasise his Crisis, he does so in no less a way than by killing off his Protagonist.

It is *Othello*, however, that makes one of the profoundest studies in Shakespeare's dramatic method. As will be seen more particularly later, he was never concerned with construction as a thing in itself. It was never he himself that wrought the construction wherein to place his characters; he created the characters that should themselves achieve their destiny, weaving it in a certain fashion according to the impulsion of life that drove them forward. Rumour has it that he declared that it was necessary for him to kill the eager Mercutio, for fear lest he should take matters into his own hands and ruin the play. Whatever the rumour be worth, it is apparent in his plays that the very vitality of his characters was often enough a matter of serious concern to him. In *Measure for Measure*, for instance, it is quite clear that not only the Provost, but Shakespeare moreover, had made up their several minds to kill Barnardine instead of Claudio. But by very virtue of the principle of independent volition that he received from his creator, Barnardine would have none of it. He swept them both aside imperiously. "I swear I will not die to-day for any man's persuasion," is his surly response; "if you have anything to say to me, come to my ward; for thence will not I to-day": and so Shakespeare has make shift with "one Ragozine, a most notorious pirate," whom he puts up finally for the occasion, and whom he might have put up much earlier had he any conception that his first scapegoat would have proved so unruly.

The same principle is to be found at work in *Othello*. At first it is apparent that Shakespeare is shaping his play on his usual lines of development. The First Act is given over completely to the Introduction, and it closes in the ordinary way with the clear hint of the Action to proceed in the next Act, from the mouth of Iago. Similarly the Second Act is occupied with the Action, and the famous and wonderful Third Act (in which, if ever, the wit of creation was at full race) is very clearly shaping for the Crisis. But the very wonder of the third scene of that Act transformed everything. It frustrated its own end. It burked its own conclusion. Its swell and its power to mount are such that it would be quite impossible to turn it aside for the introduction of a Counter-action. We have seen that a Counter-action has usually its roots in the Introduction, even as its antithesis, the Action itself, had; and consequently we can perceive the remnants of Shakespeare's original intention in the arrival of Lodovico and the Venetians in the Fourth Act. But the emotion he has conjured is urgent beyond that. Unlike other dramatists, he did not require that his characters should play attendant on his construction, or struggle against it. The whole action is imperious to amount to the conclusion of all things; and the news of Othello's recall to Venice adds fury to empire. So Shakespeare opens the sluice-gates of his construction, letting the whole matter boil fiercely to the end of all in Desdemona's death and Othello's self-destruction. And if, as it seems, the affair as touching Cassio and Bianca was the original portion of the Counter-action, be it noted, then, with what skill and deftness it is ordered in with the new swell of the initial action! This was no man, this Shakespeare, to have construction taught him by any!

Even in the smaller movements of his plays, as has already been seen, his arrangement of his alternations was not less deft. In both small and great, it is true, however, that his pen hung ofttimes listless in his hand. The palpable device of Prospero's opening conversation with Miranda; much of Cymbeline; much, indeed, of many of his later plays, when the effort for skill seemed often scarcely worth while, he being at a height of achievement and fortune, and spoilt, maybe, by worldly prosperity and success—arise to witness to his failures. Moreover, there were other failures that seemed forced from him, such as the effort to shape the mood for Tragedy into the fashion of Comedy—the cause of which has its place in later examination. Yet, despite these, his craftsmanship cannot be impeached of much in the way of failure.

Not a little of the criticism of Shakespeare has arisen from a profound misunderstanding of his idea of the occasion and situation of Drama. Drama is not a reproduction or criticism of Life. That is rather the business of the Novel. Drama is a transfiguration of Life; and therefore, instead of being the conveyance of a philosophy or criticism, it is itself part of the substance that philosophy must explain and criticism examine, as best they may. Shakespeare did not expound philosophy in his tragedies, however much they were bathed in thought. Philosophy must expound his tragedies, or stand condemned of having neglected some of the matter essential to the synthesis it would achieve. In this way his characters were more than men and women: they were of heroic stature. In their very transfiguration they became symbolic of Life itself. In this way, too, the scenes in which they contended were not streets, hostelries, or drawing-rooms: they were any such confined or unconfined spaces in which great issues might be fought. The stage of the Globe was a convenience for the conflict. Even as the characters were Ideal, so the scenes were Ideal.

It was something of this that the ancients sought to express by their exactions of a unity of Time and Space. It was not Realism they sought, but Idealism. The imposition of the conditions purported to achieve a state of mind in the spectator in which the sense of Time and Space held no sway; and in which, therefore, mundane circumstance being dismissed, the mind might move unhampered through scenes where Death, Life, and Love, Passion, Fate, and Beauty, the great realities of existence, hold unfettered sway. Mundane limitations are ever a shock to Drama. For instance, that Antony should be at Athens in one scene, and five minutes thereafter at Alexandria, is undeniably an unhappy shock. But the reason for the shock is somewhat subtler than is usually stated to be the case. It is not merely, that is to say, that we are irked, knowing full well that so swift a transition in so short a period of time is not possible. Rather, we are irked because we feel deeply that it ought to be possible, and are revolted at having the impossibility brought so nigh us. We recognise Illusion; we hail it, and are content to be subdued by it, knowing that Illusion is Eternity translating itself in terms of Time. But we demand that it shall indeed subdue us, and not awake our revolt. In all of which the chief matter is that it is Illusion we worship, and not Realism: Eternity and not Time. We do not demand Illusion in a Novel, for in a Novel we seek Relation: but we demand Illusion in Drama, for in Drama we seek Contention and a Reaching-after.

Now Shakespeare had his own way of achieving this Illusion; and it is our modern elaboration of scenery that has obscured his dramatic mode. For whereas the Greeks banished Time and Space by recognising them, he banished them by not recognising them. Antony did not go from Athens to Alexandria in five minutes: he merely went out from the stage by one door and entered by another. Athens and Alexandria were never in the matter. The whole concern was with the stage of the Globe, where the action did indeed take place, and from whence it was transported to the spectator's mind. Yet in this he dismissed Time and Space not less surely than did the ancients. Thus the numerous short scenes in *Antony and Cleopatra* but very little obscured the issue. In fact, numerous short scenes did not actually have any existence. The scene was one and indivisible, whereto all might have their free entrance.

Those who think that this assumption of ideality

in the stage on which the action took place, was confined to Shakespeare, and is happily (or unhappily) dismissed from modern times, can surely not have noticed some startling instances of it in the heart of nineteenth-century realism. Impermanent Drama may always be summarily dismissed; but in Ibsen there is presented the figure of one who is in issue with posterity, with results scarcely yet to be foreseen. And who ever saw drawing-rooms like his drawing-rooms? Most drawing-rooms, in houses possessed by the type and position of people whom he depicts, are content with one door. But one door will not suffice for the free access and contention of Drama, and so another door at least is provided. Moreover, in *The Doll's House*, one of those doors has a somewhat astonishing position with regard to the outer door of the hall, a position certainly not dictated by the comfort (particularly in winter) of the inhabitants, but demanded imperiously by the exigencies of the play. In the opening scene of *The Master Builder* there are three doors. But where Ibsen provided doors for the accessibility of new entrances, it is important to notice, Shakespeare's new entrances are marked by modern editors as different scenes, the main matter being that both stages were more or less idealised. This very accessibility of entrance in Ibsen does in fact often convey a shock, because of the very definition of his furniture and scenery, whereas Shakespeare, by his dismissal of definition of scenery (leaving it to be conveyed by his dialogue) dismissed the sense of shock. Who, for example, in a room with any pretensions to mundane actuality, ever saw the like of the Rat-Wife's entrance in *Little Eyolf*, or, for that matter, the second entrance of Ulric Brendel in *Rosmersholm*? It is to be feared an irate dismissal of domestics would succeed to the coming and going of wild strangers in so free a manner in, say, Ibsen's own homestead. But Drama, nevertheless, demands such free access, which in its turn demands an ideality of stage conditions; and even he who strangely chose to be haltered by realism had to make his concessions to the urgency of this demand.

This principle of stage utility must necessarily be clearly held in view before any separation can be made between Shakespeare's vices and virtues in the practice of it. That is to say, a swift removal of Antony from Octavia's side to Cleopatra's bed may quite fitly be achieved even were these two sites separated by a world's distance. The only question is whether Shakespeare has duly achieved without conveying a sense of shock. And here the majority of those who weigh and consider the matter will surely declare that the achievement is adequate and complete. The shock is dismissed (or, as a minority would say, only diminished) by the very subtle use of Cæsar's conversation with Octavia, on the one hand, and Cleopatra's conversation with Enobarbus, on the other hand, intruding between, covering, and conveying, the transposition of scene. A matter of far more concern are the years of Hermione's disappearance. Yet even this proves that, however much we may happen to disapprove, or wonder at, his result, he himself knew very well what he had in mind to do. The interposition of the Florizel and Perdita scenes, from within, and the fanciful glamour suggested by the title, *A Winter's Tale*, from without, helps to aid to the unity of effect, the unity that embraces all other unities. Nevertheless, the questionable success conveyed by these deft expedients is implied by Shakespeare himself in his introduction of Time as a chorus at the opening of the inevitably crucial Fourth Act. And when one speaks of deft expedients, it is noticeable that most of Shakespeare's quiet removals of Space and Time are under cover of the excitement engendered by the break of the Crisis.

Yet through the question of Shakespeare's craftsmanship and architectonic skill one consideration ever projects itself. As has already been said, Shakespeare was never concerned with construction as such. It was not he that reared the structure of a play. It was his characters that took it, built it, and moulded it. Consequently they were never at war with it. A certain prolific writer has stated that Shakespeare's " plot means mainly—not entirely—the evolution of character."[6] But this scarcely states the truth of the situation. It would be more accurate to say that the evolution of Shakespeare's characters mould and frame his plot. Hence they were the plot; and the construction was made by them.

In this, again, new light may be thrown on the subject by the comparison of Ibsen's method. Ibsen, succeeding to the glacial influence of Scribe and the Parisians, was deeply interested in construction, even as though it were a matter wholly separate from the people of his plays. He framed his construction, and placed his people in it, not to fare as they themselves would, but to be ordered as the plot should direct. One of his noteworthy characters, Hedda Gabler, is struggling, ever struggling, not chiefly against her foolish husband, nor against her circumscribed home, but against the cast-iron construction with which her creator has beset her. She longs to live, and to be herself; but she has to obey her ruthless master, and pass through the course he has ordained for her. Nora and Torvald, in *A Doll's House*, are by no means ready for, have by no means progressed to, the profound conversation each side of a table that is required of them at the conclusion of the play. Ibsen, before they had even begun to frame their own characters in speech, had had that scene in mind: he had ordained that they should pass through that momentous scene at that momentous moment: so down they have to sit, ready or unready, and speak the words appointed for them. So it is in many other of Ibsen's plays; after he sought preoccupation with construction as an entity, a thing in itself, which it neither is nor can be. It is a strange and interesting spectacle, this; and perplexed withal. For it is not as though Ibsen's characters had not Life. They are not puppets pushed about at their author's whimsey. They are warm with Life; but they are in war, with more or less of energy, against their author's architectonic desire. It is as though, in vulgar simile, Ibsen had corseted the rich outlines of life. The lines of such a corset might indeed have been possessed of an exquisite sense of curve and general symmetry; but it nevertheless rudely crushed the warm flesh and the healthier beauty. Whatever be the skill that may achieve " the glass of fashion and the mould of form," it is yet rather the Venus de Milo on which we choose to feast our eyes.

Now, this Shakespeare never did. Whatever be the faults that characterise his work, never did he crumple the flesh of the people of his imagination with the imposition of a preconceived architectonic. It need scarcely be said how infinitely his drama gained from this. One can gather some sense of his gain from the loss of others: from the mind's revolt, for instance, at Hedda Gabler's suicide, or the table conference of Nora and Torvald; for from both of these, so crucial are the situations, and so vital is it that our conviction in the truth of them should be complete, we are compelled to turn away in angry complaint. Distressed as we may be, in Shakespeare, at the conclusion of *Othello*, there is this ever to be said, that we know Iago, being what he was, had always to act even as he did, and that Othello was compelled to no deed save on the compulsion of his own character.

There are, however, one or two cases in which the requirements of the plot afoot and the exuberant life of one of the characters in it, fell into warfare. It has already been seen, for example, how Shakespeare had to wake a broil in which to dismiss the obstreperous and exuberant Mercutio; though it is interesting to notice how craftily he used this very thing as the agency for the attainment of his Crisis. But the outstanding example is *Hamlet*. There, if ever, Shakespeare had to keep his whole wit and imagination at full play in order to maintain Hamlet as a living soul, urged only by his own self to his course of action, or inaction, and yet to maintain what may be called the required plot intact and complete. He succeeded: he succeeded triumphantly: and yet the eye is puzzled often, thinking it has caught some lack of agreement in the perfect working of the machine. No sooner seen than gone again, it perplexes and mystifies, taunts and defies; and it is greatly owing to this that the problem of Hamlet has arisen, adding to the making of books of which there is no end. For instance, it is impossible to say that his irresolution does not bear the conviction of a consistent character; and yet it is equally impossible to deny that his irresolution is vital and necessary to the making of the play. This is only to say that the cornerstone of this tragedy, as of all Shakespeare's tragedy, was the ancient saying that "Character is Fate." Yet, more than once, when his irresolution becomes particularly difficult to understand, there comes some sudden hint and reminder that the plot at that moment is in risk of ruin save for the aid of such irresolution. It is so in the celebrated scene when Hamlet finds the King at prayer. It is so, indeed, always in Hamlet's course of action after the play-scene till his dismissal to England. It is especially so in the fact of his dismissal to England; for had he not been dismissed at that moment, the play, or his characterisation, would have come to a pretty pass indeed. And yet, having seen so much, we see more, and are reassured. For the King ordered the dismissal to England prior to the play-scene. Moreover, the very trait that Hamlet demonstrated when he found the King at prayer we remember as having earlier been characteristic of him. And thus we see Hamlet still as a living being, working out his own destiny. We are still able to think objectively of him as a full-orbed man. But we cannot sometimes help feeling how fortunate it was for the dramatist that Hamlet, consistent soul as he is, should have been so fully swayed by his tenderness of thought and perplexity of introspection at so opportune a moment. Yet it is this that is the intellectual feat in the making of him.

It is for this very reason, truly, that Hamlet was made so full-orbed and multivarious of attribute. A man of lesser complexity could not have borne the weight of the plot. It was the conclusive test of the magnificent ability of Shakespeare that this was so: on the side of his craftsmanship this was the proof of his exceeding skill, even as on the side of his art it was the triumph of his imagination. But, although the aspect of this from the standpoint of his craft cannot be forgotten, the fuller and completer understanding of it belongs more strictly to a consideration of his art.

CHAPTER V

HIS ART

DEFINITIONS inevitably become partisan. In their effort to reduce the subject of their choice to the margins of logical expression, they almost inevitably leave wide regions on each hand that belong truly to the subject and yet escape the definition. And if they endeavour to swing so widely that they embrace the circumambient borders, then they escape that logical precision that seems so proper to a definition. Therefore to speak of Art as the attempt of the individual to relate his vision of life, is not to define Art, but rather to attempt to express it. The individual is necessary; not only because of the palpable fact that without the individual there could be none to achieve Art, but chiefly because Art seems distinctively to be the expression of some or other individual's mind. Subjective Art and objective Art are merely academic phrases to distinguish the qualities of mind at work: the sympathetic mind being termed subjective, and the aloof mind being objective, whereas the qualities of sympathy and aloofness are central properties of the individual. When Æschylus sought to render intelligent the actions of gods to men, while Sophocles depicted the action with neither comment nor warmth, it was not that the latter escaped us while the former laid his soul bare to us. They both equally, in their several manner of procedure, gave us to know what sort of men they were. Each of them expressed the vision that their moods, and minds, and temperaments, conveyed to them of a multifarious life. It may happen that the withdrawal necessary to aloofness may cause a wider field of view to be embraced in the vision; and if this be at no loss to the intensity of vision, then, naturally, the Art so achieved will be greater than the other. It will not, however, be any the less indicative of the artist.

Life, its vision by the individual through the medium of his temperament, and its expression in terms of that individuality, are thus, in its widest and most accurate sense, the constituents of Art. Everything appertaining to the conception of the thing to be expressed belongs, therefore, to that which it is necessary to call Art in contradistinction (partly a true, and partly an artificial, contradistinction) to the craft which renders it in some or other form. Even the matter of the form is embraced in these wide arms. The form of an ode is proper to the matter and conception of an ode. There are dramatic themes, and there are epic themes; and if Milton had expressed his "Paradise Lost" in a dramatic form, the fault would have been one of his Art, not his craft. But had he chosen the apt form, and expressed it ill in that form, then the fault would have been one of his craft. As already said, this is partly an artificial distinction, since it is true that an adequate vision so burns and thrills the soul that it inflames the tongue to a passion of adequate speech. Yet there is truth in the distinction, despite the fact that there cannot be set a border-line to it.

So, when Ben Jonson said that "Shakespeare wanted arte," he ruined the value of his criticism for us by his fundamental confusion of thought. Indeed, it is likely enough that Shakespeare himself saw the confusion in much of old Ben's thinking, and therefore bantered the bluff old pedant easily, and went peaceably on with the thing he had to do. It is impossible to say exactly what was meant by that famous remark that the precise Drummond so sedulously made a note of: probably, had Ben been asked, he would have made his confusion clear by thundering out a lengthy repetition of the remark. Judging from his carefully recorded criticisms, however, it would seem that the major portion of his fault-finding was with Shakespeare's craft; in which matter a fair number of his barbs find lodgment, and the flinging of a number more of them proved his own lack of imaginative sympathy, without which all criticism is void. And that this was so seems evident by the following lines, " To the Memory of My Beloved, The Author, Mr William Shakespeare, and what he hath left us," from the Preface to the First Folio:

> Yet must I not give Nature all: Thy Art,
> My gentle Shakespeare, must enjoy a part.
> For though the Poet's matter, Nature be,
> His Art doth give the fashion.

Now, strictly speaking, the Poet's matter is not Nature, but his reproduction of Nature: or, more loftily and truly, his re-creation of symbols to take their place beside the appearances of Nature as clues to the colossal powers behind them both: in short, his Art. Shakespeare's various descriptions of sunrises, for instance, do not so much put us in mind of sunrises, as they put us in memory of those things that the splendour of sunrises themselves remind us of. They both prompt us to thoughts of Eternity; they both wake in us our divine hunger. Yet this Art needs to be given its fashion: and it is the Poet's craft that must needs achieve this end.

How difficult it is to disentangle the involutions of the two can be seen from the fact that, in a certain sense, versification is a matter of craftsmanship, whereas characterisation is a matter of artistic conception. Yet, in Shakespeare's drama, characterisation is, and can only be, expressed in versification, and cannot be known outside of it. Hamlet, for us, is what he says; and what he says depends on the skill with which Shakespeare was able to employ the medium of words. To say, therefore, that Shakespeare's characters at the outset of his dramatic career tended to artificiality, growing to a height of power at the later midmost of his course, and concluding with a subtlety and mental energy difficult to understand, is truly another way of saying that this was the course taken by his powers of versification: and contrariwise. This is not sufficiently taken into consideration when thinking of Shakespeare's work. The criticism is often levelled at him that he is too fond of an elliptical construction of sentence. Yet how otherwise was he to express a character, such as Hamlet, whose stormy passion of thought was such that his very ideas merged into one another, losing their logical sequence and method. And to fault Hamlet for an elliptical way of thinking would be rather like faulting him for the Destiny into whose toils he had been caught.

Nevertheless, it is true that Shakespeare's use of emotional stress in speech (what is meant when he is spoken of as overfond of elliptical constructions, bombast, an eager leaping from metaphor to metaphor, and vivid imagery) serves other turns than merely to express abnormal characters. It is a thing exceedingly difficult to say, and yet not oversay; but often it is evident that a violence of monologue or dialogue has a certain business to achieve in the mind of the spectator, over and above its use as an expression of a character. Were this regarded as Shakespeare's deliberate preparation for some or other urgent scene, it might perhaps legitimately be considered as a function of his craft; but it is actually

Shakespeare's subconscious method of striking us to emotional sympathy with the Action, and thus it is more truly a matter of his Art, belonging, as it does, to his very conception of things.

A very noteworthy instance of this is the following passage, spoken by Macbeth, so often, so keenly, and so adversely criticised. It begins, "If it were done when 'tis done, then 'twere well it were done quickly," and proceeds to a rapid statement of his responsibilities touching the king, who has honoured him, and who is now his guest. Then it flies off thus :

> Besides this Duncan
> Hath borne his faculties so meek, hath been
> So clear in his great office, that his virtues
> Will plead like angels, trumpet-tongued, against
> The deep damnation of his taking-off;
> And pity, like a naked new-born babe
> Striding the blast, or Heaven's cherubim horsed
> Upon the sightless couriers of the air,
> Shall blow the horrid deed in every eye
> That tears shall drown the wind. I have no spur
> To prick the sides of my intent, but only
> Vaulting ambition, which o'erleaps itself,
> And falls on th' other side.

What is the function of this? Metaphor to metaphor succeeds in violent alternation; and the mind is whipped to an extraordinary passion of excitement. An examination of the scene soon discovers the cause of this. For immediately prior to this Duncan had been seen arriving at Macbeth's

Castle; and in the succeeding scene it is ordained that Macbeth shall slay the ancient king. To pass from one directly to the other would be to create a mental revulsion that could not help destroying the sympathy with Macbeth that is so essential to our interest in the play. Moreover, it would ruin those smoother modulations of rising and fluctuating interest that Shakespeare so largely employed in order to achieve his unity of effect. That is to say, a scene should intervene in which nothing material should happen, but which should yet attune our minds to the tragic happenings about to arrive. How this could be done better than Shakespeare does it, it would be difficult to say. Angels that plead, " trumpet-tongued, against the deep damnation" of Duncan's taking-off; "pity, like a naked new-born babe striding the blast"; "Heaven's cherubim horsed upon the sightless couriers of the air": what are these but so many flails that whip the mind into a foaming excitement, preparing it to receive any terrible thing? When Lady Macbeth proceeds:

> I've given suck, and know
> How tender 'tis to love the babe that milks me :
> I would, while it was smiling in my face,
> Have pluck'd my nipple from his boneless gums,
> And dashed the brains on't out, had I so sworn
> As you have done to this :

what is this again but a further scourging of the mind to excitement? The effect of it all is to attune our minds to the dominant that shall pervade the ensuing scene, and to lead us away from the gentler dominant that pervaded the preceding scene. Perhaps in all things, but certainly in drama, nothing is good or excellent in itself; it has its value from the service it fulfils in procuring the total effect. It is beside the point to say that the whole scene in question is so oversaturated with splendour and rapidity of metaphor that it is overweening and bombastical. The only question is, what would be the result if the whole scene were eliminated? And then, surely, the question answers itself.

To judge the value of this, it is only necessary to read a modern dramatist in translation. Ibsen, for example. The fault that characterises him in translation may also characterise him in his original tongue : or it may not : but phrased in the English speech, with metaphors few, or none, it is exceedingly difficult to realise sometimes, in the acting or the reading, that the scene before us is indeed momentous and vivid. Our emotions do not spring to the scene, simply because the speech of the characters does not attune us to their mood.

A similar use of the same agency is to be found in the scene where Hamlet and his comrades are awaiting the coming of the ghost on the battlements. The opening comments on the nipping and the eager air are strangely pent with emotion; while the subsequent shooting of ordnance within, with Hamlet's answer to Horatio's inquiry as to the cause of it, do charge the mind, for some strange and inexplicable reason, with a nervous tensity, well calculated to make the subsequent coming of the ghost a thing of terror. If drama be a mere sequence of happenings, then, truly enough, these turnings aside from the strict, severe sequence, are not dramatic. But if drama be not merely a sequence of happenings, but a sympathetic conveyance of these happenings into the mind of the spectator, then such turnings aside are of the very stuff of drama. To succeed in this prime end, Shakespeare had to employ his only medium—Words: and he charged them, therefore, with an eager and rapid use of metaphor.

This question of dramatic expression, or speech in drama, has other bearings too, in elucidation of Shakespeare, and in illumination of much else. For only by dramatic speech can dramatic thoughts and emotions be conceived. Now drama is concerned with the great moments of existence. On the stage of drama characters play in which the many may see themselves depicted, not in the sordid round of their lives, nor with the wearied pulse of their aspirations, but at their greatest, noblest, and terriblest moments, at such hours when they know themselves most themselves, the memory of which may rescue them, and keep them aloof, from that littleness which alone is failure. Clearly, then, drama, to realise itself, must express in corresponding speech. If it employ the language of everyday life, the language of the ordinary habits of conversation, straightway, then, it falls beneath its own level. It denies itself in that very act. It is in this the clear, sharp cleavage announces itself between Reality and what is termed Realism. Realism is ever sordid : Reality is air taken on great heights. The husband that slew his wife when wild with liquor, is Realism: the splendour of first love, bringing thoughts of divinity, is Reality. It may so chance that disillusion may strike past all sordid accidentals to Reality; but then there would need to be involved in it some great ideal. There is Reality in Hamlet; there is also Reality in Timon, and, in a lesser degree, in Troilus. But to the realisation of all this there is needed a purging, a chastening, an exaltation, and, at times, a sheer splendour, of speech.

Therefore those who will have it that Shakespeare's employment of language is unnatural, have still to define what is meant therein by the word natural. Who has not felt, at some supreme moment of existence, Sandra Belloni's impetuous outcry to be permitted to speak in Shakespeare's speech, meaning thereby some speech equally exalted and adequate? The graces of conversational speech are an impertinence to such moods. They are more than an impertinence : they are simply unnatural. The rarity of words can alone bear such rarities of passion : even what is known as slang may be employed with vivid and startling effect, like Henry V.'s reference to the devils that "do botch and bungle up damnation with patches."

Words full of colour can alone convey the colour of such moods; and the cadences of music and song can alone sing out the lyric of such intensities of thought. In simple ungarnished fact, these are the only expressions natural to such moods; and it is only in the memory of such moods and moments as these that we pass bravely through the jolts and bars of existence.

It is this that explains Shakespeare's choice of verse for the speech of his dialogue. That it was not, as it seems with Ben Jonson, merely a varied form of his prose, can be seen from even a cursory examination of his alternation from one to the other. As has already been pointed out, it is evident that Shakespeare's characters did not speak verse by accident or from discipline: they were conceived as speaking verse. In a sense, they came into Shakespeare's imagination speaking verse, even before he discovered, by dint of intellectual labour, precisely what verse it was they spoke. Take, for example (cleaving still to the play already spoken of), the supreme and solitary instance when Lady Macbeth leaves the use of verse for prose. It has been suggested[1] that the matter of the scene is "too sublime, too austerely grand, to admit of anything so artificial as the measured language of verse, even though the verse were Shakespeare's." But what actually is the scene; and with what does it deal? When Lady Macbeth was urging her husband to the murder of Duncan, being who and what she was, was she more unnatural then, or when she was sleep-walking? Urging the contemplative Macbeth to the determined deed, she was in full possession of all her faculties and energy; and so she gave expression to her whole nature in verse that concentrated its imagery around the one definite goal she had set herself. The deed done, the goal achieved, the horror of the thing swept on her and broke her. She was no longer herself. In her waking hours she might gather herself together, and defy the ruin of her mind. But when the Self sleeps, the agent of the Self, the Will, sleeps also. And then her broken being found its expression in broken and disjointed language, in broken and disjointed pictures and memories. Clearly verse was no agent for such a moment. Prose, the *Johannes factotum* of all save the peaks of existence, had of necessity to step in, and convey the droning querulous monotone, so wrung with pity as it is.

So it is with the terrible moment prior to Othello's swooning. The grossness of Iago's pictures, striking on the centre of his being, had shivered his mind. His being reeled at the blow. Was he then most himself, or least himself? The clear fact is that he then fell away from himself: and as he fell precipitously from the clear light in which he might have knowledge of things, to the darkness where all things were blotted, he ejaculated brokenly the sight he had had of the things that had stricken him down. How different the mood when he cried:

> O, now, for ever
> Farewell the tranquil mind! farewell content!
> Farewell the plumèd troop, and the big wars,
> That make ambition virtue! O, farewell!
> Farewell the neighing steed, and the shrill trump,
> The spirit-stirring drum, th' ear-piercing fife,
> The royal banner and all quality,
> Pride, pomp, and circumstance of glorious war!

In one he was broken and shattered. In the other sorrow has sharpened his senses so that the very smell of grasses and of distant herbs was snuffed clearly by him, and the noise of the creeping things of the earth smote on his ear with a several and distinct impact. It was not a moment that could in the nature of things last long; but while it lasted it was vivid and keen beyond expression of language. And thus it voiced itself in the rhythm and beat of verse, and a cry of poetry. It was a splendid moment, a vivid moment, a poetic moment. But in the other he rambled and stumbled through prose to silence.

Shakespeare's use of prose is very subtly indicative of his dramatic method. There are occasions when the high emotional tension caused, not by the verse, but by the employment of moods that compelled the use of verse, are so exhaustive to the attentive mind that a relief must be created somehow or somewhere. It is so after the lengthy murder-scene in *Macbeth*. The very exhaustion of the mind would have caused a continuance of that tense mood to fall into utter bathos. The knocking on the outer door, too, works the mind up to its final limit of tension. So in comes the Porter: a positively prose character, speaking the natural prose of his mind in the famous devil-portering monologue. It might be imagined that the entrance of Macduff and Lennox would resume the tension. But no! the prose mood and the prose diction continue awhile in the interlocutory with the Porter: and a little reflection shows why. For on their entrance the spectators at once prepare to resume the tension. Plainly, therefore, if Shakespeare refused to resume the higher mood on the instinct of their preparation, the additional half-relief this would convey to them would be so grateful that when later he did indeed reintroduce the tension he could not fail to carry with him a rested and eager audience. And be it noted how the tenser mood is resumed. After their parley with the Porter, Macduff asks, "Is thy master stirring?" and the words are easy and negligent in cadence. Then the whole mood is tightened and braced by the firm step of metrical tension: "Our knocking has awaked him; here he comes": and forthwith the mood flames high again.

In Hamlet, again, it is obvious that when he speaks to the Gravedigger, or with the Players, he should speak in prose. The matter is prose. They are of a piece with the many prose characters in

Shakespeare who speak their native language. A far subtler matter is the well-known Nunnery-scene. For what is the scene? Ophelia has been won by that effete old intriguer, her father, to play a part, and to demonstrate to the watchers behind the curtains that it is Hamlet's love for her that has distracted him. Naturally she is anxious to lift the mood to poetry: and in so far as she truly loved Hamlet it would be true poetry, though in so far as she remembered the part she had to play it would have to be a bastard and mock poetry. For his part, Hamlet loved her: and so as he opens the dialogue he speaks at once in the purity of the loftier mood: "Nymph, in thy orisons be all sins remembered." Naturally she turns to him and speaks in the same tongue, though it rings on the false note of formality: "Good, my lord, how does your Honour for this many a day?" But he had not expected this: she had withheld him from her, by her father's edict, "this many a day," and he half expected a rebuff from her. He is preplexed. Yet he continues the mood with "I humbly thank you." Then all at once his perplexity breaks into suspicion: for some strangeness in her manner, some rustle of the curtain, has caught his attention. At once the poetic mood in his mind is broken; and the metrical march of his sentence subsides into a "Well, well, well." There is no more poetry in the scene for him: it is flat prose, coarse prose, brutal, disillusioned prose; but always prose. It is not so with her, however;

and she seeks to resume the mock poetry. But
with a ruthless blow he crumbles the poetic edifice
to the dust, it being but a mock, sordid thing.
"Ha, ha! are you honest?" asks he; and with that
word the poetry is gone, till, on his exit, she resumes
it in a very tender and frailly genuine concern at his
ruin of mind. There is probably no scene in all
Shakespeare in which this exquisite adjustment of
prose and metre express so truly the inner realities
of the minds at work in the dialogue.

There are, indeed, a lengthy procession of
characters in Shakespeare, the natural speech of
whose mouths is prose. Headed, it is, by fat Sir
John, and brought up gallantly by honest, if something obtuse, Dogberry and Verges, Sir Toby Belch,
own cousin to Sir John Falstaff, though without
the philosophy, his dupe, Sir Andrew Aguecheek,
the egregious Malvolio, Bottom, and his histronic
confederates, Bardoph, Nym, Pointz (not Pistol,
for he was a would-be poetic, a strutting braggadocio,
discontented with his prose estate), Parolles, Lafeu,
Launcelot Gobbo, Launce, Touchstone, Autolycus,
and many another rogue, and many another clown,
to say nothing of the more stolid characters strewn
about, to support the action at awkward moments;
and they are all conceived in prose, born in prose, and
urgent with life in prose. There are two, however,
that must be withheld from their place in the company: and these are Benedick and Beatrice. To
these a rebirth is granted. Born in prose, Love

visits them; and they pass to poetry. But the rest are born in prose, and live all their lives in that medium. In the case of those who have no lives to live, but only parts to play, the servitors, soldiers, and other such accessories, it is easy to understand why they should stand so completely in prose. As said, they have no lives to live, and therefore have never the opportunity of springing to the intensity of poetry, whatever their potentialities be. But the others awake a matter of deeper interest.

It is to be noted that nearly all of these are either humour in themselves, or the cause that humour is in other men. Now while it is possible that wit may on occasion rise to intensity, humour is broad and relaxing. Humour lays its arms akimbo and laughs merrily out; or it holds itself strangely aloof, while soft lightnings play through the mind. Humour does not knit the brow, or hold the passion in suspense. Humour is stranger to all the deeper, fiercer throes: and at their faintest touch it is fled past all recall. So it was with Benedick and Beatrice. When Love finally came to them, it became necessary at once to draw them up into the general plot of the play, for, not being the central interest, there was a fear of their being of no interest at all, the interest of humour having departed from them. Even the suspicion (frail suspicion though it was) of a deeper interest is sufficient to empty half the splendour out of Falstaff in *The Merry Wives of Windsor*. Wisely, and on an excellent instinct,

Shakespeare kept the fat old knight free from love itself, even though his monarch might have wished to see him smitten thus. But the suggestion of love was there: and by that token we know the Falstaff of Windsor for a slender mockery of the unquenchable Falstaff of Eastcheap.

Humour being, then, the thing it is, its expression must needs be prose. This is not necessarily the case with other phases of comedy. Mercutio, for instance, is an example of a comic character; but with him the comedy is that of wit, in which it might be said that the humour is neither broad nor tender, but light, compact, and brilliant. There is also a comedy that is light, subtle, or graceful; for the expression of which the nimbler tread of metre must be invoked, as Molière well knew. Melancholy, too, demands the compactness that slow verse can give it: as is exemplified in the case of Jaques, for all that his melancholy was couched in humour. But humour, humour intact and pure, is conceived in the breadth and ease of prose, and must therefore be expressed in that medium. The Art of all Drama is to express each emotion in its natural and apt diction; and even as passion in Tragedy, or beauty and intensity in Comedy, the peaks of existence, demand Poetry, so the laughing, sleek, undulating valleys of humour, broad as they are, and relaxing withal, seek to find their vent in Prose.

It is here a proper distinction suggests itself, both from the inherent nature of the matter, and from

Shakespeare's practice in it. Humour, be it said, is one of two things: or rather, humour is to be gleaned from two manners of people. They are those who are themselves the genuine creators of humour; and there are those who, unhappily for themselves, are the cause of humour in others. Falstaff most justly claimed to be both: "I am not only witty in myself," said he, "but the cause that wit is in other men." Of the former kind are the clowns who wag their baubles through the plays: of the latter kind are Pistol and Parolles. There is no humour in either of the latter; but they are the abundant cause of humour in other men. For the cause of humour in other men is their very pretension. They would be other than they are. They would eschew prose, and speak poetry. They would mimic the high and heroic; and the humour in others is to expose their pretension; to prick the bubble of the would-be poetry, and expose them for frail prose-creatures after all.

Thus it can be seen what accord there is, in the main, between the proper conception of Shakespeare's characters and the language in which they speak. How much this truth of conception meant to his work may be discovered from a reading of his historical plays. Their interest is at best remote. Many of the kings are very far from being kingly persons—unless there be the cynic to respond that kingly persons are of a truth habitually of this wise. But poetry is lofty speech; and since, therefore, Shakespeare puts into their mouths such diction as should have characterised them, they and their matter are exalted into interest. For, from the standpoint of Drama, neither kings nor commoners are of interest, save in the light of the destiny, tragic or comic, in which they are framed, and to which they contribute. Bombast is all too often on their lips, and the speech of their mouth is frequently a fustian ambition; but bombast and fustian are an indication, if an inverse indication, of the things of which they are bombast or fustian. Indeed, the points require only to be shifted a little, and what had seemed bombast and fustian before, is at once to be seen interlaced and intertwined with the deeper matter. Poetic speech on the lips of an unpoetic person is compact of that pretension we call either bombast or fustian. But it needs only a slight reconstruction for the mind to see the person through his speech, and to identify him with his speech; in which case the thought of fustian is lost. And it is such an interest as this that saves the latter part of *Richard II.*

This question of diction in Drama is the prime matter of all interest, since it is words, and words alone, that form the expression of Drama. And when, therefore, we find such a man as Shakespeare, so subtle in his choice of medium and character, and so pure in his conception of both, couching the more noteworthy of his characters infallibly in poetry, the situation is one that demands investigation. One cannot help remembering that the earlier splendour of Drama with the Greeks was also couched in poetry. And one cannot help being struck by the fact that, in modern days, the chief fact that hampers Ibsen in his struggle with permanent fame, is just this, that his characters are couched in prose. He himself felt this. If *The Master Builder* contains any allegory of his own dramatic architecture (and the suggestion seems too obvious to be missed), even as the Master Builder deliberately turned from the building of churches to the erection of humble dwellings, so Ibsen turned from poetic conception in Drama, in *Peer Gynt*, and *Brand* to the prose conception of *The League of Youth*, *The Doll's House*, and *Ghosts*: and even as the Master Builder determined thenceforward to put spires on to his dwellings, so Ibsen determined to put poetic meanings, by the agency of symbolism, on to his prose plays, with the result of *Little Eyolf*, *John Gabriel Borkman*, and *When We Dead Awaken*.

Now, symbolism is but a mechanical conveyance of the poetic idea. It is not Poetry. It is not Life. In symbolism, understood as such, the thing symbolised never happens: it is only symbolised. Symbolism is generally a confession of failure on the part of the artist, as though he had not enough emotional power to give us actuality. In the realm of pigment both the failure and strength of symbolism is very clear. For the sudden passionate ardour of a kiss, is Love. It needs no symbolism to convey the idea of Love: it is the warm, tremendous reality: it is Love itself. But such portrayal of a kiss needs to bring conviction in every line and colour of it; it must fail nowhere, at peril of our disgust and contempt. Obviously, then, a single maiden, with red roses wreathed in her hair (the red rose being the symbol of love), is an unspeakably simpler task; and so it can easily be seen how the latter method could rapidly amass a numerous school unto itself, energy and strength of imagination being gifts spread neither widely nor freely on the earth. Nevertheless, the limitation of pictorial art is such that symbolism not only has its place, it has its abundant excuse. But in Drama it is different. Drama so freely invites the hot pulse of Life that the mechanical conveyance of ideas is at once felt to be a frigid impertinence. It might be said that there is no one symbolic idea ever used in Drama, or ever likely to be used in Drama, that could not be better conveyed by the direct presentation of actuality. Would a dramatist convey the futility of Man in the toils of Woman? What need, then, to suggest it by the aid of external hints when the tremendous thing itself can be seen in *Antony and Cleopatra.* Is it the external encompassing and futility of Death? What, then, of the end of King Lear? Would we know what transpires when we dead awaken? Then, if we thought aright, the fact that we stand and approve the dead Desdemona, failure though she be, and reject and spurn Iago, were he never so successful, would provide us the clue to this. For, since it is apparent that we do not approve and condemn according to the finding of this world, it is equally apparent that we are taking our stand according to the finding of another world.

But it is noticeable that what is called symbolism is nearly always imposed on a prose medium. It is as though, the poetic actuality be missing, the dramatist must convey it by the hints and mechanism of symbolism; as though, the stronger lineaments being missing, Drama is driven to the necessity of tricking itself out in the meretricious habiliments of artifice. It is to the credit of Ibsen to say (what cannot be said of other of his contemporaries) that he ever avoided the weakness of making his whole play dependent of symbolism. He employed it, whether freely or scarcely, rather in the way of adventitious aid. But he was driven to it, as he himself seems to have seen, by the very fact that he had earlier foresworn the poetic conception of Drama, and scarce knew what to do in face of his later discovery that it is the seemingly useless cathedrals that man cleaves fast to, as the perpetual poetry of his soul, rebuilding and discarding his dwelling-houses even as he lightly esteems his prose. He placed steeples on his dwelling-houses; he kept his prose conception, and decked it with poetic additions: and in that act he stood out in sharp contradistinction to Shakespeare, the very body of whose conception was poetic, and who therefore had no need of poetic adjuncts.

In all this the meaning given by its adherents themselves to the word symbolism had been adopted. In a sense it is of course true that Shakespeare is full of symbolism. The picture of Lear faced and thwarted by the strength which he himself has brought into the world; Cordelia first, then Goneril and Regan, defying him just as he had often defied his enemies, even because they were his daughters and had his blood in their veins—that is a fine symbolic idea. Hamlet, placed in midst of a perplexity where not only was his own character his undoing, but where he was chiefly futile through his very virtues, not his vices — that, too, is superb symbolism. But, in that sense of the word symbolism, they are symbolical in precisely the same way as the mighty curve of a horse's neck is symbolical of strength: simply because it is strength. Which is quite another thing from the symbolism, technically so-called, which is so little identified with the thing it would express that it often demands a considerable initiation into the symbols it employs. Nor must the method be confused with the suggestion of autobiographic parallels with the action afoot. No one would confuse David Copperfield with symbolism; and no one may therefore confuse *The Tempest* with symbolism. Symbolism, like Poetry, is only concerned with abstract ideas: only, while Symbolism seeks to suggest them by mechanical contrivance, Poetry is conceived and born of them.

Thus it is interesting to see a later age reaching after the greatness of Attic and Elizabethan Drama, and failing simply because it either had not the courage or the strength to conceive of Drama poetically. Shakespeare so conceived. He might strew his plays with prose characters. Many of his purely poetic characters might fall into prose moods. Both were very fitting; and both showed a very shrewd insight into the nature of the poetic: but the major portion of his creations thought, spoke, and lived in the strength of poetry. And to say so much of him is to say that he struck past the toys of Time to the substance of Eternity, past impermanencies to the permanent. It only remains to see how he treated the permanent.

A little reflection soon shows both why and how it has come about that great Drama has ever expressed itself in the music of Poetry. Psychologies apart, the constitution of man's expression divides itself mainly into two wide divisions: intellectual and emotional. The distinctions are real in spite of the fact that they often intermingle; and intermingle not only in substance but in function also. That is to say, not only is emotion often cast in the form of intellectual pain and joy, and not only does intellect know its own emotional throbs and excitements, but emotion may be compact of itself and yet have the option of expressing itself by its own medium or by the medium of intellect. Anger, for example, is the emotional expression of a man's soul.

But in translating itself into action it may employ one of two methods: it may choose its own emotional method by means of a straight and lusty blow; or it may choose the intellectual method of a stinging phrase. Similarly an intellectual conception, such as the equality of the sexes, may express itself in the forms of its own medium, in argument, or in the forms of an emotional medium, in strife.

But though they intermingle, as all things in Life are compelled to mingle and lose their entities, the distinction between the emotional and the intellectual is not artificial, but very real. It is possible for them each to have its function unimpinged from start to finish by contact with the other: or rather, to put it more accurately, since the basis of a man's life is emotion rather than intellect, while it is possible for emotion to move through its whole ambit without contact with the intellectual, it is only rarely and remotely possible for intellect to have its being apart from emotion. Nearly every intellectual conception first started in the emotions. Also nearly every intellectual conception concludes in, or produces, a desire that derives its weight and power from the emotions. Man is a creature of emotion. He trusts, and believes in, his emotions. He may be convinced of the logical truth of an intellectual conception; he may believe himself securely housed in the faith of it; but in the moment of crisis he will always act on the instinct of his emotions, even though these rebut his intellectual beliefs at every point. It is true, he may not happen so to act, on rare occasions; but then he forthwith becomes the more a machine and the less a man; he stands in peril of alienating himself from humanity. He may even be right in so acting; but then the general acclamation will be, and his own subconscious discomfort will attest, that, were he right never so much, he was yet right in a wrong way. Which is another way of saying that the thing of health in a man is his emotion and not his intellect.

Drama, therefore, being concerned with the conflict of men, whether among themselves, or against Fates, Destinies, and Systems, is built out of the emotions that rule men. Drama being a microcosm of Life, must be true to the powers that impel and sway Life. It may be possible for Drama to depict the primal and ever-potent emotion of some man or men insurgent against the cold chains of intellectual conception. But it is not possible for Drama to be built out of purely intellectual conceptions, because then the oppositions and conflicts that would arise would not be the oppositions and conflicts of Life but of Argument. Moreover, the intellectual conception that won in the end of all would at once be suspect, because the conclusion would be unavoidable that the dramatist had conspired to its victory having in mind a subtle didactic axe to be ground. Whereas the exaltation

HIS ART

at the end of the greatest Drama arises from the fact that, the assortment of factors being what they were, the conclusion in question was inevitable. Which can only arise from the free impact of the emotions, even though in their expression they saw fit to employ the highest intellectual refinement and subtlety.

Now, the obvious speech of the emotion is Poetry. It is even the habit of men when some or other prose is largely suffused with emotional power and colour, to speak of it as poetical prose, or, maybe, the prose of a poet; as though, in the manner of Milton of old, the writer has forsaken his authentic method of expression and written with his left hand awhile. In such prose, the greater the stress of emotion the more marked are the rhythms that beat through it; for the voice of emotion cannot but speak in its true numbers even though it has to force them through the hindrances of an alien bondage. The long, stressful lives of men themselves could well provide the text for the fitness of this. In the great and critical moments of their lives, in the moments when they most realise themselves, that is to say their high, dramatic moments, the moments when their lives become Drama, such as puberty, first-love, marriage, child-birth, death, what an overwhelming mass of men take either to the writing of Poetry or the reading of Poetry! Therefore, to say that Drama has expressed itself in Poetry is only to say that Drama has expressed itself in its apt and natural language. And it is this that explains the incontestable fact that Drama, frail in dramatic power but couched in Poetry, is acclaimed as more notable than Drama strong in dramatic power but framed in Prose. It is the instinct of men discerning the fitness between manner and material.

This being so, it is more than interesting to find that the historic origin of Drama is in support of its identity with Poetry and the Emotions. Whether or not Greek Tragedy is to be identified with the Dionysian revels,[2] it is at least evident that it largely arose thence, being an expansion of the dithyramb composed for that occasion. And it is singular to note how, if it sprang not from a direct connection with Dionysus, it sprang at least from some sort of opposition to Apollo. Now, Apollo was god of the reason, even as Dionysus was god of the impulses; or, to maintain the distinction given already, Apollo was god of the intellect as Dionysus was god of the emotion. And the emotion in this case ranged itself in conscious or subconscious hostility to the intellect (let the Dionysian revelry declare with what abandon!); Poetry ranged itself against Prose, took up the wild tumult of the dithyramb, expanded a plot about it, and so reached forward to its amazing blossom of glory in Æschylus, Sophocles, and Euripides.

Such an attestation of Shakespeare's truth of instinct in conceiving of Drama poetically would be difficult to overvalue. There is no doubt that he gave not a little thought to the subject, for some of his passages from prose to poetry, and from poetry to prose, point with more than ordinary clearness to the transitions of a thinking mind; yet in the main it was instinct rather than thought that led him to it. With a mind such as his, probably the thinking mind followed up the discoveries of the instinct, enlarging, expanding, and experimenting on them. Moreover, a further curious result of such an attestation arises in the fact that whereas Shakespeare's poetic characters are nearly always and inevitably dramatic, his prose characters are seldom so. Falstaff is not, strictly speaking, dramatic. The interest in him is the interest of a jolly interlude. When he became more dramatic, in the *Merry Wives*, he became less Falstaff. Nor was good Sir Toby; nor was Bottom, despite his histrionic ambitions; nor were the many Clowns, with a wonder of exception in the Fool attendant on Lear. In truth, it was Shakespeare's own peculiar discovery that the deft distribution of undramatic matter through a tense dramatic interest, strengthened the movement tremendously by varying its rate of pace—especially under the special conditions of the stage for which he wrote.

At the cost of reiteration it seems necessary to repeat that the question at the moment is not merely, if even mainly, one of characters into whose mouths poetry or prose is put. With nearly all Ben Jonson's characters we cannot but feel that it is largely immaterial as to whether they spoke verse or prose. The Alchemist, for example, was, we feel, the Alchemist much as he now is, in the initial prose that Ben told Drummond he always first "wrote his verses in." King Lear, Hamlet, and Macbeth, Romeo and Juliet, even Beatrice and Benedick, are, however, of a wholly different nature. In prose they would simply not be the people we know them now to be. It is a thing impossible to define; but it is a thing quite unmistakably real to the imagination. The essence of the matter lies in the conception of the thinking mind. Shakespeare conceived poetically or in prose, as the case may be; with the result that his characterisation rings inevitably, in the main, in the language chosen. Ben Jonson, on the other hand, conceived in prose, the final verse form being a transliteration from the original; and it is possible, therefore, for the imagination to put its penetrating edge between the characterisation and the language it is framed in. And it has been seen that Æschylus, Sophocles, and, in a lesser degree, Euripides, conceived as Shakespeare conceived and not as Jonson conceived; and of them one could say, as one could not say of Jonson, that their power was compact of the tense power and stuff of Drama. That is to say, whereas in Jonson one is striking the hardness of the intellect the whole time, in Shakespeare one is impressed by the full-orbed power of the emotion.

It is ever so, turn where one will. It might perhaps be thought that there could be no higher achievement of the intellect than Hamlet. Yet the problem of Hamlet is not an intellectual one, but one deriving from his emotions. All Hamlet's acute mental stress was an appearance in the mind of the storm-tost emotion below. On the one hand, there was the acute grief arising from the death of his father, the suspicions that his quick intuitions sprang to from the strangeness of the event, the deep sexual abhorrence caused by his mother's speedy marriage with her own brother-in-law, with the final enormity in the course of nature caused by his father's appearance to him in ghostly shape. These were in themselves sufficient so to overwhelm his emotions, as a son and a man, that his brain reeled under the effort to express, and, at the same time, restrain, the urgent fury that it had to form in language, and so convey into the field of Drama. But to these things there were added further difficulties that assailed him on the other hand. Honour is a function of the emotion; and Hamlet was instinct with honour —the very violence of his behaviour sometimes only attesting it the more. In striking at the King without a full assurance of his guilt, was to him not only to strike at the legal monarch of the realm, but also to seem as though he was seizing a pretext to strike for the throne, he being the next in succession. Even when he knew that he could no more be called to account by the people, at the moment of death, he yet took up the responsibilities a susceptible honour laid on him, and bade Horatio "report me and my cause aright to the unsatisfied." Moreover, to strike at the King was to strike at his mother; and, apart from the fact that she was yet his mother, he knew not whether or not she was involved in his father's death.

To speak of Hamlet as being either sane or mad, therefore, is much to misconceive him. If to be mad means to be mentally deranged, then he certainly was not mad. But if to be mad mean to be mentally overburdened, then he certainly was mad: and the overburdening came from his overwrought emotions. It is in this sense madness always comes to the men of Shakespeare's mind; and, it may be said, it is in this sense that madness comes upon a good many men that people the broad earth. But to confuse it with insanity is a confusion indeed. Insanity is an intellectual derangement; while such madness is a storm waked in the mind by a gusty and perplexed passion. The former has a distinct and sharp cleavage from, it is even violently opposed to, a condition of health: the latter grows out of a normal condition as inevitably as a mountain may ascend from a valley; and it may even be evidence of a condition of health. With Hamlet it was so. The poignancy of his position arose from the fact that his perplexity dated from the very fineness of his susceptibilities. He falls in and out of normality, like a wave in and out of the sea, according to the stress of the conditions about him. The contending passion of his emotions hold a poise in his mind; on the one hand, an insurgent filial affection, with its attendant grief and emotion of revenge; and, on the other hand, his honour, and the doubt it raises as to the necessity of a clear, undeniable proof of guilt: with the result that, whether his mind flame high as the result of an abnormal excitement, or subside into its normal tenour of passion, the balance of contention makes it impossible for him to take action one way or another.

For this poise to be removed, that is to say for action to become possible to him, it is necessary, firstly, that he should prove the King's guilt upon him, or let the King prove it himself, and, secondly, that he should prove his mother's innocence. With these emotional restrictions removed on the one side and the other, it would then be possible for the passion for revenge to rush forward and translate itself into action. And this was just what transpired in the event. When the King had proved his guilt, not alone to Horatio and himself, but before the whole Court, it is Hamlet's thought at once to discover if his mother had been an accomplice in the guilt. It is this that explains his seeming hesitancy when he sees the King on his knees. A good deal of the misunderstanding that Shakespeare has met has arisen from the fact that his critics have omitted to take into consideration the fundamental factor swaying the action of his characters; and that is, the great emotional waves that fill them to overflowing. There are many such instances; and this is one of them. For instance, what is the emotion swaying Hamlet at the moment he sees the King on his knees? Whence has he come? Whither is he going? Then the truth transpires. He has just come from the scene in which the King has convicted himself; and he is actually on the way to discover whether his mother was an accomplice in the crime that so stinks in his nostrils. That is to say, a continuous act is proceeding in his soul, that act being the clearance of the double obstruction between his urgent passion of revenge and its fulfilment. His mind is, therefore, impetuous to conclude its business; whereas to slay the King would not only impede the conclusion, perhaps frustrate it for ever, but would, moreover, be to take action before the moment was ripe for it. Yet he is also in a tense state of excitement; and so, in in the manner of him, his abnormality flames high, and he unpacks his soul with words whose very hideousness and abandon of pictorial imagination are a proof of the wild flames surging through him. It is not that he is indecisive. It is rather that the moment for decision is not yet, a further clearance of obstruction being forward. "My mother stays," he says: "this physic but prolongs thy sickly days."

And so he goes out to shed his soul of its emotional mood; intending later to return and complete the business in orderly fashion.

Once in his mother's presence, however, action is thrust upon him. He is not ripe for the action; and yet the unripeness is not so much. For it is plain in her manner and her speech that, however guilty she be of weakness and indecency, she is yet innocent of complicity in her husband's murder. So when he thinks the King is hidden behind the arras, he does not hesitate to lunge at him with intent to kill him. But it is not the King who lurks there. It is Polonius, the would-be astute old schemer. He had slain an innocent man. That very fact, with the extraordinary excitement it produces in his sensitive mind (an emotional stress that has the very shape and colour of madness), threw him into the King's power; and so the intended action is made impossible for him, firstly, because his strangeness of behaviour has discredited him, and, secondly, because, before this moment of discredit has passed, the King has dismissed him to England.

Thus, by regarding this crucial part of the play from the standpoint of Hamlet's emotion, a perfect and intelligible sequence evolves itself. Viewed from the intellectual standpoint it seems indeed criss-cross, strange, and contradictory. But when it is once seen that there is one complete emotional wave at work, uttering itself in its own elliptical poetry, a wave that must spend itself before other and more purposeful emotions take its place, the mental sequence is clear to the understanding. And how true this is may be seen from an examination of Hamlet's behaviour on his return to Denmark. It is no more abnormal: for the emotional stress is over. Emotional obstructions, too, of honour and filial kindliness are gone; and there is only the relentless destiny to be achieved. Therefore he is quite calm about it, seeking only to find the occasion.

Poetry is infinitely true to life in this very fact that it springs from the emotion and not from the intellect. Intellectual action always has an inward coherence and compactness, while emotional action has this only from without. In recalling his actions to memory man is, more frequently than not, in perplexity at them. And for an exceedingly simple reason. When his actions were achieved his whole being was tense with emotion, suffusing his intellect with its own co-ordination. At the moment of recollection the emotion has passed away, and the alert intellect can only see the outstanding discrepancies of conduct with consequent wonder and perplexity. It is this very process that is repeated in intellectual criticism of plays, such as Shakespeare's, that are compact of emotion. The only just rectification of this is to dismiss the intellectual analysis and to recover the emotional sympathy.

A strange and outstanding example of this proffers itself, of even greater illumination than the case of

Hamlet. A poet, whose calm mind is, perhaps, little apt to enter into or understand the emotional storms of Shakespeare's mind, has but recently given it as an example of Shakespeare's faultiness of detail that Othello should have been permitted to give credit to Iago's suggestion of Desdemona's infidelity, when it was obvious that there had been no time for her hinted intimacy with Cassio.[3] The criticism, as criticism, is well placed. There certainly was no time for such infidelity, much less for the grossness of desire with which Iago painted it. There was not even any colour in circumstance for him to base his charges on. All this is admitted. It is even in this wise that the mass of men look back upon their lives and regard some strange inexplicable crisis when actions were taken that later hours fail even to conceive.

What, however, were the factors in the case? Here was a great Moor, strong, virile, and gross withal, who for the first time in a well-lived life had been brought into the closest daily contact with a young beautiful girl, who was pure, and without knowledge in the ways of men. He was full of vigour and health, with even an exalted nobility of character, yet, by the nature of him, gross and passionate. She was tender, sensitive, and pure. It would be invidious to elaborate the situation further. It is sufficiently obvious to see that in the early days of these new conditions he would necessarily be sexually raw and inflamed. This was the emotional mood of him: one of the factors of the situation. The other factor was a man who reveals throughout the play that extraordinary divination of moods and men that characterises the rare men of this earth; men whose intuition is like a reflex of the mind. Moreover, he was a man who, before ever Othello appeared on the scene, proved to us that he delighted to paint in words the filthiest and most vivid pictures. Now men who have this first attribute, the mystical quality of divination, are inevitably men with an irresistible instinct for power; and it was this instinct for power that made it almost inevitable that he should seek to trip up so superb a specimen of humanity as Othello. He might not see it himself; he might even seek to find other explanations for his conduct; but, the conjunction of circumstances being what they were, he being who he was, and Othello being in the mood he was, he had to assert himself and claim the prey given him. It was as instinctive as the swift glance and unerring accuracy of a hawk, past all reason of restraint or explanation.

Thus Iago never once sought to prove his case. He was never once concerned with linking up a circumstantial chain of evidence. The whole bent and power of his mind was exercised in keeping the inflammation he had produced in Othello's imagination from dying away. This was the task he set himself; not the proving of Desdemona's guilt If once Othello's raw emotions relapsed from their passion of excitement, then, not only had the whole plot failed, but Iago stood in actual peril of his life—the spice of adventure that gave the whet of excitement to his mind. Whereas, if he could but manage to maintain this abnormal inflammation, then it was as sure as the sequence of inevitability that Othello, being the man he was, would either slay himself or Desdemona. Violence of some kind would be the only means of relief.

Note Iago's method of procedure in that wonderful third scene of the third act. When he first broaches a faint hint of infidelity in Desdemona, Othello is harassed and perplexed indeed, but yet master of himself. He remains so till Iago does the one thing that in his present mood is so deadly: the one thing, too (and this is the bitter irony and terror of it), that Iago was of all men the most fitted to give, as his earlier conversations indicate so terribly. Iago becomes gross. He suggests that Desdemona in marrying a black man gave proof of her indecent desires. His own choice of words suggests grossness.

> Not to affect many proposed matches
> Of her own clime, complexion and degree,
> Whereto we see in all things nature tends;—
> Foh! one may smell, in such, a will most rank,
> Foul disproportion, thoughts unnatural.

Thus his grossness has struck Othello's sexual rawness. At once he bids Iago go from him; for a terrible fire has spung up in his blood, that wants, not proof, not evidence, but only time to subside. But it is Iago's business to see that it never has time to subside.

We have already seen that in *Othello* Shakespeare largely departed from his usual framing of the five-act construction. Here we have the reason for it. An antithetical movement in the Fourth Act would mean that Iago would not be enabled to keep at full heat of passion this hideous fire that he has waked in Othello's mind. So the construction is thrown aside in order that the issue between Iago and Othello should be waged to the finish.

When next the two meet Othello has largely recovered himself. That is to say, his passion has turned from sexuality to red anger against Iago. He demands proofs. Does Iago give them? Not a bit of it! That is not his line of procedure. He has to strike Othello's grossness again; and so, in answering his impetuous demand for proofs, he says:

> Would you, the supervisor, grossly gape on?
> Behold her tupp'd?

"Death and damnation! O!" cries Othello, as his whole soul sickens at the picture, and his blood flames higher than ever. But Iago is not a man to leave his renewed advantage at that. He goes on coldly to describe the imagined bedding of the two with the utmost detail of circumstance and description.

It is all over with Othello at this. Iago had described Desdemona and Cassio as being "as prime as goats, as hot as monkeys"; and long after, after the visit of the Venetians, after his striking of Desdemona, he calls out wildly "Goats and monkeys!"

All this is not a matter for proof. Even the handkerchief is not used so much as proof as a suggestion of great intimacy. It is Iago's terrible insistence, apt and natural as it is to his mind, on this theme that makes it so impossible for Othello's brain to hold his emotion that he falls into a swoon. And Iago's conversation with Cassio while Othello looks on, is only intended to inflame further this sexual mood by the function of suggestion. To say that there is no proof of, nor time for, infidelity, is to say truly; but it is to touch the play nowhere. Drama, like life, is compact of emotion, and while the intellect requires proof and plausibility, the emotion only requires a sufficient actuation. And the combination of circumstances provided more than a sufficient actuation for Othello's character.

When Shakespeare built character he always built thus—save, of course, in his earlier days of experimentation. He conceived the inmost of his characters, and, holding truly to that, let their outward consistency fall in order as it might. In this, as is plain, he was true to life—which is to say that he was true to that larger than a merely logical synthesis that life represents. Such a character as, for instance, Brutus is paradoxically conceived: but the paradox is not one of perversity, it is one of truth; that is to say, it is not one of restlessness, but rather one of repose.

Not that he was always thus. In fact, he grew into it as he grew in imaginative power. In *Love's Labour's Lost* there is but little emotion, and therefore but little poetry, and therefore but little drama: what there is being, as clearly as one may discover, due rather to the 1597 revision than the much earlier original. Most of the Biron and Rosaline scenes, for example, belong to the later revision, as can be seen not alone from their general temper as opposed to their context (which argument, though fair, would seem at the moment somewhat like special pleading), but also from much internal evidence. One such instance is provided in the Fifth Act, following on from line 827. There is, to begin with, a five-line question and answer between Biron and Rosaline as to the nature of his punishment. Then when this is concluded, and a similar business has proceeded between Dumain and Katharine, and Longaville and Maria, the original question and answer between Biron and Rosaline is resumed, only now considerably amplified with emotional matter. In which, it is clear, we have the two separate layers of the two separate writings.

In its original form the hard intellectuality of *Love's Labour's Lost* is obvious. In fact, it has been well called the characteristically intellectual effort of a clever young man, meaning thereby that inexperience caused him rather to rely on brain-function without the suffusion of emotion, than on brain-function as the wise and deliberative shaping of a rich and powerful emotion. So, too, in *The Comedy of Errors*. Critics have fluctuated between the several appellations of comedy and farce for this play. And with justice. In the adjustment and movement hither and thither of the two pairs of twins the play relies on a purely intellectual ingenuity, whereas when the deeper interest of Adriana and Luciana, or Ægeon and Æmilia, intrudes on the scene, the emotion is carried far nearer comedy. In the other play which was probably acted at the same occasion at Court, *Richard III.*, we can see Shakespeare working away from this artificiality in a truly characteristic way. To break the bonds that tie him in this his first really individual effort, he relies on a sheer excess of strength in his chosen monarch. He does not wholly succeed; though he does indeed convey a strong impression of emotional power in Richard's very fury of intellectual strength. But he does so far succeed that *Midsummer Night's Dream* is coloured with emotion. Indeed, he succeeds in breaking his bonds only too well, for in *Richard II.* the emotion is somewhat over-maudlin to be wise. But in *King John*, chiefly in the last two acts, strength has reasserted itself; and in *Romeo and Juliet* it stands out in such full power and splendour that there can no more be any fear for the future of this dramatist, the more particularly when it is seen that he has also acquired the subtlety of letting his prose characters have their say in their native tongue.

He could not yet, however, permit his conceptions to have their free and unfettered sway. He had still to discipline his characters to convention, for he had elected to frame them in the ways of comedy. Orlando and Rosalind could not love like Romeo and Juliet, for there was the gentle divinity of pastoral comedy over their heads to subdue them to itself. Nor could Orsino and Viola, Sebastian and Olivia, prove too resolute a quartet, for the divinity of the comedy of manners hung overhead with main intent to expose so fatuous an egoist as Malvolio. But the mood could not last long. With Hero a stronger note already comes in, curbed and stifled though it be on one hand by the immortal Dogberry and on the other hand by Beatrice and Benedick. In his next play, *All's Well that Ends Well*, the volume of emotion has grown so insurgent in Helena that it makes mockery of the intellectual artifice of Comedy, ruining the play, and holding itself up to more than the possibility of misrepresentation. It is for this reason, looking at the play from one standpoint, that Coleridge could speak of Helena as Shakespeare's "loveliest character," and later, regarding the play from another standpoint, declare that "it must be confessed that her character is not very delicate, and it required all Shakespeare's consummate skill to interest us for her." The truth is that what happened to Helena might very easily have happened to Hero in *Much Ado about Nothing*. In the earlier play the artificial divinity of comedy was sufficient to subdue Hero, whereas in the latter play it was not sufficient to subdue Helena. The emotional strength of Shakespeare's characters was rising in power, and was throwing down a very severe challenge to the god of Comedy.

In Comedy the destiny of the characters lies outside of themselves, in an intellectual conception called the Comic Spirit. However powerfully they may be actuated by emotional power, their characters must nevertheless be subdued to the requirements of the divinity they are called upon to serve. In Tragedy, on the other hand, the destiny lies in the characters themselves; or, rather, in the emotional concatenation that their coming together has awaked. Looked at thus, it is easy to see that a strong emotional concatenation might very easily, in fact would most indisputably, pluck the destiny away from an artificial conception, and carry it forward itself. And this is exactly what happens. Hero is as much as Comedy may subdue. Helena is somewhat too much. Whereas Isabel in the next comedy that follows, *Measure for Measure*, is altogether too much. In fact the day of emotional freedom had already dawned, for *Hamlet* had in actual sequence of writing already preceded *Measure for Measure*.

In the latter play the artifice of Comedy raised its brow in a final effort to reassert its sway. Futilely, however. When in his last of days Shakespeare returned to what seemed like Comedy, in *Winter's Tale*, *Cymbeline*, and *The Tempest*, it was yet not Comedy he returned to. It was rather Tragedy, in the end of which Fortune graciously interposed, and, without too undue a disturbance of the conditions the characters themselves has brought into being, adjusted a gentle conclusion to all things.

In the meantime, however, right on from Hamlet to Coriolanus, there was neither a Deity of artifice to serve, nor the possibility to be entertained of the intrusion of a gentle Fortune. In its stark strength, in this his height of achievement, Destiny was neither above nor beyond, but with the characters. Emotion had asserted itself in full power; and therefore, in the truth of the ancient saying, "Character was Destiny."

Yet the elaboration of this belongs rather to a consideration of what may be called Shakespeare's Thought, which lies behind his Art even as his Art lay behind his Craft.

CHAPTER VI

HIS THOUGHT

WHATEVER its origin in history may be, whether it sprang from the Dionysian revelry, or whether it sprang from the ancient instinctive desire for ancestor worship, or whether, as is more likely, the latter was its mental origin and the former its effective origin, it nevertheless remains a fact that Tragedy, and particularly Shakespearian Tragedy, is a supreme and strange paradox. The persistent instinct of man regards it as the highest of all Art, despite the fact that, seemingly, Beauty, the first instinct and last goal of Art, is continually frustrated in it. It regards it, too, as the highest of morality, in spite of the fact that Righteousness, even as Loveliness, is ever subdued, or baffled, by malice or distortion. The paradox it presents may well be seen when it is contrasted with Melodrama, in the present meaning of that word. In Tragedy, Othello and Desdemona die, while Iago lives; if Edmund dies, Lear and Cordelia die too, while Goneril and Regan live; Hamlet dies, to be succeeded by a man in whom our interest is of the slightest; and in each of them, what may be called the moral problem seems to remain as unsolved as at the outset of the play. In Melodrama, the hero triumphs gloriously, while the villain meets his more than well-merited judgment. Moreover, in Melodrama the villain is as much of vice compact as the hero is of virtue compact, and thus there is no possibility of moral indecision. In Tragedy, however, the hero may be a Macbeth, who, for all his deeds, compels our sympathy, and demands our unity of interest with him. In a word, in Melodrama the moral issue is clear, whereas in Tragedy it seems perplexed and inexplicable: in Melodrama, right is ever triumphant, while wrong is ever punished, and the conclusion is therefore such as our moral instincts would desire, whereas in Tragedy right is ever conquered by an evil that may even happen to win gloriously. And yet Melodrama is held to be the lowest of Art and the lowest of Morality, whereas Tragedy cries out undeniably as the highest of Art and the loftiest of Morality. The first does not impress us, and may even move us to expressive mirth, whereas the latter ever purges and exalts and refines our truest emotions. And yet the first gives us a clear and patent morality, whereas the latter baffles us at every point.

It is in Shakespeare's main tragic period that this is best seen: that is to say, as already stated, when his creations swelled to such strength of emotion that they firmly took their Destiny out of the hands of the artificially created Divinity that rules Comedy, to work it out themselves. For reasons shortly to be examined, *Romeo and Juliet*, his only other tragedy, has nothing of the baffling perplexity that dominates all the plays from *Julius Cæsar* up to, and including, *Coriolanus*—though the latter play has already a hint of the settlement that is to ensue and manifest itself in Shakespeare's concluding period of thought, in *Winter's Tale, Cymbeline,* and *The Tempest.* It is not possible to say of *Romeo and Juliet,* as one must inevitably say of the later plays, that the tragedy is not so much in the disastrous end as in the portentous conjunction of characters. In *Romeo and Juliet* the catastrophe might have been avoided by a variety of possible methods; it would even never have arrived save for an extraordinary sequence of accidents and coincidents. Therefore it is not so much baffling as merely calamitous. The sorrow of a calamity is direct and sudden; it may wound the whole being, but its nature is not such that the soul is driven into an examination of the profound perplexities of Life, Death, and Destiny. If a soul does so, it is because that soul is given to doing so. A calamity is as sharp as a blow; but it does not haunt the mind like a situation. Now, the later tragedies are not calamities; they are situations. The tragedy there is not so much in the end of all, as in the terrible conjunction of characters at the beginning and all through the play.

It is this that harasses the thought. It would do so even if the conjunction were such that some or other vice was awaked in what may be called pivotal character of the situation, so fetching a house of ruin about his ears. It is something of this that creates the tragedy of *Macbeth*. But when it happens, as repeatedly it does happen, that the house of ruin owes its downfall, not to an active vice but to an active virtue, then the perplexity is supreme. Something of this is to be discovered in *Hamlet*. If the habitual reading of this play be accepted, that Hamlet was ruined by a fateful and inherent lack of decision in his character, the tragedy is not the less terrible. But there is another reading of the play. Those who insist on the customary reading forget that in all circumstances other than that of his revenge he has decision enough and to spare. There is no lack of decision when the Ghost appears to him. There is no lack of mental decision in his handling of Polonius, or Rosencrantz and Guildenstern. There is no lack of decision either in the matter of the King's letter, or when the ship that was to convey him to his death had to "put on a compelled valour" with the "pirate of very warlike appointment." Above all, there is no indecision in his deportment or procedure when safely back in Denmark. He knows then what he has to do; and, with the melancholy characteristic of him, he is firmly resolved to complete it. From this it appears that what seems like indecision in the early portion of the play, is really the honourable desire not to let his mere hatred of the King prick him into a capital action against an innocent man, to prove that the apparition of his father was no heated fantasy, and, above all, not to take action till he was assured that his action would not involve his mother. In other words, what ruined him was not a weakness, but rather a thing of strength, not a vicious indecision but an honourable sensitiveness. And this makes Tragedy terrible and bewildering.

The tragic quality of the situation may be discovered by placing a man like Othello in Hamlet's position. Here was a man of camps rather than of courts and universities. The subtler virtues have long since been whelmed in him by the necessity for bold decisive acts. He could well say of himself that "to be once in doubt is once to be resolved," for his resolute and various way of life had demanded such an attitude of him at peril of very existence. In the issue, the finer things of thought and tenderness had gone from him. The man who could be raised to such a passion that to slay his newly-wed wife was the only way of relief for him, was little likely to have held his hand at shaming his mother or weighing the chances of guilt when his instinct of wrong done summoned his hatred against a man. Knowing the people of Denmark behind him, one swift blow furiously struck would have ended the matter for him. Even so would King Lear, too, have dealt with the situation. Or imagine Hamlet in Othello's position! His sensitive instinct would at once have recoiled from a man of Iago's cast of thought, and so the Ancient would forthwith have stood revealed for what he was. Furthermore, that sensitive instinct would never have doubted a man like Cassio, to say nothing of Desdemona. To say that Hamlet would have unravelled and exposed Iago's intrigue is to say far too much. The truth is that, with the leading character in each play transposed, the several situations would never have arisen. Long before the elder Hamlet has even thought of revisiting the glimpses of the moon, his brother would have gone to meet him in the shades. And Hamlet would even have preferred a perfumed Osric, though he were civet cat twice over, to a man of Iago's outlook on life.

It is impossible to believe that a man could have merely put out a continuous bundle of cross purposes and correspondences such as this without any supporting thought in them all, something that ran through them with a linking unity. And this is made all the more impossible of belief when, amid all this seeming rage of cross purposes, one character here is heard crying out in startled wonder:

> Our indiscretion sometimes serves us well
> When our deep plots do pall; and that should teach us
> There's a Divinity that shapes our ends,
> Rough-hew them how we will;

or when another can be heard declaring stoically, "The wheel has come full circle: I am here"; or when some further one, in a vivid light of new illumination on the ways of men as compared with the way of God, can be heard crying out on those that " play such fantastic tricks before high Heaven as make the angels weep." The man who wrote such tragedies, strewing them with such vivid perceptions of life and after-life that they have become texts for philosophers and thinkers, must needs have been a man who had thought long and deep, and whose thoughts must have been occupied with matters of far more moment and permanence than the pleasure of an Elizabethan audience, important though that might have been. It is not likely that he crushed his thinking into a co-ordinate scheme. It is certain that he did not do so in his dramatic practice: which is as much as to say that he did not do so in his private opinions. One way or another this is so. If it be said that it is quite possible for a man to cleave fast mentally to certain opinions, and yet pourtray wholly different matters in his dramatic practice, then the contrary principle comes into operation: that it is impossible for a man to pass his being through the severe mental discipline of such a creation as the tragedy of *King Lear* without it leaving an effect upon his private opinions. An identity of dramatic and personal thought would soon be achieved by this inverse method, after the writing of several forceful plays, even if it were not already in existence.

Yet, though this thought may not have been framed in an arbitrary co-ordination, it nevertheless is by no means devoid of system. It has that sure sign of an organic constitution: its growth can be traced. It is possible to discover an orderly evolution of thought, a systematic progression of ideas, passing up from the immaturity, the straightforward crudity, of the early plays, through an increasing involution to a perfection of subtlety in his fullness of intellectual power, and then a gradual coming of roundness to the parts, till the whole thought seems burdened with such a feeling of ripeness that the reader, even before he learns that the Magician has decided to bury his wand, has it borne inevitably upon his thought that there is coming an end to things. And yet, through it all, there can be seen a single dominating thought from his first of plays even to his last, however it may have developed in subtlety by reason of the journey it has had to pass through.

For example, it has been seen that the earliest play of his that can definitely be traced is *Henry VI.*, which Edward Alleyn produced at the Rose in Southwark early in 1592. That he mainly served a patriotic purpose in it is obvious both from the conduct of the historical matter in it, and from its reception with the people, to which Nash bears testimony. It was this same patriotic purpose, probably, that led to the continuation of the historical series. It was but little likely that a rising dramatist would, even if he could, afford to neglect the fact that he had struck on a dramatic vein of richest ore ; and when, in addition to this probability, it is seen that he did indeed actually prosecute the series that he had begun, and that he concluded it with a play such as *Henry V.*, it is clear that the mundane motive was not lacking. And in *Richard II.*, where the weakness of the King might seem to make such an appeal a matter of doubt, there is given to Gaunt some lines touching "this little isle, this England," that cannot have failed to have stirred the blood of yard and room alike.

But that this was not wholly dictated by patriotic purposes is equally clear from his choice of material. Indeed, as one traces the actual line of subjects chosen, it is at times almost possible to see his development of idea. The continuation of the three parts of *Henry VI.* into *Richard III.* requires no explanation, the latter play being virtually a continuation of the one interest, with its proper conclusion at the threshold of Tudor ascendancy. Yet Shakespeare goes out of his way to demonstrate that these four plays are linked together in his mind by more than a merely historical sequence. Through them all, in sheer defiance of historical truth, Margaret flits to and fro like a figure of doom. As she passes in and out she is more than merely Margaret, Queen to the sixth Henry, King of England. She is a symbol in Shakespeare's hands, indicating that through all those constant fluctuations of interest there is a Destiny that has a goal to achieve. Kings may come and kings may go, York and Lancaster may vary the interest of mundane affairs by a see-saw that advances the real sequence in no way, but Margaret remains as proof of a deeper and more real progression. The waves of the sea only rise and fall, they do not progress: it is the water that progresses through them, utilising them. And so it is here, Margaret being the symbol of that progression. It is impossible to read the third scene of the First Act of *Richard III.* without feeling that this thought was forcibly present in Shakespeare's mind. He was not unaware, of course, that after the battle of Tewkesbury she was imprisoned in the Tower till she was ransomed by her father, in 1475, when she removed to France to live with him till her death. He knew that her intrusion to Richard's altercation with Elizabeth was impossible; but he had need of her; and so she comes in, not as a woman, but as a symbol of an implacable Destiny. Thus her curses are not the curses merely of an angry woman, they are the pronouncements, as she says herself, of a prophetess; and as she passes out we are not surprised to hear the cool diplomat, Hastings, say, "My hair doth stand on end to hear her curses," for somewhat of the same thing is in our own thought. Her own phrase for the situation is given in that famous fourth scene of the fourth act. "Right for right," says she; and later:

> I had an Edward, till a Richard kill'd him;
> I had a Harry, till a Richard kill'd him:
> Thou hadst an Edward, till a Richard kill'd him;
> Thou hadst a Richard, till a Richard kill'd him.

And as the three women sit and lament together, the whole scene is an allegory. We can see very evidently Shakespeare's thinking on the subject; and

we know that in all the resounding history he is
seeing not men as men only, but men as pawns
moved hither and thither by fates and destinies.
Already we can hear the unripe dramatist hinting
the Divinity that shapes men's ends, even though the
men in question, in their effort to rough-hew them
as they would, stay not at violent resolves, but
actually take in hand sword and halbert, and press
matters to the issue of bloody battles.

In this Shakespeare's thought (and such gropings
are clearly the result of conscious thinking) is neither
complex nor subtle; it is even a little crude and
obvious, though it wears the semblance of subtlety
from the fact that it has to be worked into the
history by way of a manner of allegory. Yet it is
sufficient to indicate that something in his subject
had struck a secret affinity in him, and that he was
awake and alert for an interest deeper than that of
the mere historical pageant. There were two things
in this that had caught his attention: one was the
destiny that set about to achieve its own end in
calm contempt of, or even by the use of, the little
querulous men who struck for themselves and themselves
only; and the other was the figure of Margaret
that moved hither and thither, in defiance of
historical likelihood, as a kind of symbol of that
destiny. Now criticism is divided in its voice as to
which was the next play in his historical series that
Shakespeare put his hand to. Some stand forward
for *Richard II.*, and some for *King John.* The

masterly characterisation of King John in the concluding two acts of the play bearing his name, under the influence of an avenging conscience, as contrasted with the altogether more straightforward characterisation of Richard II., serves to lead to the conviction that *Richard II.* preceded *King John*. In the former play the characterisation is subtler than that of Richard III., but it has not the complexity of the last two acts of *King John* (the first three acts being no more than a varied chronicle), which therefore leans forward in the direction of the yet distant Macbeth. But whichever of the two be taken, its derivation from *Henry VI.* and *Richard III.* may be seen without difficulty.

If it be *King John*, then Constance is seen at once in direct relation with Margaret. Mothers both of them, whose sons have had their lineal rights to kingship baffled, with consequent imprisonment and violence to their bodies, their lives are spent in curses on the several usurpers that have something dark and prophetic about them. That is to say, they both are clothed in the likeness of fate, though one is wild and dark like a fork of lightning, as Margaret, or furious and implacable like a tropic sun, as Constance. Both of them, in temporal power, are helpless; but both of them shine with victory in the end, even though they themselves are not in presence to wear the laurels of victory, because they both have been robed in the priestly vestments of real authority by that Destiny that never swerves

in the goal it strikes forward to achieve. Of what
sort that Destiny is may be gathered from the later
development of this central thought of Shakespeare's;
but to see that it sprang, in these early plays of his
dramatic range, from the womb of mother love, is to
see that it is moral, not in the untender, colourless
meaning of a much abused word, but in the full
lustrous beauty of its inward expression. The impulse
is seen as humane, not mechanical; generous and
splendid, not utilitarian. It is vital to have this
said: for it is necessary to see that in Shakespeare
morality was an impulse, not a system, and more a
passion than a fascination.

This is seen if *Richard II.* be turned to. Even as
King John dated from one of the two things that
had caught Shakespeare's attention in *Henry VI.*
and *Richard III.*, so *Richard II.* dates from the other.
King John had dated from the symbolic figure of
Margaret; *Richard II.* dates from the Destiny that
Margaret stood for. In the *Henry VI.* sequence
and *Richard III.*, Shakespeare had seen Red Rose
and White Rose rise and fall like alternate puppets,
while a single wave of Destiny flowed on through
it all to a conclusion seemingly preordained; and
therefore, looking before and after, he searches
back to see whence these strange things began. He
found it in a figure where weakness was gifted with
the power of charm. It is not the present business
at all to discover if Shakespeare's interpretation of
Richard's character accords with the relation of

history—though in this Shakespeare has his right to his interpretation as we to our judgment. Even if his characterisation seemed wholly wrong it would demand careful examination, for it is seen to be the base of every one of his historical dramas save *King John*. And as we examine it we see that its principle of interest is one that he seems as yet unconscious of, but which is to develop into a factor of considerable importance in his later work: for Richard, a figure not without his graces, is placed in a position in which those graces appear as vices, and actually develop into pronounced vices. As king, Richard is unlovely enough; maudlin even, though that is graced over by the pseudo-poetry in which it seeks to express itself: but as a private citizen he rises often to the pathos, and even awhile to a manner of true dignity.

He was wholly unfitted for power. That is to say, he was misplaced; and thence arose a coil that it became Shakespeare's business to follow out to the end that he had already depicted on Bosworth Field. In contradistinction to Richard, Henry of Bolingbroke arose; a man eminently fitted to command. In truth, he was so well fitted to his place that there was no dramatic interest at all in him once he had obtained the throne he struck for. Therefore when he was taken up in the play in two parts bearing his name, Hotspur had to be developed to sustain the interest, and the good fat knight, Sir John Falstaff, had to drink sack, and

HIS THOUGHT

hold Reality at bay with the nimble spirit proper to him, or waked by that beverage of his choice. But even here Shakespeare cannot avoid the deeper interest sprung in him. Who can help but think of the Destiny working through men, when we hear this man, who through sheer fitness for the place he claimed, had snatched it for his right, exclaim:

> Can'st thou, O partial sleep, give thy repose
> To the wet sea-boy in an hour so rude ;
> And in the calmest and most stillest night,
> With all appliances and means to boot,
> Deny it to a king ? Thou, happy lowly clown !
> Uneasy lies the head that wears a crown !

Throughout the whole of the scene that this introduces, it is easy to see Shakespeare looking beyond men, and their qualities and ambitions, and exclaiming in the words he puts into Henry's mouth :

> O God! that one might read the book of fate,
> And see the revolution of the times
> Make mountains level, and the continent,
> Weary of solid firmness, melt itself
> Into the sea ! and, other times, to see
> The beachy girdle of the ocean
> Too wide for Neptune's lips ; how chances mock,
> And changes fill the cup of alteration
> With divers liquors !

It was in some such words as these that Prospero afterwards spoke, in that rich cadence of his that has rung itself to perpetual memory ; and in one, as in the other passage, it is possible to discover the obtrusion of Shakespeare's personal preoccupation with the main problem of his thought. Mutation and permutation were all about him, in men and in things; and he grappled with it ever in the effort to see the drift of it, and to embrace it in a synthesis that should give it meaning. In a sense, and more actively than is frequently thought, all his Drama was an attempt to "read the book of fate."

It is impossible to turn aside to Falstaff, who roves this play with broad philosophy. Yet his attitude to life, as the reverse reading of the shield, has an importance too obvious to be missed. Destiny may drive its chariot through the ways of men to its allotted goal, but the ways of men are not less important in themselves because they seem to serve as means to further ends. As will be seen more clearly later, it was just this constitutional balance of Shakespeare's mind that makes his thinking carry so far. Fate, as the expression of the prescient will of God, preoccupied him; he "took upon him the mystery of things"; yet if he became thereby one of "God's spies," his spying was not in the council-chamber of the Most High, nor did he pretend to unravel the secrets of the Almighty. When he spied, he spied on earth. He only took reckoning of the counsels when they worked themselves out in the ways of men. That is to say, his preoccupation never became an obsession; for as he looked upon earth to see the "mystery of things" work its way out through the aspirations of men, it was quite possible that some man should usurp his attention. It was even possible that such a man might usurp his attention by a buxom endeavour to hold that fate, with all the reality it brought into life, at bay. And such a man was Falstaff. He might be so close to the fate, the Destiny, that wrought its end unperturbedly, that his very companion, Prince Hal, was marked out as the prime pivot of its movement. But that did not disturb him. His whole wit was employed in the effort to keep reality at bay, Destiny or no Destiny; and he cracked his laughter at the hounds of wit with such unerring deftness that he made the steeds of the Car of Fate to seem like antics of folly by contrast. He was the balance of earth against the Destiny of Heaven; and it was peculiarly characteristic of Shakespeare that when Prince Hal was required to step into the higher chariot and turn away from his good abdominal companion on the earth below, it is with Falstaff that our sympathy remains, not with Henry, for all that Shakespeare was occupied tracing out the higher Destiny.

If in *Henry IV.* Shakespeare was hard put-to to maintain the interest, what can be said of such a subject as *Henry V.?* Hotspur has gone, Falstaff is dying, and though Pistol remains, he is not, like Falstaff, a centre of humour, but only a target for humour. But there is one obvious method of attaining interest, a method that the subject invites, if not demands—and that is Patriotism. But what is this Patriotism? What bearing has it on Shakespeare's tracing out of the Destiny that was evolving itself out of these historic portents? It is very undesirable to place thoughts in Shakespeare's mind, and then extract them thence as his. Yet it cannot be forgotten that Shakespeare had already completed the step in history succeeding to this. He has already shown us the frail weakly thing that lost all the glory and territory won in France, won by his warlike father. There is no doubt that the patriotic appeal to the audience was both genuine and effective. It is impossible to think of the characterisation of King Henry in this play bearing his name, and forget that Shakespeare had his audience very definitely in mind. Yet, on the other hand, who that has read the earlier plays of *Henry VI.* and *Richard III.* can miss the bitter irony of the vigorous patriotism of *Henry V.*? Is it likely that Shakespeare failed to see it; or that, seeing it, he failed to emphasise it? If this be thought, then what shall be said of the climax of Henry V.'s rolling patriotism and triumphant procession of victory? Let it be remembered the character Shakespeare had already given the sixth Henry, and then hear the fifth Henry woo Catherine thus: " shall not thou and I, between Saint Denis and Saint George, compound a boy, half French, half English, that shall go to Constantinople and take the Turk by the beard?

Shall we not? What say'st thou, my fair flower-de-luce?" Patriotism or not patriotism, those words are almost sardonic in their ringing confidence; and thus again we see into Shakespeare's mind; and, in this the least likely of places, discover him again thinking past men to God. Indeed, his process of work has been such, the end of the sequence having come at the outset of his labour, that now, at the crest of culminating movement, there is almost something godlike in these hints of prescience, ironic though they be, and given amidst all the flavour of enthusiasm.

Yet while this historic sequence was in process of achievement Shakespeare had not been idle in other fields. Tentative endeavours of various sorts had flowed from his pen, in farce, comedy, and tragedy; and in the majority of them it would be clearly foolish to look either for the evidences of direct thinking (such as some swift perception expressing itself in a memorable phrase), or that instinctive framework of Drama which is the most delicate evidence of a subconscious progression of thought. For example, in the *Comedy of Errors* it would be manifestly out of the way to desire constructive thought; though even there, so ripe already is his mental outlook, more than once or twice the thought overburdens the structure of the play. In *Love's Labour's Lost* his thinking is hard and unavoidable: the young man conscious of ability (as ability must always be conscious of itself), and consequently more than a little contemptuous of mere academic learning, is seen declaring his patent opinion that Life and Love are the grand Tutors, not aloof Academies and Booklore. While it is true that this has not in itself that cosmic suggestion we call moral thinking, it has, nevertheless, not a little influence in that direction. For if it be true that men are not all that comprise Life, but that there are Fates and Destinies, expressions of a High God's will and purpose, inextricably bound up with it, then Life has come to wear a new meaning. Academies, most surely in such a case, can never give us what vivid living and eager thinking can give us, for in Life we are contending with, and being moulded by, the powers that urge the cosmic Destiny. This, to be sure, is not expressed by Shakespeare; yet it is more than interesting to note how complementary his statement of belief in *Love's Labour's Lost* is with the speculative thinking in his historic sequence.

It is this speculation, these cosmic suggestions of thought, and the subconscious, or half-conscious, framework of Drama that he phrased it in, with the instinct of Art, that has the deeper interest at the moment. Therefore such a play as *Two Gentlemen of Verona* is at once withdrawn from attention. And in similar manner it would seem at first thought that the *Midsummer Night's Dream* equally well would be withdrawn from attention; but here a somewhat subtle connection between that play and *Romeo and Juliet* emerges to light, throwing a new significance into each play—a connection whose value is the better seen when it is remembered that both plays belonged to the same period of workmanship.

It has already been noted that the tragic interest of *Romeo and Juliet* differs totally in conception from that of the tragedies Shakespeare wrote in the splendour of his powers. In *Romeo and Juliet* the tragedy is that of an accident, or of a series of accidents: in the later tragedies it is that of inevitability. In the later tragedies, too, it seems as though the whole of the action suggests a conclusion that is not to be found in the play, lying beyond. But *Romeo and Juliet* is self-contained. The general release from the tragic climax, inevitable to Shakespeare, is, in the later plays, a general gathering together of the tissue that hints an unseen solution to all the evil and fury that has been abroad; but in *Romeo and Juliet* the solution is clear-set and unequivocally expressed in the amity between the rival houses, with even the promise of a pledge in gold for an eternal symbol of its perfection. A difference so radical as this can only arise from a difference of conception; and that is as much as to say that Shakespeare in his later plays had progressed beyond the axioms of thought that had stood symbolical of his mental progress in his earlier days. Or to put it otherwise: the problem of *Hamlet* is conterminous with that of *King Lear*, while the problem of *Romeo and Juliet* is conterminous with that of *Midsummer Night's Dream*, assuming the *Dream* to have its problem.

What, then, is the tragedy of *Romeo and Juliet*; and what is the element in it that relates it to a play that seems so remote from it as the *Dream*? The loves of the two immortal lovers striking athwart the hereditary hates of their respective families is a tale that needs no relation; yet a little reflection shows that the tragedy that befell them only remotely arose from the larger hate in which their love was framed. It was the killing of Tybalt (or, deeper still, the killing of Mercutio, a man who could give vent to an impartial "plague o' both your houses") that led to Romeo's banishment; and this, in circuitous fashion, led to his death. We never know what would have chanced if Romeo had not been banished, and the lovers had been able to face the enmity of the Montagues and Capulets with the accomplished fact of their marriage. One may be pardoned the belief that it was thus Shakespeare would have wrought the tragedy in his later strength. But, as it is, it is not the strength of their mutual love being overcome by the strength of the mutual hate opposing them, that makes the tragedy now; it is rather the uncanny malignity of side issues. It was malignity, not inevitability, that caused so gay a wit as Mercutio to take up the fight Romeo had refused; it was very malignity that caused Tybalt to return back along that very road "alive, in triumph! and Mercutio slain," while Romeo lamented his friend. It was no more than a kind of malign chance that thus caused Romeo to be banished on the very eve of his wedding—with the rapid pressure of Paris' suit immediately he had gone.

But this was not all. It is possible to see no more than luckless accidents in these things. But who that has read the closing act — the fact that Balthazar should have so narrowly outsped Friar Laurence's message, the fact that Friar Laurence's message should have so closely missed Romeo, the fact that Juliet's potion should have lapsed its power immediately after instead of immediately before Romeo's death, and all of these not only in the mere happening, but in their cynic precision of mistiming— but has had his mind oppressed with the thought of sardonic spirits hovering around these luckless mortals and bringing all their plans to nought? As will later be seen, the characters in the maturer tragedies were responsible beings working out their own ends according to the pre-allotted destiny of the situation in which they were placed. But in *Romeo and Juliet* there are no responsible beings. All of them, but chiefly the lovers themselves, seem led aside by the course they would take, by mischievous spirits that frustrate their clearest plans. How much this is so can be seen if it be remembered that when old Capulet heard that Romeo was a masker in his house, early in the play, he takes it peacefully enough, and will not have the general gaiety disturbed. It is hard to think that such a man (or Montague, for that matter) would have made a very effectual pother with an accomplished marriage before him. But it lay not in his charge to do much. He, with his hate or goodwill, and the lovers, with their love or folly, seem only like puppets moved hither and thither at the direction of the nimble spirits that haunt the air, or the Destiny whose agents such spirits may chance to be.

Seen thus, the connection with the *Midsummer Night's Dream* is clear; for in that play the whole basis of the action is not the responsible volition of the mortals who find the interest, but the aerial spirits that hover about them, directing them, chiefly the satirically mischievous Puck. Helena and Hermia, Demetrius and Lysander, even a substantial portion of good clay such as Bottom, all matter nothing; the action is invested not in them, but in the Fairies that trick them about to fulfil their stranger ends. Whatever they do or say we can hear a song, merry, but not free of satire, floating above them:

> Up and down, up and down,
> I will lead them up and down:
> I am feared in field and town;
> Goblin, lead them up and down.

Demetrius may think he loves Hermia; but it is decreed that he shall love Helena, and therefore it must be so. It is all a very merry sport, laughter-making withal: but there is all the time a keen edge running through it; as though the creator of this wild dream had seen things that he chose to drape thus in the semblance of fantasy. It is not strange to remember that even at this time he was working out a historic sequence in which much the same kind of futile volition on the part of mortals was proceeding; and it needs but a darker outlook for the whole action to devolve itself into drama like *Romeo and Juliet*, where the satire of the immortals becomes tragic instead of playful. Well might Theseus, the cold man of reason, who can see no further than human beings, and who therefore cannot apprehend the immortals that trick them into their pre-allotted destinies, declares in his amazement:

> I never may believe
> These antique fables, nor these fairy toys.
> Lovers and madmen have such seething brains,
> Such shaping fantasies, that apprehend
> More than cool reason ever comprehends.
> The lunatic, the lover, and the poet,
> Are of imagination all compact:
> One sees more devils than vast hell can hold,—
> That is the madman: the lover, all as frantic,
> Sees Helen's beauty in a brow of Egypt:
> The poet's eye, in a fine frenzy rolling,
> Both glance from heaven to earth, from earth to heaven;
> And, as imagination bodies forth
> The forms of things unknown, the poet's pen
> Turns them to shape, and gives to airy nothing
> A local habitation and a name.

It was so he dismissed it, bewildered at the wildness of the tale he had heard; but even through his own speech we can catch a sight of the dramatist who was regarding him whimsically, and who saw more than he did, not being preoccupied with mortal men merely, seeing beyond to fates and destinies.

In all this it is important to notice that a Divinity mingles freely with the characters deployed in the action. All Drama is concerned with a Divinity by the very needs of the case; for it is impossible to depict the fortunes of a combination of characters without giving the whole the purposeful direction of a Divinity above them. It may be possible to call that purposeful direction the dramatist's conscious philosophy: yet this is only to phrase the same thing otherwise, for a philosophy purports to be the apprehension of God and His working. Didacticism apart, whether the philosophy be within the limits of a conscious synthesis, or whether it be too vast for a mental synthesis, it is nevertheless a fact that in serious Drama it is impossible for a dramatist to depict his action without introducing into it somewhat of his own attitude towards God. In ancient Drama the God was not so much identical with the machine of the play, but rather at the end thereof. Speaking generally, the action in Greek Drama began long prior to the actual opening of the play; and the play might be said to begin when the action came within striking distance of the Divinity that was to conclude it. The God was within the machine; but being at the end of it, he seems to sit there in function as a judge, one who was to apportion praise and blame, and generally to adjust the necessary equity.

Now, in the plays of Shakespeare already considered, in the historic sequence, and in *Romeo and Juliet* and *Midsummer Night's Dream*, the Divinity is not only in the play, but contained within the limits of it. That is to say, the action in *Romeo and Juliet* does not begin prior to the opening of the play; the opening of the play opens the action. Perhaps it is for this reason that the action is interfered with all through by the Divinity above it. An illustration may make this clear. The conclusion of a Greek Drama may be said to be caused by the God suddenly stepping out of the machine, and adjusting and apportioning judgment for an action with which he has had more or less to do. But in Shakespeare's plays hitherto it is rather that the Divinity at all times actively promoted an end he had ever had in view. Therefore, even in a tragedy like *Romeo and Juliet*, the play is concluded with itself: the interest is not projected into the infinite Beyond, as in *King Lear*. The play, that is to say, is not so much cosmic as mundane. Romeo might "shake the yoke of inauspicious stars from this world-wearied flesh," but the conclusion of the play is, nevertheless, that the houses of Montague and Capulet are henceforth to live at peace, and that he and Juliet are to lie beside each other in golden effigies for all Verona to wonder at.

In this, it is to be noted, the play is shaped more like a comedy than a tragedy. The action is concluded at the limit of the play; and though we turn away sorrowful, we turn away with our interest completed: we are not left baffled with a strange exaltation as at the end of the later tragedies. Something had to transpire in his workmanship and thought[1] before *Hamlet* and *King Lear* could be achieved. And the first thing toward this end had to be that the Divinity no longer should arbitrarily interfere in the action. He might hover above the action; the action might always suggest him, as it was necessary that it should always work in the sight of him; but he and the action must be things separate. For if he and the action be identical, then misfortune in one will appear like malice in the other; as in the case of Romeo when Friar Laurence's letter missed him. If they be separate, however, then misfortune and temptation will not be malign, but rather a test of virtue; as when a clean heart and a vicious intellect were tested by a witch's word in Banquo and Macbeth. For there to be any interest in God there must be free-will in Man, would be a philosophic statement of the case. And Drama is philosophy in action.

Now, if Shakespeare's next period of work be examined it will be found that this was just what is in process of evolution. His two years at the Rose, and his four years at the Theater and Curtain, cannot be said to be much more than his dramatic pupilage; even though it rose to triumph, as pupilage is wont to rise, in Falstaff, *Romeo and Juliet*, and *The Merchant of Venice*. It was not till the erection of the Globe that he might be said to have turned mannerism to manner; although in the early days of the Globe he still clave more or less closely to inspiration provided by older plays. At the Globe he began the series of comedies that opened with *Much Ado about Nothing*, and afterwards, under compulsion of a swelling stress of emotion, ushered in the later tragedies. It becomes urgent, therefore, to discover how the Divinity that was active in its direct intrusion in the first period, withdrew itself from such intrusion to become the ultimate goal of the action in the second period.

Precisely what this meant may be seen by comparing *The Merchant of Venice* with *Much Ado about Nothing*. Demarcations of intellectual territory are ever artificial, and this is no exception. Yet it has this virtue, that *The Merchant of Venice* is perhaps the greatest of the plays prior to the erection of the Globe, and one of the last of them, moreover; whereas *Much Ado about Nothing*, while much inferior as a play, yet dates forward, not backward. What, then, form the Crises in the two plays; for as the Crises are, so shall the plays be also? And thus a curious difference transpires, almost bewildering in its fitness with a preconceived expectancy. For the Crisis of *The Merchant of Venice* is the reported loss of all Antonio's ships at sea, which is just such a malign stroke from the Divinity in charge of the play as one might expect from the author of *Romeo and Juliet*, and the *Midsummer*

Night's Dream: whereas the Crisis of *Much Ado* is the strange villainy of Duke John. One arises from circumstance; the other from character. It is true enough that the character is so strange and unaccountable that its interference seems almost a mechanical irruption of circumstance; but this is even what one might expect in view of the fact that the Duke John is Shakespeare's first farewell to the older order of things. He is the first step away from the mechanical identity of Divinity and action; that is to say, he is the first step toward human purposefulness: and therefore it can easily be understood if in his human purposefulness there was not a little of mechanical intrusion. But when attention is turned to those worthy citizens Dogberry and Verges, his unwitting abettors in the Crisis, it can be seen at once that the step forward is not indecisive but vital: that beyond doubt we are to be done with malign intrusions from above, and that the future is to lie with the purposes and characters of humanity, with its frailties and follies, with its vices, and even perhaps its virtues, for the achievement of Destiny; even though Divinity may lift human action into strange significance by the throb of its pervading Will.

Once this is seen, however, the question immediately arises: Where, then, is this Divinity to be found, if it is thus to be dismissed from the course of the action by the purposeful acts of humanity depicted in varying characters? And the answer to such a question comes from a consideration of the type of play that now engaged Shakespeare's attention. For it is to Comedy he turns; and in Comedy the presiding Divinity has imposed upon him the function of conclusion. He, it must be admitted, is but a frail Divinity at best. There is very little cosmic or actual about him. He is half of social grace compact: sometimes, even, wholly so compounded. Moreover, by the laws of Comedy that govern his existence, it is required of him that he smile perpetually; and sometimes this is a very painful effort. His rulings are the rulings of artifice; and so it comes about that too often he robs of vitality and power the characters whose arbitrament he is charged with. If their actions seemed to be so full of earnestness and power that they are like to escape past his place on earth to a higher heaven, and so to scorn his adjudication that all things shall end happily, then he strikes them down to earth, within the scope of his voice; and too often, then, the characters whose actions are thus treated have difficulty in maintaining the unity that compels our interest. Sometimes a character bests him (as did Shylock), and then his play is undone as Comedy. More often he succeeds in besting a character (as with Helena), when his Comedy is saved at the expense of its interest.

Yet, however artificial he may be, and therefore however unreal his interest may be for awhile, it is important to notice two things about this presiding

Divinity: firstly, that his place is now, even as in ancient Greek tragedy, at the conclusion of the play; and secondly, that his function there is as a Judge. No longer is he permitted to intrude arbitrarily with the action of a play, as with *Romeo and Juliet*: he may only influence it by the fact that it must conclude itself where he sits at the termination of the five acts. Everything must synchronise there. Nothing must escape beyond, under penalty of failure.

What this meant will be seen shortly, when failure is to be recorded. But a caution imperiously raises itself to insist that Shakespeare's thoughts upon Life and Destiny can never be conveyed in anything so artificial as Comedy—such comedies, for instance, as *Much Ado about Nothing* or *As You Like It*. That is undoubted. The fact of an expectant Divinity at the conclusion of the five acts, waiting for all the issues awakened to converge at his feet, must needs so foreshorten the psychology, and so restrict the characters thereby, that unreality is supreme: whereas the business of Thought, whether conscious or instinctive, is the quest of Reality. That has already been seen. Which is to say that the true worth of these intervening Comedies is the linking up of the reading of Life in the historic sequence and *Romeo and Juliet* on the one hand, and the great tragedies on the other. Nevertheless, there are certain aspects of Life that can only be rendered in the stiff fashion of such artifice. What else had so mordant a philosopher as Jaques in mind when he declared roundly:

> All the world's a stage,
> And all the men and women merely players:
> They have their exits and their entrances;
> And one man in his time plays many parts,
> His acts being seven ages;

and thus on? To a full vision of Life such Comedy, however artificial, was necessary; particularly when it is remembered that without it the flagellation of such fatuous egoism as that of Malvolio's would be impossible. It was not only the transition from one direct reading to another direct reading; it was, in *As You Like It*, the relief of overburdened earnestness, and in *Twelfth Night* a corrective of pompous folly.

Yet it is true that the chief interest at the moment of such plays as *Much Ado*, *As You Like It*, *Twelfth Night*, and *All's Well that Ends Well*, in the direct progress of Shakesperian thought, is to demonstrate the change that has befallen the function of the Divinity of Drama. Previously the Divinity had intruded in, and had even actively propelled, the action that was forward. Now, however, he awaits the action at the conclusion of the play; not interfering with it, but demanding that it shall converge at his feet. Yet it is to be noticed that his place at this end of the five acts is held on a very precarious tenure. In truth, it becomes more and more precarious as play succeeds play. As has already been seen, emotion and power of character are swelling apace. In

Much Ado there is but little thought; and thus the Divinity is enabled to settle all things, and conclude the interest satisfactorily. In *As You Like It* Orlando takes the place of Claudio; and therefore the action is driven forcefully so near the conclusion that Oliver and the Duke Frederick have to make some lightning changes of disposition to get it through in time. Whereas by the time we reach *All's Well*, the patchwork at the conclusion is so disastrous that it is clear to see that the Divinity must soon be thrust forward by the swelling strength of the characters of the play, and driven off his post at the end of the five acts to some position in the further Beyond. In this way the Divinity would no more be within the play. The characters would be free to swell great and strong, to play out their destinies as they might; and as the play with untrammelled vigour concluded its visible course, it would reach forward to, and suggest, the adjudication of the Divinity that stood beyond, waiting with penalty and bounty in his hands. And whatever was thus suggested as the judgment to be given Beyond would be purging and exalted inasmuch as it would be the achievement of untrammelled and unhindered reality in the course of the action.

In the great tragedies this is just what happens. It cannot be too strongly enforced that in all this there is no hint that Shakespeare consciously was achieving all this. That he was consciously occupied with thoughts on Destiny (Destiny being Divinity in action), there can be no doubt. But whether he consciously removed the Divinity from his identity with the action to a situation at the conclusion of the action; and whether he consciously made strength of character so to thrive that the Divinity was thrust forward to his place in Eternity—is not the question at the moment. He may have wrought his work so. It is infinitely more likely that he did not; for an artist is far more moulded by his work than an active moulder of it. What he does is generally not known by him till after he has done it. His doing of it makes him aware of what he has done. The more important matter at the moment is that Shakespeare's work did indeed take this course: it is a subsequent matter to discover how far he was aware of his achievement. To cite four examples in evidence of the procedure: in *Romeo and Juliet* it is clear that the Divinity of Drama was identical with the action of it; in *Much Ado* it is equally clear that human agency was responsible for the action, and that the Divinity awaited the action at the conclusion, somewhat in the manner of Greek Drama, to adjust and finish it; in *All's Well* it is as clear that a certain fierce strength in Helena has given so powerful a drift to the action that for the Divinity to retain his place he had to make a considerable patchwork of the conclusion, and that if Bertram had only had the strength, ungainly though it seem to be, of Helena, instead of being the puppet he is, no conclusion could have been adjusted, which is to say that the Divinity would either have been dissipated or thrust forward beyond the limit of the action; and it is equally clear that this is just what has happened in *Hamlet*. To *Hamlet* there is no conclusion. There only remains to see whether the Climax suggests a conclusion, that is to say an adjudicating Divinity beyond, or whether it is mere dramatic anarchy.

Before this can be done, however, and as introductory to it, it is more than interesting to note the precise position that *Hamlet* occupies. It is the chief landmark that points the end of a series that has its Divinity within the limits of the play, and indicates a newer series in which the Divinity is relegated elsewhere. Nevertheless, it must be noted, in the chronological order of writing, it was undoubtedly immediately preceded by a tragedy, *Julius Cæsar*, and it was probably, if not immediately, at least very shortly after, followed by a comedy, *Measure for Measure*. An examination of these reveals a very curious state of affairs. For while *Julius Cæsar* is in strict sense a tragedy, that is to say while in it the resolution of the issues in contest are in fact relegated to a higher Court, yet it has a strange affinity with the comedies it succeeded to, in the fact that the conclusion is far more complete than in any of the tragedies it was destined to usher in. Partly this was achieved by the fact that the last two acts, that is to say, the Counter-action and the Climax, are in such marked contrast to the opening three acts, that they may be said to set-off and balance the initial interest. There is indeed the suggestion of a higher Court; but then there is also the satisfaction of a lower Court. The death of Brutus may call in the necessity of a further settlement; but the adequate revenge of Cæsar is the very thorough prosecution of a present settlement: whereas in *Hamlet* there is no vestige of present settlement: Hamlet's death, with the deaths of his uncle and his mother, waive the whole issue away to further fields. But similarly, even as the preceding Tragedy has part of the settlement of Comedy in it, so the ensuing Comedy is ruined by the fact that it is Tragedy undilute turned arbitrarily to Comedy. It is not too much to say that the conclusion of *Measure for Measure* is incomparably worse than the conclusion of any reputable drama yet conceived. And why? Simply because the Divinity is forcefully dragged in from his position beyond the play (a position lately acquired) to his sometime position at the limit of the five acts. The result is a psychological foreshortening in the concluding movement so inconceivable as to be absolutely unreal. The characters were shaping their destinies for a far-seen and dimly-glimpsed Divinity: but the Divinity suddenly appeared immediately before them; and so they dropped their destinies, and became merely puppets. The action had in prospect a distant settlement; but an immediate settlement was violently demanded of it; and so it gave over Reality, and botched up the necessarily violent conclusion. Nothing could better prove the real nature of the change that had preceded.

But this is to say that there is indeed a further Divinity: a Divinity in the Beyond. This is to say that it is not dramatic anarchy that has appeared; but that the action contains within itself hints of the Divinity it serves under. And the question arises: Is it possible to discover from the tragedies of what sort that Divinity is? In what may arbitrarily be called the first stage, the Divinity was, from his identity with the action afoot, either mechanically righteous, in the Histories, or mischievous, in *Midsummer Night's Dream*, or malign in *Romeo and Juliet* so far as the lovers were concerned, though it had an ultimate goal in the union achieved between the Montagues and the Capulets. In the second stage, by reason of his arbitrary position at the termination of the action, and his consequently automatic demand of the characters that created and propelled the action, he was artificial. But now the action is free, the characters are unhindered, with permission to what of power they may desire; and the Divinity is relegated to some point beyond the limit of the earthly accent. In all of which the action is, as Drama should be, an allegory of Life; and we already begin to see why it is that the persistent instinct of Man has ever regarded such Tragedy as the highest of Reality, meaning thereby the highest of Beauty and the highest of Morality.

In *Othello*, for instance, the tragedy that succeeded *Hamlet*, there is never any anarchy; we are never out of the eye of a Divinity. So pure a flower as Desdemona may be crushed in the ruin of sexual rage. A man with such an extraordinarily fiendish cast of mind as Iago may live to think in triumph of the ruin he has caused. He may even be given, to close our memory of him, six short words in such superb defiance of danger that we are won to a kind of admiration of him.[2] Nevertheless, we are never left in doubt of the Divinity that rules the play. In the light shed about the play we feel that an appeal has been made to something in us that we call our faith; and so we take our stand with, or accord our sympathy to, Desdemona and not Iago. If the play were all, then we should have to take rank with Iago against Desdemona; for the play shows him to be in unchallenged victory over her. But the play is not all; the play but shapes for something beyond; and so we take our stand according to the judgment of the Divinity beyond. We believe what we cannot see; we trust what we cannot prove: and so we are exalted and purged in our outlook on life.

It is this that finds the centre of interest for the period of Shakespeare's great tragedies. No doubt it had its roots in the tough business of his life.

There are not wanting varied indications of this.
The man who made a prince to say,

> For who would bear the whips and scorns of time,
> Th' oppressor's wrong, the proud man's contumely,
> The pangs of disprized love, the law's delay,
> The insolence of office, and the spurns
> That patient merit of th' unworthy takes,

even at the risk of dramatic impropriety, was manifestly one who had received the rancour of this earth's moral topsy-turveydom into his soul. It is this topsy-turveydom that provides the very stuff of his tragedy. Through all his plays, from *Julius Cæsar* onward, he wrestles with it; and his reply is never that of evasion. If we hold fast by Desdemona and reject Iago, it is not that their common Creator gave us a patent and unavoidable clue as to which way his affections lay. Indeed, it is Iago that engages Shakespeare's utmost power and sympathy. Desdemona is in no way elaborated. The whole situation is faced with an unswerving allegiance to Life. Villains and heroes are banished as the fictions of cowardice; and men and women appear, compact of many parts. Virtues and vices are disregarded in favour of complex psychologies; and judgments give place to sympathy. Even the utmost rigour of the earth is faced in a tempest of tears. "Patient merit" is overwhelmed terribly, while "the unworthy" stands by with words of courage and superb defiance on his lips. Yet the issue is really never in doubt with us. We rank ourselves as of the host of Desdemona, for all that she is strangely frail and ignorant, and for all that Iago is somewhat superb in his triumph. Hamlet's failure to conclude the thing he had set his hand to, may exasperate us; and we may admire the decisive attitude of Claudius as an effective contrast: moreover, in so far as the course of the action may aid us, they both may pass from our sight in the ruthless equality of death: yet it is Hamlet we esteem, not Claudius. Whether or not Shakespeare was himself "grappling amid the eternal verities," the issue to us is not uncertain. The very perplexity seems to make it clearer. Through all the smoke and dust a light shines; and then we begin to see that the ray is cast through the play by some lustrous glory beyond it.

It is in this connection an axiom of Shakespearian criticism takes a new significance. More than once it has been pointed out that Shakespeare, throughout all his tragedies, refuses to conclude at the moment of the climatic outbreak; and we have seen that the conditions of his stage demanded of him that he should remove living and dead from the sight of his audience, except when such exceptional conditions as befell Othello enabled him to withdraw the Climax behind a curtain. Now, it is improbable that so astute a craftsman as he should fail to perceive the excellent opportunity this gave him of hinting the Divinity he would not introduce on to the arena. And in his practice we find that this is

even so. "Now cracks a noble heart," says Horatio.
"Good night, sweet Prince, and flight of angels
sing thee to thy nest." "O Spartan dog," says
Lodovico to Iago; "more fell than anguish, hunger,
or the sea! Look on the tragic loading of this bed."
And to us the contrast is an effective clue. "This
was the noblest Roman of them all," says Antony.
But stout, faithful old Kent is even more explicit.
Says he of Lear:

> Vex not his ghost: O let him pass! He hates him
> That would upon the rack of this tough world
> Stretch him out longer.

And as we hear such words, we cannot but remember
that other man who had just said, "The wheel is
come full circle: I am here." Similarly, the unity of
soul that mocks at all ill, and provides the centre of
interest, in *Antony and Cleopatra*, is very clearly chosen
by Cæsar for our last memory of the two great lovers:

> She shall be buried by her Antony:
> No grave upon the earth shall clip in it
> A pair so famous. . . . .
> . . . . . . Our army shall
> In solemn show attend this funeral.

So he speaks; and in his words we catch the conscience of the play. In fact, it is not Cæsar that
speaks. Cæsar would not so have spoken. He is
only indicating the judgment of the further Divinity.
He is doing what other characters, with more or
less of actuality, are doing throughout all the

tragedies. He is not gathering together the stray issues of an unconcluded play; but he is showing how they might be gathered together in a judgment that waits beyond. It is this that gives the true calm to the mind; not merely the relief of tension. And it is a calm born of thought and patience; a fortifying calm. By it we are transported above the fury of circumstance.

It can very easily be seen, then, how it is that Shakespeare avoids that simplicity of issue characteristic of Melodrama. Such simple issues are born of the need for a settlement within the limits of a play. It is only complex issues that demand an exalted and prophetic outlook. One is crude, and therefore subject to derision; whereas the other is purging and stimulating morally, because it demands the faith of something that does not appear. It is not that in one Morality is present, and that in the other Morality is dismissed (although, in a sense, and inverted from its present application, this is so): it is rather that in one there is no occasion for Morality, since all things are so patent and mechanical, and that in the other there is always an appeal for Morality in the teeth of circumstance. For without faith there can be no morality in action.

With what vigour and equity—indeed, with what penetrating insight—this is couched in Shakespeare's Tragedy can be seen by an appeal to *King Lear*. We pity Lear, we love Cordelia, as we are revolted by Goneril and Regan. Yet when we come to reflect on the play it is with something of mystification that we discover that what has urged our pity, our love, and our revulsion is all one and the same thing. For what is King Lear but a man full of bodily vigour, strength of will and superb self-confidence? He is great and strong; and well he knows it. It was certainly with no thought of abnegating his prerogative of command that he desired to make over his kingdom to his daughters. He intended still to rule; and his sway was to be all the supremer since it was not bothered by the adventitious trappings of power. And so it would have been: save for one thing he had not thought to reckon on. There was not a man or woman in the kingdom but would have bowed to the empire of his will, were they clothed in kingship never so much. But what he omitted to think of was the fact that even as he was strong so were they strong who had sprung from his loins. He had not thought of that. He had reckoned without himself in his daughters; and what broke him was that they, beginning at the strongest and concluding with the weakest, defied him and pitted themselves against him. First came fearless and crystal-clear Cordelia; then came crafty Goneril; and wild-cat Regan concluded the action. It is true to say that King Lear himself broke himself; and that there was none other that could have done it. Yet it is bewildering to notice this same instinctive defiance of authority translate itself into such a variety of effective action. Nothing could better frustrate a simple adjustment of vices and virtues; and so equal is the vigour with which the father and each of the daughters is depicted that the initial bewilderment gives place to a subsequent poise of thought that baffles any pert adjudication of thought. The whole various family bundle is so tied together by this one uniting strand of temperament that it becomes impossible so to separate it that judgment may easily follow the separation. Thus our sympathy is attained. We are enabled to understand the founts of action in each of them; we recognise how inevitable it all seems to be; and so we are saved a trite allotment of moralities. Nevertheless we are never once in doubt as to the main lines of a further adjudication: which is as much as to say that we attest the truth in it by the truth in us, and we approve them both by their agreement.

A distinct difficulty, therefore, was presented to Shakespeare by his choice of subject in *Macbeth*. Here the central act in the character of his interest is one of crime: a crime, moreover, the more revolting in that it demanded violence by a man awake to a man asleep, by a man full of vigour and strength to a man old, gentle and tenderly attractive, kindly intentioned withal. Were Duncan the centre of interest the perplexity would not be so deep. But Macbeth is the centre of interest; and so we notice that Shakespeare begins by

s

bringing in a subsidiary aid, and concludes by departing in large measure from the practice prevalent in his other Tragedies—in truth, it is doubtful if the strangely hesitating conclusion to this tragedy has ever yet met the attention it deserves.

For it is noteworthy that Shakespeare evades the responsibility of criminal decision in Macbeth by throwing it on to his wife, who thereafter figures little in the play. It is true enough that in succulent Holinshed it is carefully stated that Lady Macbeth burned "with unquenchable desire to bear the name of queen"; but this scarcely accounts for so extraordinary a scene as the seventh in the First Act. For Lady Macbeth so to have burned it was not necessary that Macbeth should have looked before and after with such imaginative fury. Moreover, it is also true, and deeply true, that in this Shakespeare struck one of his most startling intimacies with human nature. For Lady Macbeth's strength was just the feminine strength of seeing the one thing before her; and that one thing so fiercely and intensely that all things else were banished from existence. Therefore when, after the deed was done, she broke, she broke fiercely and sharply, like a tense string snapt. But Macbeth's weakness was just his masculine strength of seeing not only the one thing, but a thousand things besides. Therefore he never broke: he was haunted and hunted to mental ruin.

Yet in this very fact it is easy to see that our sympathy with Macbeth is largely achieved by the fact that he was pricked to his deed by one who thereafter leaves him the centre of interest. Subtly and deftly, yet undeniably, the centre of interest is shifted in the course of the action; and by this fact our sympathy is achieved and retained.

Thus too with the conclusion. Even as in the course of the Action the centre of interest is shifted from Lady Macbeth to Macbeth, so in the Counter-action and Climax the centre of interest is gradually shifted from Macbeth to Macduff. For if Macbeth was not wholly responsible for the death of Duncan, he certainly, and he alone, was responsible for the deaths of Banquo and Macduff's wife and children; and therefore he cannot retain our sympathy, for all his subsequent torture of imagination. It is for just this reason that we are not permitted to behold the deaths either of Lady Macbeth or her husband: a thing not often remembered. It is not difficult to discover why. When we see Hamlet, or Desdemona, or Lear, die, our thoughts are at once projected to the ruling Divinity beyond the play; but to see Macbeth die would be to see the Divinity standing within the limits of the play. So we are refused the sight; and instead of the sight we have the memory of words which serve instead to signify the further things.

> To-morrow, and to-morrow, and to-morrow,
> Creeps in this petty pace from day to day,

> To the last syllable of recorded time;
> And all our yesterdays have lighted fools
> The way to dusty death. Out, out, brief candle!
> Life's but a walking shadow; a poor player,
> That walks and struts his hour upon the stage,
> And then is heard no more: it is a tale
> Told by an idiot, full of sound and fury,
> Signifying nothing.

Such words, with their utter world-weariness, grip our sympathy far more effectually than the sight of his death; moreover, they project the interest more surely beyond: and since their utterance makes his death sympathetically imperative, the sight of his head awakes memory of them, and they therefore come to us as a closing note.

Yet it is clear the interest is quite different from that of Shakespeare's other tragedies; which may cause us to wonder how Shakespeare came to choose the subject. Then we remember that Middleton co-operated in the writing; and an immediate question is started as to whether Middleton has anything to do with the choice of theme. It is certainly far more a Middleton subject than a Shakespeare subject.

Nevertheless, even here the action does not meet its settlement within the borders of the play. By just so much as Macbeth wins our sympathy and tenderness, by just so much do we require a subsequent judgment to balance the interest he has awoken. Yet as the tragedies proceed in their course a change can be noticed coming over them;

and it is *Macbeth* that makes the border-line of distinction. In *Hamlet, Othello,* and *King Lear* the conclusions are about as perplexing as they well may be. Everything ends in disorder and disaster; scarce anything is resolved on this earth, all things, even subsidiary perplexities, being dismissed to a further court for settlement. But in the tragedies that succeed *Antony and Cleopatra* and *Coriolanus,* the ends are far more peaceful owing to the fact that they fall to more of a conclusion. They are in no way so perplexed. In *Antony and Cleopatra* the judgment beyond, as has been seen, is plainly hinted at, and so in a measure achieved. In *Coriolanus* the end is not one of perplexity but one of rest: Tullus Aufidius' words, together with something in *Coriolanus* that altogether loses our patience, make the end seem something complete in itself. And this gives us the clue as to wherein the difference exists, and how Macbeth contributes towards it. For Hamlet, Othello, and King Lear are compact of a deep irony; they are the subjects of an extraordinary cast of Fate. What brings them to ruin is not the vice in them, but rather something that might well have been the agencies of nobility and virtue on all occasions other than the situations that faced them. Hamlet's honour it is that trips him; with Othello his undoing springs from a splendour of passion that was untimely touched to sexual rage; and Lear comes to nought because he has brought daughters into the world that partake of his own defiant blood.

But Macbeth falls through crime; Antony is undone by a viciousness in his blood; and Coriolanus is so unbearably haughty that he scarce ever achieves our sympathy. Therefore the end of these last three has something of present judgment in it. Yet it is not a whole solution. It is as though the Divinity were half seen, half wrapt in mist.[3]

The connection, thus, between the onward course of the great tragedies and the concluding period of Shakespeare's work is not difficult to see. It needed but a very little tenderness of circumstance for Coriolanus to have avoided his seeming Destiny; whereas neither Hamlet, Othello, nor Lear could have come to any other end than they did, the circumstances being what they were. The Divinity being beyond the action it is possible for viciousness or weakness to avoid judgment within the action; whereas a virtue so caught between the forks of perplexity that its very exercise is to plunge itself further into difficulty, is foredoomed to catastrophe. Moreover, our very sympathy with the nobler part of a vicious character, that was one of the very agencies in propelling the Divinity beyond the play, calls out in demand of the possibility of a kindly destiny for him.

Nevertheless, Coriolanus does not escape his doom. But Leontes, in *A Winter's Tale*, does. So, too, does the somewhat less faulty Pisanio in *Cymbeline*. And it is interesting to notice how, in each case, this is done. For the Divinity beyond seems now to have its representative participant in the very action. In the opening of Shakespeare's work the Divinity itself intruded in the action; and its intrusion wore by necessity somewhat of a malign or mischievous aspect. Now, in the close of his work, it does not intrude in the action; but in each of the two plays mentioned appears a character so rich in forgiveness, and so fully and perfectly orbed, that there seems only the word Divine to suit the occasion. Hermione in the *Winter's Tale*, and Imogen in *Cymbeline* may, in a workaday hard world, move us to wonder or impatience; but their perfect poise and serene beauty are glimpses caught on earth of a Divinity beyond. And thus, by them, the fury of occasion is avoided for Leontes and Pisanio.

It is as though Shakespeare's mind became so absorbed with the preoccupation with his Divinity (and Destiny, which is Divinity in action), that all the shows of Time became merged in it. All the fury of circumstance became swallowed up of Beauty, whether it expressed itself in the mature experience of Hermione and Imogen, or whether it emerged in the tender wonder of Perdita and Miranda. It was indeed a "fierce abridgment," or rather a mellow abridgment, having "to it circumstantial branches, which distinction should be rich in"; but it was the abridgment that occupied him now, not the distinctions that engaged him in *Hamlet*. There is something rich and matured in it; and we can already catch hints of the vision in which he seems to have framed somewhat of a personal message and a closing expression.

> These our actors,
> As I foretold you, were all spirits, and
> Are melted into air, into thin air:
> And, like the baseless fabric of this vision,
> The cloud-capped towers, the gorgeous palaces,
> The solemn temples, the great globe itself,
> Yea, all which it inherit, shall dissolve,
> And, like this insubstantial pageant faded,
> Leave not a rack behind. We are such stuff
> As dreams are made on, and our little life
> Is rounded with a sleep.

In such words as those the Divinity is already become a Reality; and the Earth is seen as a transient show merged in an eternal Destiny: a Destiny that seems more patent to Shakespeare's thought than the present and frail example of its course. It is difficult to imagine anything more complete than this; and therefore it is difficult to imagine anything that could be added to it. Shakespeare's Thought has taken its complete course from its early efforts to find Reality to a fully-orbed expression of it: and it only remains to see in how far this expressed the maturing character of the man as he moved through his days on the earth.

CHAPTER VII

HIS PERSONALITY

IN the course of the present Study it has been possible, having once set out the nature of its inquiry, firstly to trace out the tenour of Shakespeare's life. In this the necessity of logical sequence made it imperative that it should be set out in lines, and taken through courses that have not hitherto been usually associated with it; and it was found that all the side issues of circumstantial evidence joined in approving the sequence that was chosen. Having seen so much, it became necessary at once to seek behind this for that which provided the pivot and zest for the life that was lived; and so the Stage for which he wrote was examined with some care in the light of the work he placed on it. Similarly, behind his Stage lay the Craft with which he used it and its possibilities: a Craft which moulded his work in certain fashions and certain forms. This, too, was studied; and it was discovered that, far from being the careless craftsman that modern criticism would report him to be, he was, in truth, deeply occupied with the fundamental questions of construction and dramatic sequence. It was seen that he had a firm principle on which he modelled his Drama: a principle that he clave to, and often wrought to surpassing beauty, despite many seeming failures; and a principle, moreover, that the highest modern craftsmanship has failed to achieve, despite its thought for technique. Again, behind this lay the Art with which he filled his craft; and it became evident that his choice of Poetry for the phrasing of his characters was no mere chance, but the very essence of his Drama. Then, since it seems impossible to couch Drama without conveying something in the nature of a philosophy—or, to phrase it otherwise, since it seems impossible to envisage life without giving it a form and fashion indicative of reflection, conscious or sub-conscious—it became necessary to proceed once more further behind his Art to the Thought that gave it its outline. Then, also, it was seen that his Thought flowed in orderly sequence from first to last; from tentative immaturity to full-orbed ripeness. And thus we have approached so closely to the man himself, that it has become necessary to take the only step further back that it is possible to take, and to discover of what sort he was, what was his character, and how it shaped and moulded his life and his work.

Truly speaking, we have been clinging on the borders of Shakespeare's personality through the major portion of this Study; so that now it becomes only necessary to speak the thing that the accumulation of facts has hinted. It is this fact that is missed by those who would have it that Shakespeare's work is no indication to this character. The leading, if not the only, lance in this camp declares that "an author gives in his written page an expression of what is in him. He can have nothing else to give."[1] Precisely! If an author were enabled to give other than that which is in him, then difficulties might arise. But since an author does give "an expression of what is in him," then we may know what is in him by the expression that he gives. He does not "summon out of nothingness all manner of emotion"; he summons out of himself just that manner of emotion proper to himself. And it is by this we know Shakespeare. Even those who are most vociferous in denial are yet most assured of the manner of man he was. They would unhesitatingly deny the ascription to him of "The Canterbury Tales," on the one hand, and "Epipsychidion," on the other. That is to say, their attitude against such an ascription would be that the manner of emotion in such poems was not proper to Shakespeare, and that, therefore, he could not call it into being: in fact, that, whoever or whatever he was, he was neither like Chaucer nor like Shelley. Yet how is it possible to assert what a man was not like except on the basis of a more or less clear knowledge as to what he was like? And such knowledge is gained by an acquaintance with the distilled idiom of his mind in his work.

This distinction between what a man is, and what

he is not, has in fact been the basis of a considerable part of the misunderstanding. It is said, for example, that we cannot know Shakespeare from his works, because in his works he gives us no clearly-cut or sharply-defined philosophy of the universe. But this is not a denial of his personality: it is an expression of it. He gave no clearly-cut or sharply-defined philosophy of the universe simply because, to the exceeding enrichment of his life and thought, he had no clearly-cut or sharply-defined philosophy of the universe, which is another way of saying that he was of a nature opposed to a hard dogmatism of thought; and thus, that he either perceived a synthesis too vast to define, or that he dismissed syntheses altogether.

Similarly, it is sometimes forgotten that attributes are not characteristics, though they may indicate the presence of characteristics. For instance, it is a fact that throughout the great tragic period of Shakespeare's work, one of the prevailing notes towards the whole sex-question is of an absolute nausea and abhorrence. It is the keystone of Othello's tragedy; Hamlet is saturated with it; Lear in his madness reverts continually to it; and there is a variation of it underlying *Antony and Cleopatra*. It is also a fact that in Shakespeare's concluding period the prevailing note is an exaltation of woman so pronounced as to be almost precious. Coriolanus' "gracious silence," as has been seen, led to Hermione and Imogen, to Perdita and Miranda. Now, were one to regard these several attitudes as characteristics of Shakespeare, they might well be found so contradictory as to defeat the possibility of a union between them ; such a union as would be necessary for them both to consort in one personality. Then it would be necessary to say that Shakespeare chose them from without instead of producing them from within. But if they be regarded, not as characteristics, but as attributes of a characteristic, then they at once fall into unity and perspective ; indeed, they become the revelation not only of a personailty, but they also hint the development of a personality. The characteristic in this case would be an extreme sensitiveness to the subject of sex : a nature that could rapidly be attuned to all musics wherein sex was the dominant. Then both the abhorrence and the exaltation become phases of the one thing, and are seen as clear indications of the character of the man behind them. Something sexually obnoxious to the man, in the earlier of the two periods, has evidently touched his extreme sensitiveness ; and he has as evidently in the later period found refuge from his revulsion in letting the same sensitiveness lift woman into some rarer glory, in which she may realise her sex without exercising its functions.

This in its turn raises another important fact in the estimation of Shakespeare's personality. It must not be forgotten that Shakespeare was not only a man who lived upon earth, but also a man who grew upon earth. As he lived his life experience befell him, moulding and altering him. He was not at the time when the Globe was built what he had been when he and his companions reopened the Theater in the autumn of 1594. Therefore if his works are to be searched for an indication to his personality their chronological sequence must carefully be borne in mind. It would be manifestly absurd to discover some or other trait that seems clearly to hint the man in, say, *Love's Labour's Lost*, and then to decide that it obviously cannot hint the man inasmuch as some other such evidence has been discovered in *The Tempest* which seems to point in the opposite direction. It must be remembered that the writer of *Love's Labour's Lost* was a young man full of eagerness for life, and almost propagandist in his faith of the tuition of Life; whereas the writer of *The Tempest* had had his tuition of Life, and therefore had his attention fixed, not on Life, but on the great sleep that rounds our little Life.

An instance where the force of this might aptly be remembered is in the ascription of the word "gentle" with regard to him. If Ben Jonson be the foremost to apply the word, he is far from being the only one. Too much has been made of the use of the word "sweet." On most of the occasions on which this epithet is used, it seems rather to apply to his versification than his personality; where it has an obvious reference. Yet its use certainly tends to bear out the application of the word "gentle." Nevertheless such an ascription might be applied in a very confused way if its correlations were forgotten, or if its biographical application were not taken into account. For example, for a man at the crest of success to be described as gentle is one thing; but for a young man, full of vitality, eager with ability, and in conflict for an adequate recognition, it would be quite another. In the first instance the attribute of gentleness would be a very proper proof of his nobility and true dignity; in the latter instance it might smack somewhat of sycophancy; it would certainly wear an aspect perilously like those acts of ingratiation that Shakespeare himself was not slow to condemn in his later work. Yet, however this be, the fact is that there is no proof that in his early days he won a name for gentleness. There is rather proof to the contrary.

This first hint we have as to Shakespeare's personality is in Greene's famous reference already treated of. And this is instructive in many ways. For a man's character may often be discovered when it is seen how he strikes his contemporaries. But to this it is necessary that the character of the contemporaries be known. It is a strange earth this; and it takes many kinds to fill it; but it may frequently chance that one man's hatred may be not less a proof of excellency than another's love. Now we have a conceivably fair idea as to Greene's character; and we have a rough, yet workable, idea of the other participant in this 1592 fray, Henry Chettle. We know the first as being irritable, quick-tempered, and irascibly insistent on his rights as a dramatist known and approved; and we know the latter for a somewhat genial, good-humoured man, in no way mightily convinced of his own prowess, and therefore the more apt easily to admit the prowess of others. It was the first who, in his quick anger, spoke of Shakespeare as an "upstart crow beautified in our feathers": in which words can be heard very distinctly the reverberation of some controversy over the play *Henry VI.* in which Greene had been worsted. It was Chettle who, later that very year, expressed his regret at having been the publisher of this evidence of Greene's biting hatred, with the declaration, "I am as sorry as if the originall fault had beene my fault, because myself have seene his demeanour no lesse civill than he is exelent in the qualitie he professes, besides divers of worship have reported his uprightness of dealing, which argues his honesty, and his facetious grace in writing that aprooves his art." Now, apart from the direct reference given here as to Shakespeare's "uprightness of dealing," the situation thus created between Shakespeare, Greene, and Chettle throws quite another, and probably more valuable, light on Shakespeare's personality in the days prior to his recognition and prosperity. For it would appear that to a man like Greene, who seemed desirous of setting him back whence he came, Shakespeare's manner was that of an "upstart crow." That is to say, gentle or ungentle, Shakespeare had no intention of being put down by any man; for if he had not stoutly opposed Greene's attitude the elder dramatist would have found no cause of anger. He probably withstood him to the face, seeming not a little bumptious in the proceeding. But to a man like Chettle, who probably readily admitted him to terms of equality, his demeanour seemed "no less civil than he is excellent in the quality he professes," meaning thereby his acting. Which is an allegory of his life. When Shakespeare had won to terms of at least equality with all, he displayed his true instinct of honourable courtesy and an easy and tender grace. But while he was kept out of his own, there is no doubt he displayed all that consciousness of ability, and anger at baulking, which in a young man wins the name, not of gentleness, but of bumptiousness.

There are other evidences of this: evidences that stretch through the course of his life. If the tale be true, for instance, that Shakespeare organised a company of boys at the Cross Keys to tend horses during a performance, which company came to be known as "Shakespeare's boys," this does not altogether suggest mere gentleness. It, to be true, is no proof to the contrary; but it certainly is proof of an instinct for command and authority, not to say consciousness of ability. Moreover, in the years immediately following this the Sonnets came to be written; and who that has read them can have failed to notice the continuous hints of Shakespeare's disgust at seeing ability and work kept out of its own:

> As, to behold desert a beggar born,
> And needy nothing trimmed in jollity,
> And purest faith unhappily foresworn,
> And gilded honour shamefully misplaced,
> And maiden virtue rudely strumpeted,
> And right perfection wrongfully disgraced,
> And strength by limping sway disabled,
> And art made tongue-tied by authority,
> And folly, doctor-like controlling skill,
> And simple truth miscalled simplicity,
> And captive good attending captain ill.

These are not the words of a merely gentle character, nor are they the words of a snob bowing down to all that calls itself authority. They are the words of a man strong in himself, conscious of his worth, and conscious, too, of the excellence of the art he professes, in something very like anger and indignation at seeing inability reposing on authority. We are reminded inevitably of two other passages written subsequent to this, each unsuitably phrased by the character who speaks them. We have already seen that it is not Hamlet but Shakespeare who speaks of

> The whip and scorns of time,
> The oppressor's wrong, the proud man's contumely,
> The pangs of disprized love, the law's delay,
> The insolence of office, and the spurns
> That patient merit of the unworthy takes.

Similarly, it is not Isabella but Shakespeare who gives out this splendid scorn:

> Man, proud man,
> Drest in a little brief authority,
> Most ignorant of what he's most assured,
> His glassy essence, like an angry ape,
> Plays such fantastic tricks before high heaven
> As make the angels weep.

He himself said of himself, in Sonnet 62, that "sin of self-love possesseth all mine eye"; yet, even if this be set aside as poetic mannerism, there is no reason to doubt but that he was quite sufficiently self-assertive where his worth was not recognised. In his later days this was probably allied to the wisdom and dignity born of experience; but in his younger years it doubtless did not scorn ungentler methods.

In addition to this, there are not wanting signs to show that he had a severe, even inexorable, sense of fitness. The argument for this from his works may be a doubtful quantity to rely on. But there is no doubt the argument is sound, one way or another. For example, it might be possible to say that a man could cause the death of Lear, despite the fact that the King was so near a deep joy in his old age, and yet not be inexorably minded. Yet it would not be possible for a man to achieve this without some manner of bent in that direction; and it would be yet more impossible for him to complete the achievement without being influenced in a relentless direction. And when one remembers that it was not only Lear who failed so pitifully, but Desdemona, Hamlet, Ophelia, and a number of others, who cannot have failed to win their Creator's love, the feeling that there was something severe and inexorable present, but not generally recognised, in Shakespeare, is intensified. Then one remembers that there is a certain episode in Shakespeare's life that has not received the attention it deserves. The facts surrounding the episode, and from which it may be derived, are these. We know that in 1598 Ben Jonson, who for some years previously had written for the company managed by Alleyn and Henslowe, had the first play we now know of, his *Every Man in his Humour*, acted by the Lord Chamberlain's company at the Curtain; and the story goes that the author had already been turned away, when Shakespeare, hearing the altercation, intervened, read the play, and accepted it for the company. The story rings true to what we imagine Shakespeare to be, and not less true to the fact that we know that subsequent to this a warm friendship existed between the two. Be this as it may, however, the second fact is, that Ben Jonson's next play *Every Man Out of his Humour* was acted the following year at the Globe by the same company. Now, this play was a somewhat acrimonious attack on certain playwrights, and ushered in what has come to be known as "The War of the Theatres." We know, too, that after this play Ben Jonson left the company, and wrote for the children's players at the Blackfriars. We cannot say of a surety that this arose because Shakespeare, one of the householders of the Globe, came forward firmly to his friend saying that brawling must cease, and that if Ben wished to continue it he must be gone. But we do know that a play called *The Return from Parnassus* was written a few years after this, and we have already heard its reference to Ben Jonson as a "pestilent fellow," and the apparent zest with which it records the fact that "our fellow Shakespeare hath given him a purge that made him bewray his credit"; we know, moreover, that Shakespeare acted in *Every Man in his Humour*, but made no appearance in the later play; and it is an inference hard to overlook that something of this kind occurred. It is to the lasting credit of both Shakespeare and Jonson that it does not seem to have left any permanent stain on their friendship. Jonson was one of the two who saw the last of Shakespeare; and stout Ben left the record behind him that he "loved the man, and did honour his memory on this side idolatry as much as any." But it is fairly clear that in this whole episode Shakespeare proved himself to be firm, inexorable, and masterful; and when it is remembered that the object of his attentions was a man who had slain a man in duel the previous year, the matter is thrown into yet clearer relief. Indeed, a somewhat penetrating light is thrown thereby on to two phases of Shakespeare's personality. For he is seen as a lover of peace and concord, of gentle means to the end of amity; but he is also seen as a man who could be quite relentless in insisting on his gentle desires. It is a rare combination. And taken in conjunction with such things as the death of Lear, it is peculiarly arrestive.

One remembers, for instance, how remorseless was Hamlet in the cross-examination to which he submitted his mother: how almost ruthless he is in his dismissal of frail Ophelia. One remembers with what pitiless decision Othello goes to the immolation of his lily-fair wife, with the severe words held before him, "It is the cause, it is the cause, my soul." One remembers Macbeth's words when he hears that his "dearest chuck" is dead: strange words, "she should have died hereafter; there would have been a time for such a word": quite intelligible at so stressful a moment; yet severe, nevertheless. In the Ben Jonson episode, and the death of Lear, it is Shakespeare himself who is relentless; in these several instances it is his creations that are relentless; but viewing them together, it is easy to see his characters dating this attribute in themselves from a similar attitude in him.

There is another characteristic in many of his characters that can definitely be traced back to their creator. We remember that Iago speaks scoffingly of Othello thus:

> The Moor is of a free and open nature,
> That thinks men honest that but seem to be so.

Hamlet, with all his swift penetration into the motives of men pitted against him, and with all the mordant humour with which he could thwart guile with guile, was also a man of this nature. It does not need his wholly different uncle to tell us that

> he, being remiss,
> Most generous and free from all contriving,
> Will not peruse the foils.

It is not much that Hamlet shares with the Moor: yet he certainly shares this. We feel that it is just how Othello would have behaved himself: carelessly to accept the first rapier, and say negligently, "This likes me well. These foils have all a length?" It is this "free and open nature" that provides the whole base of Timon's tragedy. In fact, it would seem that when Shakespeare desired to phrase any character that should inevitably enlist our sympathy, he could not help but give him firstly and foremostly this indescribable nobility, this "free and open nature." A lengthy list arises to instance the assertion: Romeo, Falstaff, Henry IV., Henry V. (apart from his dastardly rejection of Falstaff, and his somewhat priggish appearances in *Henry IV.*), Antonio, Orlando, Brutus, Hamlet, Othello, Lear, Timon, Antony, Coriolanus (in fact, and necessarily, all the heroes of the tragedies), Posthumus, and Prospero, not to speak of many minor yet lovable characters. It is therefore not surprising, though it is illuminating, to hear Ben Jonson say of Shakespeare, in Iago's very words regarding Othello, that "he was, indeed, honest, and of an open and free nature."

Now, even as it was necessary to point out that Shakespeare's "gentleness" did not at all imply that he lacked self-assertion, bitterness or extreme severity, so here it is necessary to insist that Shakespeare's "open and free nature" does not at all mean that he failed to remember an injury that had been done him. There is somewhat of a confusion of thought in this regard, owing to the fact that men find it difficult to think of more than one thing at a time. It is forgotten that human character is not only complex in its construction, but paradoxically conceived. To understand it, therefore, the intelligence must needs think paradoxically: must, in fact, in no way be distressed at finding seeming contradictions consorting happily together. For example, there is no doubt that when Brutus describes himself to Cassius we are enabled to overhear Shakespeare in self-revelation.

> O Cassius, you are yoked with a lamb,
> That carries anger as the flint bears fire,
> Who, much enforced, shows a hasty spark
> And straight is cold again.

But this does not mean that, if Brutus and Cassius had both survived the battle, the former would have turned quite so much to the latter's judgment in later affairs in Rome. And if Cassius had not shown a contrition somewhat difficult to understand by reason of its violence, Brutus might have been a lamb never so much, and yet Cassius have been given cause, at some later date, to remember their quarrel. So with Shakespeare.

Several incidents in his life serve to illustrate this. Perhaps the chief is his attitude with regard to his wife. Yet, since this depends on indirect, and uncircumstantially supported, inference from facts, that might perhaps be made to yield remote inferences, it would be well to turn first to another method that gives a lesser latitude of deduction. It has already been seen that when Shakespeare left Stratford in 1587 the causes that induced him to this step were several. The prime cause seems certainly to have been his indigence. The active cause, if adequate weight be given to several independent traditions, would seem not less certainly to have been the fact that he fell foul of Sir Thomas Lucy, who owned extensive game-preserves near Stratford; which preserves, or rather the " venison and rabbits " on which preserves, had received Shakespeare's predatory attention. " For this," we have already heard Rowe say, " he was prosecuted by that gentleman, as he thought, somewhat too severely; and in order to revenge that ill-usage, he made a ballad upon him, and though this, probably the first essay of his poetry, be lost, yet it is said to have been so very bitter that it redoubled the prosecution against him to that degree that he was obliged to leave his business and family in Warwickshire and shelter himself in London." The good purport of that shelter in

London was a considerable artistic and earthly prestige; and it might therefore be thought that Shakespeare would good-humouredly waive the memory of past bitterness. Not so. Some fourteen years thereafter he was back in Stratford to set up his own earthly tabernacle at New Place. And memories were stirred in him. Moreover, at that time he was occupied with the varied adventures of a certain Sir John Falstaff; and so when it came to the turn of that fat knight to gather levies for the northern campaign, nothing would suit Shakespeare but that he should go into the West country, not so much for the purpose of gathering together "the cankers of a calm world and a long peace," but rather that he should meet there a certain Justice Shallow. All through the latter part of *Henry IV.*, whenever Master Shallow puts in an appearance, there is the subtle feeling that there is a caricature afoot. From that play it is, however, impossible to say whom the caricature is driven at: though doubtless good Stratfordians, such as saw the play, were never in much doubt over the matter. But when Justice Shallow appears again in *The Merry Wives of Windsor*, all doubt is set at rest. Sir Thomas Game-Preserving Lucy had on his coat-of-arms "three luces hauriant argent," luces being an ancient name for pike-fish. Therefore Justice Shallow's coat is described as having a "dozen white luces in it," whereat Sir Hugh Evans comments more sagely than civilly that a "dozen white louses do become a coat well." Thus the caricature is fixed beyond reasonable question; and doubtless, if we had any discovery of Sir Thomas Lucy's private character, we would find the portrait of Justice Shallow quite sufficiently cutting to ease Shakespeare's shrewd memory. Certainly to speak of such reprisal as revenge would be much to misinterpret Shakespeare's mood. It was probably too equable for revenge; it was rather such a keen sense of equity as humour itself depends on; but therewithal it is another testimony to the inexorable severity that blent with the other things, with the gentleness, good-humour, and free and open nature that went to the construction of Shakespeare's personality.

It is this strange balance and proportion of qualities that is so baffling in any examination into the constituents of Shakespeare's personality. The qualities are themselves by no means indefinable. The stouter difficulty is to discover how far they are contributory to the higher unity compact of them. For example, there is a species of mind cast in a contradictory mould. Whatever the enunciation be, in possession of an argument, they may safely be trusted to oppose it. Often this is no more than whimsey or perversity; yet often it is unwisely mistaken for such. It is as though the enunciation of an argument, rendered partial by the very necessity of economy in statement, brought to such a mind the proper complement of that point of view in the larger truth we all serve. At once, therefore, it was induced to violent opposition for the maintenance of equity. Now, in Shakespeare's mind and personality these opposing complements were not asserting themselves in these alternations either of struggle or perversity. They proceeded forward equally together. The total result might have been gracious or ungracious (judging from the attitude of his contemporaries, it was, on the whole, exceedingly gracious); but the deeper importance is that the man was neither one-sided nor swayed violently to alternative issues; rather, he was, through the general tenour of his days, variously compounded; which is to say, that he was equably poised. In arguments at the Mermaid, for instance, he would probably either be silent, because he saw the wider issues of the debate, or, if good sack were in him, engaged in the lighter word-play that Fuller credited him with, because over-earnestness in discussion could but inevitably narrow the issue, and so destroy the truth of it.

Surely this is very often and very unwisely omitted from the calculation of critics. For example, we have knowledge of cases where Shakespeare has seemed to be entirely severe in enforcing legal measures for the collection of debts owing him. This is entirely in accord with what we have seen of certain aspects of his character; and it is quite probable that in some of the cases his levy imposed hardship. Yet we know that he was also gentle and of a kindly disposition: therefore, knowing this, we would do well not to give an overweight of attention to these cases. It would be salutary, not to say fair, to remember that by the nature of the case we can have no knowledge of any remission of debt, or of any passage of money that took the form of gift instead of debt. And this is even more important in another regard. Certain criticisms have been responsible for the impression that Shakespeare in his private life was dominated, in somewhat of the same manner as Walter Scott, by the thought of establishing a worldly position of good prestige and comfortable esteem; and that, to this end, he was willing to give the public what it demanded, and what it would pay for most liberally, with no thought of artistic truth.[2] In short, that he was not so much an artist as a tradesman.

Now, we have already seen the life of the man, and we have therefore seen precisely what this criticism has had for its basis of operation. We have seen him rise from obscurity to prominence, and from penury to what has well seemed like opulence. We have seen him purchasing a considerable holding of real estate at Stratford, establishing himself as a householder both in the Globe and in the Blackfriars, and, finally, near the end of his days, buying some property near the latter playhouse. All this has seemed highly prosperous; it has all hinted the man engrossed in the ways of sleek success. Yet actually what is the real significance of these various facts? Even were they what at first sight they seem to be, they would yet not wholly imply the man engrossed in material success. It cannot be forgotten that for the better part of twenty years, both as boy and man, he had had his life searched by the necessities of penury. It would, therefore, be but natural if, while pursuing deeper ambitions, he was carefully to erect safeguards against a possible declension into those unhappier ways. But are the facts what at first sight they seem to be? In the first place, there are two outstanding misapprehensions that have hitherto ever confused the issue. One is that calculations hitherto made of Shakespeare's probable earnings as householder, dramatist, and actor, have been much in excess even of likelihood;[3] and the other is that the story of Shakespeare's retirement to Stratford to settle down as a respectable urban gentleman, is found to subsist rather more on imagination than on fact. But there are a variety of ways of regarding the facts, that are not usually employed. For example, it is true that he purchased New Place in 1597. Yet, beside this fact, it is well to have in memory the equally important fact that he did not elect to occupy it till another fourteen years had passed. It is also true that he bought property in Blackfriars some time during the year 1613. Yet, if he were so wealthy as is sometimes said, how came it that at this late date in his life he covenanted to pass nearly half of the purchase money into a mortgage, which mortgage remained unredeemed at his death? For money was not then, as now, so irremovable a product.

Yet the light shed by his Book, direct and indirect, is of surer value. Take, for example, the parallel so often and so unhappily put forward between Shakespeare and Walter Scott.[4] The very citation should be its own answer. There are surely none who can fail to be caught by the healthy charm of Scott. Yet it is a first axiom in criticism to distinguish things that differ. Where is the affinity between Scott and the author of *Hamlet*, *Othello*, *Lear*, and *Timon*, or *Midsummer Night's Dream*, *As You Like It*, and *The Tempest*? It is as though one would ask the affinity between Dumas and Sophocles. To be told that the Waverley Novels were so many bids for remuneration is not to be told anything incredible. But can this be said of Shakespeare's tragic series? If so, then how came it that he should make lament in *Hamlet* over the children players that "are now the fashion" and who "so berattle the common stages"; that he should go on to praise plays that "pleased not the million," and that are "caviare to the general"; and then, having said so much, that he should proceed to write a series of mighty plays that were in the last remove unlike those done by the children players that "berattled the common stages," and that precisely were conceived in the fashion of the plays praised by Hamlet that "were caviare to the general" and that "pleased not the million"? For if one thing above another be clear, it is that in giving Hamlet speech upon matters dramatical, it was not the Prince of Denmark who was speaking, but Shakespeare in his own proper person. And these utterances are surely proof enough that Shakespeare's first concern was to achieve an Art worthy of himself, and that it irked him ill to do anything that would huckster his pen. Yet if they were not sufficient, the precise accord of such sentiments with the tragedies he immediately set his hand to, should set the matter at rest. For in one he is seen enunciating his critical principles, with a great scoff at the demands of his public; and in the other he is to be discovered achieving in practice the principles he had set out in theory.

But the matter wants not a reference yet more direct. There are continued passages throughout the Sonnets in which Shakespeare declares that the friend he addresses is sure of perpetual memory by reason of the verse in which he is proclaimed. The theme is rung to many changes. It may be self-effacing; as thus in Sonnet 16:

> But wherefore do not you a mightier way
> Make war upon this bloody tyrant Time?
> And fortify yourself in your decay
> With means more blessed than my barren rhyme?

It may rise to greater assurance in the next sonnet. In the nineteenth sonnet it may ring out a triumphant challenge:

> Yet, do thy worst, old Time: despite thy wrong,
> My love shall in my verse ever live young.

Or again in Sonnet 107:

> And thou in this shalt find thy monument,
> When tyrants' crests and tombs of brass are spent.

Now to dismiss these are customary conceits, because they chance to appear in Daniel, Drayton, and other English, not to include French, sonneteers, is rather too abrupt a method of procedure to commend itself to sane thought. To call a manner of expression a customary conceit is not to say that it has no root in personal conviction. To prove that every Elizabethan sonneteer declared his faith in the eternal laurels his verses were destined to pluck from the brows of Time, would seem rather to prove that the Elizabethan age was one in which poetry was held in high esteem, not that it was an age in which all the poets were fashionable rhymsters vaunting things they did not themselves believe. One would have imagined that the actual poetic achievement of the Elizabethan age would have been enough to establish that. One might have imagined, too, that it was scarcely necessary to point out that words, even the phrases of conceit, are not devoid of meaning; that they must have meant something to begin with; and that their constant exercise in the emotional labour of poetic conception would have made them, to such a man as the author of *Hamlet*, mean even more to conclude with. And certainly it should not be necessary to remark that a certain expression, repeatedly employed, from the pen of the author of *King Lear*, is likely to have a more considerable weight of meaning than a similar expression from Drayton or Daniel.

Yet if they all were dismissed, there remains the strange earnestness of such a sonnet as the twenty-ninth, part of which has already been quoted:

> When, in disgrace with fortune and men's eyes,
> I all alone beweep my outcast state,
> And trouble deaf Heaven with my bootless cries,
> And look upon myself, and curse my fate,
> Wishing me like to one more rich in hope,
> Featured like him, like him with friends possessed,
> Desiring this man's art, and that man's scope,
> With what I most enjoy contented least;
> Yet in these thoughts myself almost despising,
> Haply I think on thee; and then my state,
> Like to the lark at break of day arising
> From sullen earth, sings hymns at heaven's gate;
>   For thy sweet love remembered such wealth brings,
>   That then I scorn to change my state with kings.

There are none who have lived, and not evaded, this doughty life of Man on the Earth, but must recognise in this the delineation of indubitable experience. Overwrought and overstrained, melancholy has swept the skies of thought, with the result that one by one the soul has examined all its imagined wealth, the truth of its friends, the security of its earthly achievement, the value of its hold on deeper things, and has turned it all aside as dross,

—even that which was red gold. It has compared its possessions with this man's and that other's, with despair and disgust. At such times the melancholy has either been complete; or, in casting here and there, it has struck on something fair and pure: some treasured and stalwart friend, or some fair-cheeked child: when a soft gentle glow has thrilled the being with an impalpable calm. All this is to be found in the sonnet.

But there is to be found another thing that is more than significant. When such moods befall a man his thought flies to closest investigation of the thing most near the priceless to him. A lover questions his love; a tradesman (in the true sense of that word, as implying one who has first thought of gain) doubts the security of his profits; an artist doubts the beauty of his vision or the skill of his utterance. Now, where throughout this sonnet is Shakespeare to be discovered doubting if he had indeed "provided permanently for himself and his daughters"? Even the line which might seem to suggest this, "Wishing me like to one more rich in hope," implies the opposite in truth, since it looks to the future rather than to the present for gain. On the other hand, however, on what does his melancholy most securely fasten? Hear him then!

> Desiring this man's art, and that man's scope,
> With what I most enjoy contented least.

Who is it can think of these words that they were

written by a man who had no other thought for the work of his brain than that it should pay him well? Yet, especially when the likely date of their writing be remembered, they concur precisely with his dramatic achievement. Few will question that the Sonnets were begun after Shakespeare's establishment at the Theater in 1594, probably in 1597; and thus the twenty-ninth sonnet would come somewhere about the year 1597-8. Now this was the time when Shakespeare had most cause to enter the dissatisfaction in question. He had just completed what was probably the second draft of *Romeo and Juliet*. He had lately left Marlowe's leading-strings in *Richard III.* to attempt plays in his own manner in *Richard II.* and *King John.* He had completed *Two Gentlemen of Verona*, in which he is manifestly at a loss to achieve certainty of characterisation; and he was probably occupied in learning his art by rehandling the plays of the old Burbage company as the Queen's men for the present Burbage company as the Lord Chamberlain's men. In other words, the plays manifest uncertainty and tentative trial on every hand; while the sonnet manifests the realisation of this in the hour of melancholy. Nevertheless, he may be "contented least" with his art and his scope, yet it is noteworthy that he "enjoys it most": in which the true signature is given of the man for whom the creation of beauty and power is a joy; the artist, that is to say, irrespective, though not necessarily independent, of gain. And the result was that thenceforward he never turned back as an artist: his scope became the more, till it embraced *King Lear*, and his art became intenser, till it flamed to wonder in *Othello*.

Of the fact that he had to write for his audience, there is no question; nor that it influenced and cheapened his work. So much has already been seen. Yet he was fortunate in that his dealings were directly with his audience. He did not labour under the misfortune of later days, in having to deal with intermediaries in the shape of actor-managers and directors. This is to say, he could be true to his ambitions in Art, and temper them directly through the ordeal of the "yard." One of the results of this, in the way of instance, was *Hamlet*. So far as may be judged from contemporary evidence, *Hamlet* was a considerable success, though it is doubtful if any director or actor-manager, of that day, or any other day, would have dared to venture it as an unknown quantity. And yet there is little in it in which Shakespeare was not true to his conception of dramatic Art. The infinite pains with which he tended it, as manifested in the various versions it underwent at his hands, proves that he esteemed it highly, and meant loftily by it. Moreover, that he intended it for a more substantial end than the stage of the Globe is seen from the fact that, judging from a collation of the various Quartos with the Folio, it never seems to have been acted in Shakespeare's own day in the full form that we have it now. There is no such proof with regard to *King Lear*; but contrasting it and *Hamlet* with the average length of the other tragedies, it would seem probable that it also was not acted in the full form as now read.[5] That is to say, Shakespeare intended a wider appeal for such work than that afforded by his stage, however much he wrote for his stage, and held it before his eye as the scene on which his characters moved, thought, and spake; and in this, it is to be seen, he foreshadowed Charles Lamb's famous enunciation of dramatic creed. Yet, whether he bravely ventured the full strength of ambition, or whether he withheld part of it, giving only a shorter version of it on the stage, or whether he tempered his strength with the devices his audiences demanded of him, and which, as seen in our study of the conditions of his stage, he gave grudgingly as a thing apart, or transmuted to power, it is evident that Shakespeare was no mean playwright producing matter to the requirements of purse and audience, but an eager Artist, very much absorbed in the production of such power and beauty as should not readily be suffered to perish from memory. Probably Hemings and Condell in publishing the Folio edition were only fulfilling a charge entrusted to them by their friend when living. Indeed, it is surely preposterous that the opposite conception could have ever so far found credence as to need repetition.

How then came such a faith to win its way? And here one strikes a very subtle phase of Shakespeare's personality. He has been seen as a man quick and generous, open-hearted and free, yet with a certain aloof dignity that could be stern and severe, ruthless even to the remembrance of ancient wrongs, if occasion evoked it to activity. He has been seen as a man very apt to take his line of conduct from his opposite: to the hard man he was hard, to the gentle, gentle, to the noble, noble, and to the overbearing, revengeful: to honest Ben, even when honest Ben was most severe in his strictures on him, "he was, indeed, honest, and of an open and free nature," to cantankerous Greene he was an "upstart Crow," to buxom Chettle he was of civil demeanour and honest repute, to pompous Sir Thomas Lucy a broad and ruthless lampooner. His attitude in the Mountjoy-Bellott lawsuit bears out this impression.[6] In bringing about the marriage between Bellott and Mountjoy's daughter he appears as only too anxious to render a service that may bring general happiness. In the lawsuit that finally arose, his attitude is that of a man who will answer his interrogatories no more fully than he is bound to do; and who will remain at Stratford out of all broils, leaving justice or injustice to take its own course. In his life at the Cross Keys he was seen as industrious to succeed. His progress from the Rose to the Theater showed him as one quick to see, and strike at, a passing prospect, and convert it into a permanent success.

In the building of the Globe, and the subsequent continual changes in the householders' shares, he appears like a man who, having won his advantage, was not fretful to push it further, though fully resolved to maintain it. In other words, the prevailing note in him is one of extreme sensitiveness to influence and environment. This is seen in a variety of ways. Take his attitude to the commonalty. He is often spoken of simply as either democratic or, more frequently, undemocratic; when in fact this very sensitiveness in him denied simplicity in him, and made him complex. What are the facts? When he regards the sufferings of the poor and the erring, he is angry and bitter, as in *King Lear*; when he is presented with their bodily presence he is offended at their breath and odour; and when he sees them in the "yard" from one of the "rooms," he describes them in *Coriolanus* as "many-headed." So with men of rank. If they accord him gentleness, and treat him frankly, he will grant them fully, only too fully, the esteem of their fortuitous dignity. If they slight him, he can be very stiff. It was this sensitiveness that made him in the Sonnets (as will later be seen more fully) so quick and fond with the grace and beauty of a young man. And when his mistress submitted to the caress of his friend, the sensual disgust stirred in him reeks through play on play.

Now, with a man of this nature there is one quality that is bound to emerge in his work. An element will appear that will look much like mental sloth; and which, though primarily not mental sloth, might finally produce it. He will revolt at detailed attention. To work, he will need to work at pressure of imaginative heat; but having once written a thing it will jar on him after to endeavour to recover the similar heat necessary to its detailed examination. It will be easier for him to scheme in large than to work in small. A *King Lear* will come more apt to his mind than a polished lyric: and if a lyric came not complete in a single wave of emotion, he would dismiss it and proceed with other matters. Thus a scene will engage him more than a speech of it; and this speech than one of its lines. Not that fine speeches and memorable lines are foreign to him. In truth, they are his abundant riches. But they came not of themselves so much as in the course of a larger endeavour. They were not wrought: they were pulled-off. They were the result of a sudden flame in the imagination on its way to a further goal.

In other words, we have returned to the criticism with which this study launched itself, having tracked it to its source. Shakespeare's personality was such that he could not work in detail: his way of work had to be in large; it had to be prodigal; it had to be wasteful. It might look like sloth; but it was in reality the result of an excess of mental activity. In a sense, so complex is personality, it was both, even as a man may continue to walk because he is too fatigued to make the mental decision to hail a passing conveyance. He was too slothful to take pains because he was too urgent to proceed. In time this would grow to a philosophy with him. Even as he gave contending forces fullness of power in faith of a loftier synthesis, so he may have come to see that waste was functional. His later plays certainly seem to hint this. It may even be that he passed such dramatic faults as Prospero's explanation of their appearance on the island to Miranda, in the half-thought that some strange and hidden beauty might emerge from it.

Yet, whether it grew to a philosophy or not, it is plain that Shakespeare was very prone to such carelessness. And it is clear to see that this way of work was a strict function of his personality. He was ambitious; but he was more ambitious to conceive largely than to polish infinitely. It revolted him to turn back and face a completed piece of work. It dissatisfied him for further work. If he ever rewrote a play, it was after a considerable space of time; and then, instead of repassing it all through the alembic of his imagination, he altered here a little and there a little, leaving old and new in a mingled indiscrimination—sometimes, indeed, as in *Love's Labour's Lost*, even putting down a refurbished speech to follow the speech it was a refurbishment of. Now, while critically and truly this is seen to be a strict function of his personality, it is obvious to see that, were it not examined critically, it might easily seem like the carelessness of a man concerned, not with an Art worthy of himself, but with the gain to accrue from any work that was good enough to find favour. And as the bulk of men are zealous to seek an excuse for mental sloth, such criticism, once pronounced, would very soon find a general acceptance.

This sensitiveness in him, however, explains not only much that is perplexing in his work: it explains the course and tenour of his life. He had once tasted of an acute poverty; and it must needs have struck something like a fear through his blood. This very sensitiveness would make him subject to acute waves of melancholy; and at such times he would fear above all else a reversion to such ancient unhappiness. It might even paint his dreams. Hence he would be careful to secure himself against this in a variety of ways. He would seek varied investments, so that no single catastrophe might possibly whelm him: which is precisely what we find Shakespeare doing continually. But it would not only affect him negatively: it would affect him positively. Comfort would affect him; the entertainment of friends would make a sure appeal to him; the amenities and dignities of station could not fail to flatter his emotion, even while he searched their lack of reality. And all these things he strives for. If to put a fool in a play would aid such an end, he will put the fool there; but he will not account the fool as part of the play if he does not catch his imagination. He will give him separate scenes, as in *Othello*; or he will find him tags at the end of scenes, as in parts of *King Lear*. But he will not suffer him to mar his work in any essential.

In all this a very clear and engaging personality presents itself. And as we examine his plays we find that precisely such a personality is ever emerging in them. Romeo, for example, is such a man; so is Hamlet; and in those two, as criticism has not been slow continually to aver, Shakespeare has probably put more of himself than in any of his characters. Both of them may be called sensual: though, while with the earlier character it is, as we should expect, tender, eager and melancholy, with the latter the tenderness is painful and the eagerness and melancholy have turned to disgust and morbidity. Yet to speak of them as sensual is not so much to speak of a characteristic, as to mention the attribute of a characteristic. They are sensual because they are both highly sensitive; and because, therefore, the beauty and love of women have power to sway them absolutely. They are both sensitive to friendship: quick Mercutio in the one case, and firm Horatio in the other, staunch hearts both of them, call out in each something that is more like love than mere friendship. Both are melancholy; both are highly susceptible to honour. Both, be it particularly noted, have also something ruthless in their outlook on life. In Romeo this is decidedly felt, though it makes no more emphatic an appearance than the prompt dismissal of Rosaline and his impatience with the somewhat fatuous Count of Paris. With Hamlet, however, this takes a very emphatic appearance. With a foolish old man like Polonius he is impatient and cynical; with a frail flower like Ophelia, inasmuch as she has failed him, and become the dupe of her diplomatic father, he is ruthless and bawdy; with his mother he is dignified though earnest, and honourable though determined, but he is quite inexorable in searching her soul for guilt; he is ironical always with two such dunces as Rosencrantz and Guildenstern, and when he dismisses them to their death at his ordaining, it perturbs him not at all; for, says he,

> Why, man, they did make love to this employment;
> They are not near my conscience; their defeat
> Does by their own insinuation grow:
> 'Tis dangerous when the lesser nature comes
> Between the pass and fell incensed points
> Of mighty opposites.

In contrast to this, with Laertes he is open and hearty, affectionate even; for Laertes may be a foe, yet he has cause for enmity, and he is honest withal. It was not so with the others; and so they never show the tenderness which was ever his first instinct, and which he gave in such abundant measure to stout Horatio. In this he was Romeo grown older, and embittered by experience; which is to say that in the meantime Shakespeare himself had grown older, and had been embittered by experience. For Romeo, though he never had occasion so to act, was yet capable of all this. The capability in him, even as the actuality in Hamlet, was again not a characteristic, but the attribute of a characteristic; that characteristic being a certain aloof dignity, which we have seen to be so severe a line in Shakespeare's own character.

In yet later years, when the storm that had broken through the Tragedies had made an end, a gentler mood came over him. This is only to say what can clearly be seen, and what has already been discovered, in the general aspect of the plays that succeeded to the Tragedies. Yet it is only fair to say that this must needs have been the result of a definite softening of this same severity in Shakespeare's mind. The question may be put in this way: How would Hamlet (Hamlet being Shakespeare's fullest discovery of himself) have acted toward one who had severely wronged him, had he struggled through his hour of strife to a later serenity? Now in his later plays there is to be found a character who wears Shakespeare's portrait upon him; and since he is not only symbolic of Shakespeare in other ways, but had actually had a grievous wrong done him, which he is discovered as being in the power to revenge, it should be interesting to note his course of action. Prospero is sensitive, frank, and melancholy, with ever a strain of severity; also, even as he bade farewell to his magic so Shakespeare, in the play in which he

HIS PERSONALITY

appears, also completed his Book. Moreover, having been deeply wronged, he now holds his malignants in his power. How, then, does he define his attitude? Note the following dialogue, and see how aptly, in the progress in the characterisation from Hamlet to Prospero, the progress in Shakespeare's emotional outlook is declared. It is Ariel who tells him of his enemies.

> Your charm so strongly work 'em,
> That if you now behold them, your affections
> Would become tender.
>
> *Prospero.* Dost thou think so, spirit?
> *Ariel.* Mine would, sir, were I human.
> *Prospero.* And mine shall.
> Hast thou, which art but air, a touch, a feeling
> Of their afflictions, and shall not myself,
> One of their kind, that relish all as sharply,
> Passion as they, be kindlier moved than thou art?
> Tho' with their high wrongs I am struck to the quick,
> Yet with my nobler reason 'gainst my fury
> Do I take part: the rarer action is
> In virtue than in vengeance: they being penitent,
> The sole drift of my purpose doth extend
> Not a frown further. Go, release them, Ariel:
> My charms I'll break, their senses I'll restore,
> And they shall be themselves.

It is to be noticed that such relenting sprang not from instinct, but came of reflection; and we feel that it was thus, if at all, that Hamlet would have found it possible to forgive such a knave as the King, or such a very old fool as Polonius. Moreover, with this breaking in severity there is to be noticed in Prospero a feature new in Shakespeare's characterisation: and that is a quick irritability, born of over-strained nerves, at sudden intrusions or interruptions. Apparently the tempest that had whelmed through Shakespeare's life had not left his health untouched.

Yet, taking the Prince of Denmark as Shakespeare's completest declaration of himself, there is a side of Hamlet's character that we find neither in Romeo nor Prospero. It is, in fact, in few other characters, simply because there is sufficient timber in it for the separate creation of whole characters. Whenever, for example, Hamlet handles Polonius there is always the hint in the air of Falstaff. Sometimes there is the very Falstaffian cadence; as thus: "Let her not walk i' the sun: conception is a blessing; but as your daughter may conceive,— friend, look to 't." Once at least it is almost startling. It is when Hamlet mock-seriously hales Polonius to and fro, beginning thus: "Do you see yonder cloud that's almost in shape of a camel?" There is a mordancy in Hamlet that is never in Falstaff; but it is just so that we feel Falstaff, in the melancholy that afflicted him after Henry's rejection, would have searched the secrets out of men. Hamlet is more than Falstaff; for he includes Falstaff more than Falstaff includes him. Yet they each have much of the other in them. What they do not share in common is Hamlet's sensitive nobility on the one hand, and Falstaff's robustious search for pleasure and defiance of reality on the other. This is only as we should expect it to be in the course of Shakespeare's life. Yet it would be interesting to conceive a character whose conception stood midway between Falstaff and Hamlet: a character that, as it were, had half shed Falstaff and half grown into Hamlet. Such a character demands no imagining, however. His prototype exists in Jaques. Then we remember that the creation of Jaques was just about midway between Falstaff and Hamlet in order of writing. And so again we are enabled to see Shakespeare recording in the creation of his characters the growth and development of his own personality through the course and tenour of his life.

At once, therefore, the question is raised as to what it was that produced this singular line of development in Shakespeare: a line that takes, from one aspect, its course through Romeo, to Hamlet, and so on to Prospero; and, from another aspect, through Falstaff, to Jaques, and on to, and past, Hamlet. And seeing that this question has raised itself from the plays, it is obvious that it must find its answer outside the plays. That is to say, it must seek its answer in the Sonnets. Now, it is neither fitting nor necessary to examine the Sonnets with elaboration or detail. That has already been done more than adequately: they have been examined minutely, they have caused derision, they have ruffled perplexed brows, they have been harried

to and fro, up and down, they have been chased
through and through in the search for new portents
and strange chimeras, until interest in them has been
wellnigh whipped flaccid.[7]

Nevertheless, a clear and continuous story emerges
from them. It is true that no positive proof exists
that this story is the story of Shakespeare's own
life; though there is collateral proof that it must
needs have been. That sonneteering was a conventional exercise is true enough; but that Shakespeare's sonneteering was no conventional exercise
is sufficiently obvious from the fact that the story it
tells is no conventional story. The same argument
dismisses the thought that the Sonnets, if not conventional, were at least occupied with a fiction; for
the story is not only unconventional, it is decidedly
unpleasant; and therefore it was little likely to have
provided the burthen for a sequence of Sonnets, unless
that sequence were indeed occupied with an undeniable, if undesirable, relation of actual life. But
when it is found that the story provided by these
Sonnets is precisely what is needed to render intelligible the progress of Shakespeare's personality
as evidenced in his characterisation, then surely it
is evident that both the characterisation and the
sequence in the Sonnets are both parts of one whole,
that one whole being Shakespeare's expression of
himself.

The first series of Sonnets, that is to say, all the
Sonnets 1-126, in the unfolding of such a story,

become of value primarily as the basis on which the remaining Sonnets (save the last two, which are perfunctory) erect their interest. In them, in one way and another, Shakespeare is heard addressing himself to a man very much his junior, who is so beautiful that Shakespeare's susceptibility has been awoken to an ardency of affection not so rare on this earth as may be thought, and certainly not unexpected of the creator of Antonio and Sebastian in *Twelfth Night*, or Antonio and Bassannio in the *Merchant of Venice*. The first sequence (1-19) rings perfunctorily in its appeal to this young man to marry. He may have been urged to this by the young man's parents; but it is clear that he is not much concerned in the matter. But suddenly a change occurs. It is as though his first sequence was his introduction to the young man; who now captured a sudden and fierce affection in him. For no sooner are we clear of the last of the perfunctory Sonnets than we plunge into a series in which the poet begins by hailing his friend with the following strange and complete abandon :

> A woman's face with Nature's own hand painted,
> Hast thou, the master-mistress of my passion.

After this there is only this one note. Whether he has to send his affection from a distance (26), whether melancholy (29), or the silent thought that succeeds to melancholy (30), immerses him, or whether he goes out with his company on tour

(43-52), it is all the same. Even if the young man disappoints him grievously by some or other "sensual fault" (33-5), it makes no difference; he is soon brought to the acceptance of all blame, or at least to the acquittal of his friend (36-42).

Now, it is here we strike the first hint of the trouble. His friend may leave him awhile (56 and onwards); some other poet may win the attention and favour of him (78-86), and it may bring coldness between them (87 and onwards); it may even bring so deep an estrangement that Shakespeare may cease writing these Sonnets to his friend for awhile (see 100-103), and have subsequently to pen something like an apology (109 and onwards): but it is here the centre of difference is discovered. The first sequence is dismissed with Sonnet 126, and the subsequent sequence (127-152) is addressed to a woman, dark and hot, who was Shakespeare's mistress, and who has played him false. Contrasting this latter sequence with the Sonnets 33-42—and especially 40-42—the strange story is easily discoverable. Apparently Shakespeare's fair young friend and his dark, hot mistress have met, and, apparently at her instigation, they have each played him false with the other. And it is this that revolts his whole being.[8]

Thus we see that it was in the mood of Romeo and Falstaff that Shakespeare loved his young friend. Soon after the unfaithfulness occurred we find

Jaques; and when Shakespeare's naturally reflective nature has carried the mischief through his whole blood in sheer disgust, we find Hamlet. Moreover, it would seem that the silence and estrangement that is conveyed in Sonnet 100 was caused by the young man rejecting Shakespeare in favour of Shakespeare's mistress; and, therefore, that it is this that is occupying Shakespeare's thought when he depicts Henry's harsh and inexplicable rejection of Falstaff. Certainly the unfaithfulness of his friend created a bitter melancholy in his mind, even as the lustfulness of his mistress created a sexual abhorrence in his emotion. The two things were doomed for ever to banish from Shakespeare's personality the possibility of another Romeo or another Falstaff. Things have changed the earth for him; and there are hints enough to indicate the change. There is the rejection of Falstaff, for instance. There is also the fact that at this time Shakespeare took up his old play *Love's Labour's Lost*, rewriting it, and describing the cruel Rosaline in it precisely as we find the dark mistress described in the Sonnets. Moreover, there appears a brooding power of thought and emotion rising in the plays.

Reading the Sonnets together with the Plays in this manner it is possible not alone to discover Shakespeare's personality in his characters, but also to discover it all the more surely inasmuch as we are enabled to see the tragic happenings that are moulding and embittering it. The two lines of progress through Romeo and Falstaff to Hamlet come to wear a vivid significance; and we can understand now what seemed perplexed before, the meaning of this rising tide of sexual abhorrence through the plays. "To a nunnery go!" can be heard remotely through Jaques, and actually through the strange interest he has chosen for plot in *All's Well.* In what Hamlet terms the incest of his mother we can hear an echo of the intimacy of relation that his own mistress has sought and permitted. His own sexual tenderness is the centre of power in Othello's mood. In Lear's madness this same thought haunts his mind. And in *Antony and Cleopatra* we find Shakespeare describing his dark mistress, in Cleopatra, precisely as he had described her in the *Love's Labour's Lost* of 1598, and the last sequence in the Sonnets; even as in Antony he describes his own helpless bondage at the wiles of his mistress, a matter to which he gives a more explicit reference in Sonnets 137-138.[9]

The storm that this woke in Shakespeare's mind was too terrible long to continue. It wore itself to an end; and as it dies low we are enabled to hear the echo of it in that strange characteristic we have already noticed dominating the later plays: the insistence of woman's faithfulness and truth in Imogen and Hermoine, and the exquisite delight in girlish purity in Perdita and Miranda. It is Shakespeare's method of recalling health to his blood and beauty to his mind. It is his recovery of his soul.

So Shakespeare stands revealed to us, not only as an ambitious and earnest Artist who mastered his craft with careful thought and unflinching zeal, for all the prodigal bounty of his way of work, but also as an eager susceptible man to whom friendship might be a passion and love a torment, and who, when these failed him, and failed him with one another, was torn by a tempest of fury. The natural melancholy, to which his brooding temperament was so often subject, only abetted this the more; and thus it took more than the form of distress, for it was endued with bitterness. Yet it permitted him to swell to a height of passion and power that enabled him to take in his imaginative grasp such mighty tragedies as those that stretch from *Hamlet* to *Antony and Cleopatra*. We have seen him come up to London as a young man overburdened with poverty, the weight of family responsibilities, and, it may be, bitter prosecution. He wrought hard, and he worked diligently, and as he wrought and worked it was evident to see that this was no common Artist. Yet his very careless abandon, his large wastefulness, and his aversion to detailed workmanship, filled his work full of faults. What he needed was something that should give his mind concentration. Something was required in order that his personality should gather its breadth together to flame to a towering height. This his private tragedy gave him; and so, in play on play, he demonstrated not power only but achievement also, not only space and possibility, but might and magnificence. And yet, when he flamed to his height, he took all his breadth with him: which enables him therefore to remain the perpetual and profitable study of the artists of all time.

NOTES

CHAPTER I

INTRODUCTION

1. G. B. Shaw, "Authorised Biography, 1911," p. 268

CHAPTER II

HIS LIFE

1. Maldon MS. See "Life," by Sir Sidney Lee. 6th edition, p. viii.
2. This seems a fitting place to speak of the indebtedness every student of the stage history of that time must owe to the labours of Frederick Gard Fleay. His "History of the English Stage, 1559-1642," in particular, is more valuable than repeated citation can ever exemplify; and this, despite ofttimes its strange disorder, despite at times its unverifiable untrustworthiness, and its capricious whimsey. Fleay had, what Shakespeare has not often been blest with in his biographers, and what is of the highest moment in all biography, an extraordinary sense of divination, a sense that he supported with indefatigable labour, but not always with judgment.
3. Sir Sidney Lee, with others, declares that Shakespeare "naturally drifted to London" in the year 1586 (*op. cit., circa*, p. 32), looking for work; that he *probably* lived with a native of Stratford for a time; and also *probably* joined the players at "The Theater or The Curtain." There is not a vestige of proof for all this; nor a hint of

reasonable inference. The account as given in the text, therefore, is an entire reconstruction of this whole period, among others, and is taken directly from the accessible facts. Why a web of fancy should ever have been spun when a clear and logical sequence links up the reputable facts, must remain a mystery.

4. This is obvious from the "Short Treatise of the English Stage" that Richard Flecknoe adds to his "Love's Kingdom" (1664). It is interesting in itself; but as a side-support to the reconstruction given in the text it is peculiarly luminous.

5. See Halliwell-Phillipps' "Illustrations," p. 7. To speak in praise of Halliwell-Phillipps at this time of day would seem as much an impertinence as to condemn him. Yet when one comes to consider in him the utter lack of that divination without which biography is void, his discovery of the rarest facts without any appreciable idea of their relation, not to speak of his sentimental judgment, it is not so easy always to give fit weight to his patience of discovery.

6. See the *Athenæum*, March 26, 1904.

7. See "Memoirs of Edward Alleyn," by T. Payne Collier, Shaks. Socy. Pubs.

8. See "History of the Stage," by F. G. Fleay, pp. 83-4.

9. See *Ibid.*, p. 86. Also "Early London Theatres," by T. F. Ordish, pp. 147 and 164.

10. See Halliwell-Phillipps' "Outlines," 6th edition, 1-332.

11. "History of Stage," Fleay, p. 134; and "Early London Theatres," Ordish, 68.

12. H. C. Beeching in "Stratford-on-Avon Shakespeare," vol. x., Appendices.

13. See "Life," Sir Sidney Lee, *circa*, pp. 200 and 210.

14. These were discovered by the inexhaustible patience of Professor C. W. Wallace, and published in *Harper's Magazine*, March 1910.

15. Here again one has to rely on Professor Wallace. See *Century Magazine*, August 1910. All this matter is

NOTES

shortly to be published by him in a book "entitled Shakespeare, the Globe and Blackfriars."
16. Professor Wallace again. See the *Times*, October 2, 1910, and also the *Century Magazine*, August and September 1910.
17. See "Shakespeare as a Groom of the Chamber," by Ernest Law.

CHAPTER III

HIS STAGE

1. It is strange that one should have to dismiss the only sketch of an Elizabethan stage that purports to derive itself from a contemporary account. I am referring, of course, to what is generally known as the De Witt sketch, but what should more accurately be called the Van Buchell sketch, since it was drawn by Arend van Buchell from the account given him from memory by his friend Johannes de Witt, the latter having been on a visit to England. Apart from the fact that we have no guarantee that Van Buchell faithfully rendered De Witt's idea, the latter himself has laid himself open to serious question. He declared that the subject of the sketch in question, the Swan playhouse, was "built of flint . . . and as to shape seems to be an imitation of Roman work," whereas it is as sure as any can be sure that no Elizabethan playhouse (with the possible exception of the private Blackfriars, which was in fact, in its exterior semblance, akin to a large dwelling-house) was built of stonework, however much the wood was painted to resemble stonework. But when, in addition to this general insecurity, we find the sketch itself self-contradictory, and, moreover, that it fails to take account of, or render intelligible, many of the plays that have come down to us, while we cannot but value many of the hints it gives

us, we must dismiss its total or general claim to accuracy. This is not the occasion to place the arguments against it. Two, however, may be mentioned. Firstly, for reasons mentioned in the text, it is obvious that the outer doors should in some way face each other. In the sketch they are cut in a level wall facing the audience; so that, when soldiers were required to pass from one to the other, to complete this manœuvre they would have fetch an ungainly circle on the stage. Secondly, the audience is represented as being in the gallery. Would they, then, be required to make room for Romeo and Juliet when the lovers came out with the dawn; or would they be specially cleared for the occasion?

Apart from a somewhat careful examination of this question from an independent standpoint, I must confess—and very gratefully confess—my indebtedness to Dr Victor E. Albright's book, "The Shakesperian Stage" (Columbia University Press, 1909), and to Mr Archer's article on "The Elizabethan Stage," in the *Quarterly* for April 1908. The first of these, except for some points of difficulty, gathers together a fund of detail, the importance of which it would be very difficult to exaggerate, whereas the latter has all the perspecuity one is accustomed to associate with that author's way of thought. Other books and articles that render important aid, even though that aid cannot always be accepted, are: "Some principles of Elizabethan Staging," by G. F. Reynolds (Chicago, 1905); "Trees on the Stage of Shakespeare," by the same author, in *Modern Philology* (October 1907), and the article in *Modern Philology* for June 1905, on which Dr Reynold's book was based; "Elizabethan Stage Scenery," by Mr C. C. Stopes, in the *Fortnightly Review* for June 1907. Also Fleay's various works, to which reference has already been made.

2. I need scarcely say that I refer to that brilliant and astute journalist, A. B. Walkley, who, in his "Drama and Life,"

seems to be grieved to think that dramatists should be so retrogressive as to think of reverting four hundred years back to the conditions of Shakespeare, and who, when he has sufficiently recovered from his grief and horror, arrays himself in all his urbane and witty charm for the purpose of taking dramatists back well over two thousand years to Aristotle.

3. William Archer, *vide supra*.

CHAPTER IV

HIS CRAFT

1. See Ben Jonson's "Timber and Discoveries," xxi., Temple Edition.
2.   Do.   do.   cxvi.
2.   Do.   do.   lxv., Note 9.
4. This is the fundamental point of view that Dr Bradley overlooks in his treatment of the subject in his "Shakespearian Tragedy." Hence he is driven to the anomaly of regarding Goneril, Regan, and Edmund as, constructionally, the leading characters in *King Lear*. To those familiar with Dr Bradley's work I need scarcely express my indebtedness to his pellucid thinking on this whole matter, though, in fairness to myself, I am obliged to insist on my independent point of view. Professor Baker's objection to Dr Bradley, in his "Development of Shakespeare as a Dramatist," is surely beside the point. A good story well told means an arrangement of weights; and an arrangement of weights implies places where the weights are not.

It will be noticed that I have used the words Introduction, Action, Crisis, Counter-action, and Climax, employing them in their usual meanings as typical of the five movements of Shakespeare's Drama. Professor

Lewis Campbell would call them Opening, Climax, Acme, Sequel, and Close. (See his "Tragic Drama in Æschylus, Sophocles, and Shakespeare.") Were one to revert to the stricter meaning of the words, and were the confusion that this would engender desirable, I imagine it would be necessary to phrase the five movements thus: Introduction, Climax, Crisis, Anti-climax, and Catastrophe—though this would perhaps tempt some or other wit to rejoin that an Anti-climax always leads to a Catastrophe.

5. Perhaps it is necessary to point out that in none of the editions of *Hamlet* that have come to us from Shakespeare, neither in the several Quartos nor in the Folio, is any demarcation set between the Third and Fourth Acts of *Hamlet*. There is no doubt that this is owing to the fact that the play was subject to more than one revision at Shakespeare's hands. Yet, whatever be the cause, the result is that most modern editions have various opinions as to where the boundary line should be placed. If Shakespeare's general method of construction offers any solution, however, there seems very little reason to doubt that Hamlet's exit with the words, " My thoughts be bloody, or be nothing worth," is also the exit of the Third Act, and that therefore the new act opens with the entrance on to the scene of the new protagonist, Laertes.

6. Professor Saintsbury. See "Cambridge History of English Literature," vol. v. Article on Shakespeare.

CHAPTER V

HIS ART

1. See Professor W. H. Hudson's note to the scene in the "Windsor Edition" of Shakespeare, *Macbeth*, page 90.
2. See Nietzsche's "Birth of Tragedy," Professor Ridgeway's

"Origin of Tragedy," and the review of the latter in the *Times*, with the correspondence that followed.
3. I refer to Mr Robert Bridges' article in the Appendices to vol. x. of the "Stratford-on-Avon Shakespeare."

CHAPTER VI

HIS THOUGHT

1. I need scarcely say that, all through, I am concerned with Shakespeare's thought rather as expressed in, and fashioned by, his workmanship, than as embedded in it. The highest value of artistic achievement is that it is a spiritual discipline to its workman: it teaches the Artist infinitely more than it may ever teach readers or spectators.
2. How splendid they are in their self-command! "I bleed, sir; but not killed."
3. I have omitted *Timon of Athens* in this, for the obvious reason that Shakespeare's portion in it is so small that it seems impossible to credit him with part or lot in its architecture. He seems only to be concerned with blowing to fury Timon's bitter disillusionment with life, leaving the play otherwise as it came from other hands. Perhaps it was done by another hand for his company; and when he saw it, it touched a kindred mood in him, with this result.

CHAPTER VII

HIS PERSONALITY

1. The quotation is from Sir Sidney Lee's Address to the English Association in 1909, entitled "The Impersonal Aspect of Shakespeare's Art." The best substantiation of the claim that Shakespeare's character cannot be known is, of course, the same author's "Life."

2. It is to be feared that Professor Dowden's "Shakespeare: His Mind and Art," was chiefly responsible for this. But it is a principle that dominates the writings of most English critics, the attribution being an English characteristic.
3. See Sir Sidney Lee's prodigal surmises in his "Life" (p. 203 and following), and compare it with Professor Wallace's more careful calculation from authentic documents in his articles in the *Times* (October 2 and 4, 1910) and the *Century Magazine* (August and September 1910).
4. Perhaps the least disingenuous instance is the delightful close to Chapter xvi. of Sir Sidney Lee's "Life," from which my quotations are made.
5. In this I should perhaps be careful to point out, what ought to be obvious, that the structure of the play was not altered. The deletion of a passage here and there for the purposes of shortening, is one thing; to make nonsense of the gradual crescendo of the plot—the construction, that is—as done on the modern stage, is quite another. And this holds good despite the fact that minor alterations of the crescendo seem to have taken place in the Third Act of *Hamlet* under Shakespeare's own hand. But this was not alteration: this was polishing.
6. See Professor Wallace in *Harper's Magazine*, March 1910.
7. The editions of the Sonnets that a reader will have chiefly in mind are, perhaps, those entrusted severally to the following care: Thomas Tyler, Samuel Butler, H. C. Beeching, George Wyndham, and Edward Dowden. Of these Tyler's is the most expansive and comprehensive, in analysis and hypothesis; one wonders if Butler sometimes had not his tongue in his cheek; Mr Wyndham's is closest in literary analysis; and Professor Dowden's is learned and analytical. But for balance, judgment, and careful examination, one turns most to Mr Beeching. The older editions, such as Massey's, are generally comprised in these. Yet an unedited edition most frequently proves the truest guide.

8. It is difficult to see how the matter is materially aided by saying that the young man was William Herbert, Earl of Pembroke (the W. H. of the Dedication) and the woman Mistress Mary Fitton. I myself am of opinion that Pembroke was the young man. I also think that the first perfunctory nineteen sonnets had something to do with the effort by Pembroke's parents to induce their son to wed the Earl of Oxford's daughter, and that these were the base of Meres' reference in 1598. But I do not think the Mary Fitton theory seems likely of truth; it certainly has no proof. Both the Pembroke and the Fitton ideas are chiefly and primarily indebted to Tyler, who worked up the suggestion thrown out by the Rev. W. A. Harrison.

This would give 1596-7 as an approximate date for the beginning of the sonnets, and would bring the meeting of the young man and the dark mistress to the year 1597-8. (Compare the opening of Sonnet 33 with the first part of *Henry IV.*, Act I. scene ii. line 221 and onward.) This would establish Frank Harris' suggestion that the 1597-98 redaction of *Love's Labour's Lost* had for its primary object the setting-out of the cruelties of the dark mistress, who was satirised and described in detail in Biron's "Rosaline." See "The Man Shakespeare." And this is the date on which the argument in the text is based.

9. See, again, "The Man Shakespeare," by Frank Harris, who treats this matter fully, in fact so fully as almost to turn the mind against his own thesis. The interest is, doubtless, important; but it is by no means all of Shakespeare. He wrongs Shakespeare much who thinks so. Nor surely does it absorb the number of plays that Mr Harris would seem to suggest.

INDEX OF NAMES

Adriana, 225
Æmilia, 225
Ægeon, 225
Æschylus, 182, 210, 212
Aguecheek, Sir Andrew, 197
Albany, 139
Albright, Dr Victor E., 332
Alchemist, 81, 212
Alexandria, 172
Allen, Giles, 41, 58, 68, 69, 70
Alleyn, Edward, 36, 37, 39, 40, 41, 43, 44, 45, 49, 50, 51, 55, 65, 70, 72, 76, 129, 236, 292
All's Well that Ends Well, 74, 76, 168, 226, 261, 262, 263, 326
Angus, 124
Anne Shakespeare (*née* Hathaway), 38
Antonio, 111, 112, 117, 120, 295, 323
Antony, 3, 172, 173, 175, 270, 278, 326
Antony and Cleopatra, 173, 203, 270, 277, 284, 326, 327
Apollo, 210
Archer, William, 332, 333
Arden (Forest), 76
Arden, Mary, 30
Ariel, 129, 319
Armado, 165
Arragon, Prince of, 117
Asbies, 30, 35
As You Like It, 74, 76, 127, 168, 260, 261, 262, 303
Athens, 172, 173
Augustus, 142
Autolycus, 197

Badger, George, 62
Baker, Prof., 333
Balthazar, 251
Bankside, 72
Banquo, 124, 256, 275
Bardolph, 61, 197

Barnardine, 169
Bassanio, 112, 113, 115, 117, 118, 120, 323
Barton-on-the-Heath, 31
Beatrice, 197, 198, 212, 226
Beeching, H. C., 330, 336
Beeston, William, 35
Belch, Sir Toby, 197, 211
Belloni, Sandra, 191
Bellott, Stephen, 66, 67
Benedick, 197, 212
Benvolio, 107, 108, 110
Bermuda Islands, 129
Bertram, 263
Bianca, 170
Biron, 224, 337
Birth of Tragedy, 334
Bishopsgate, 39, 45
Bishopsgate Ward, 41
Blackfriars Theatre, 51, 70, 75, 77, 83, 293, 301, 302, 331
Bottom, 97, 197, 211, 252
Bradley, Dr, 333
Brand, 202
Braynes, John, 42, 56
Braynes, Margaret, 42
Brend, Sir Nicholas, 72
Brendel, Ulric, 175
Bridge, Robert, 335
Bristol, 49
Brown, John, 32
Brutus, 100, 101, 102, 103, 104, 105, 265, 295, 296
Buchell, Arend van, 331
Burbage, Cuthbert, 56
Burbage, James, 41, 42, 43, 51, 56, 69, 71, 77
Burbage, Richard, 42, 43, 49, 50, 56, 58, 69, 70, 80
Burbage, T., 52
Burby, Cuthbert, 74
Burgundy, 139
Burton Heath, 31
Butler, Samuel, 336

CÆSAR, 105, 175, 265, 270
Calphurnia, 105
Cambridge History of English Literature, 334
Camillo, 149
Campbell, Prof. Lewis, 334
Canterbury Tales, The, 283
Capitol, 105
Capulet, 107, 241, 250, 255, 266
Carey, Henry, 1st Lord Hunsdon, 51, 52
Cassio, 170, 219, 223, 234
Cassius, 102, 103, 296, 297
Catharine, 246
Century Magazine, 330, 331, 336
Chapman, 81
Chaucer, 8, 283
Chettle, Henry, 288, 289, 311
Claudio, 169, 262
Claudius, 269
Cleopatra, 175, 326
Clink, 45, 66, 68
Coleridge, 6, 7, 16, 17, 19, 137, 167, 226
College of Heralds, 62, 63
Collier, T. Payne, 330
Comedy of Errors, 58, 155, 225, 247
Condell, Henry, 68, 310
Constance, 240
Constantinople, 246
Cordelia, 140, 205, 229, 271, 272
Coriolanus, 228, 231, 278, 284, 295
Coriolanus, 277, 312
Cornwall, 139, 140
Costard, 165
Count of Paris, 317
Cripplegate, 66, 68
Cross Keys Tavern, 40, 41, 51, 52, 68, 289, 311
Curtain Theatre, 69, 73, 256, 292, 329
Cymbeline, 145, 147, 171, 228, 231
Cymbeline, 82, 278, 279

DANIEL, 305, 306
D'Avenant, Sir William, 54, 55
David Copperfield, 205
Dead Hand, 10
Dekker, Thomas, 68
Demetrius, 252
Denmark, 38, 163, 233
Derby, Earl of, 36, 37

Desdemona, 99, 170, 203, 219, 220, 223, 229, 234, 267, 269, 275, 292
De Shakespeare Nostrati, 142, 150
Development of Shakespeare as a Dramatist, 333
De Witt, Johannes, 331
Dionysus, 210
Discoveries, 142
Dogberry, 197, 226, 258
Doll's House, The, 174, 177, 202
Dowden, Prof. Edward, 336
Drama and Life, 332
Drayton, Michael, 85, 305, 306
Drummond, William, 12, 141, 147, 184, 212
Dumain, 224
Dumas, 303
Duncan, 187, 188, 192, 273, 275

Early London Theatres, 330
Eastcheap, 199
Edgar, 139, 167
Edinburgh, 79
Edmund, 139, 229, 333
Elizabeth, 238
Elizabeth, Princess, 83
Elizabeth, Queen, 38, 41, 77, 79, 81
Elizabethan Stage, 332
Elizabethan Stage Scenery, 332
Elsinore, 77, 129
England, 17, 161
Enobarbus, 175
Epicæne, 81
Epipsychidion, 283
Errors, 73
Essex Conspiracy, 78
Euripides, 210, 212
Evans, Henry, 77, 80
Evans, Sir Hugh, 298
Every Man in His Humour, 69, 77, 145, 292, 293
Every Man Out of His Humour, 60, 77, 292

FALSTAFF, SIR JOHN, 60, 197, 198, 199, 200, 211, 242, 244, 245, 256, 295, 298, 320, 321, 324, 325
Field, Nathaniel, 68
Finsbury, 74, 75
Fitton, Mistress Mary, 337
Fleay, Frederick Gard, 329, 330, 332

INDEX OF NAMES 341

Flecknoe, Richard, 330
Florizel, 149, 176
Fludd, Humphrey, 66
Fluellen, 61
Fortnightly Review, 332
Fortinbras, 99
Fortune Theatre, 79
France, 139, 238
Frederick, Duke, 262
Fuller, 141

GABLER, HEDDA, 177, 178
Gaunt, John of, 237
Gentlemen of Verona, 73
Ghosts, 202
Globe Theatre, The, 8, 55, 57, 72, 73, 75, 76, 80, 84, 100, 101, 126, 127, 129, 141, 257, 286, 292, 293, 301, 309, 312, 331
Gloster, 139, 167
Gobbo, Launcelot, 113, 114, 115, 118, 197
Goneril, 140, 205, 229, 271, 272, 333
Gracechurch Street, 40, 41
Gratiano, 113, 114, 115, 120, 121
Greece, 17, 18
Greene, 36, 37, 43, 46, 47, 50, 287, 288, 311
Greenhill Street, 31
Groatsworth of Wit Bought with a Million of Repentance, 46
Grub Street, 68
Guildenstern, 161, 232, 317

HALLIWELL-PHILLIPS 330
Hall, John, 83
Hamlet, 3, 4, 9, 14, 77, 129, 130, 160, 161, 162, 163, 179, 180, 185, 186, 189, 191, 195, 196, 205, 212, 213, 215, 216, 219, 228, 229, 232, 233, 234, 265, 269, 275, 277, 278, 284, 294, 295, 303, 304, 316, 317, 318, 319, 320, 321, 325, 326, 334
Hamlet, 60, 74, 76, 81, 99, 125, 127, 128, 144, 157, 160, 163, 164, 179, 227, 232, 249, 256, 264, 265, 267, 277, 279, 303, 305, 309, 310, 327, 334, 336
Hamnet, 35, 62
Harper's Magazine, 330, 336

Harris, Frank, 337
Harrison, W. A., 337
Hastings, 238
Haterius, 142
Hathwey, Anne, 33
Hathwey, Richard, 32
Hazlitt, 19, 20
Helena, 226, 252, 259, 263
Heminges, John, 42, 45, 68, 70, 80, 129, 310
Henley Street, 31, 62, 76
Henry of Bolingbroke, 242
Henry IV., 295
Henry IV., 60, 73, 160, 245, 295, 298, 337
Henry V., 133, 191, 246, 295
Henry V, 61, 236, 245, 246
Henry VI., 50, 240
Henry VI., 36, 37, 43, 45, 47, 48, 58, 236, 237, 241, 246, 288
Henry VII., 62
Henslowe, Philip, 36, 43, 44, 45, 55, 57, 97, 292
Herbert, William, Earl of Pembroke, 337
Hermia, 252
Hermione, 176, 279, 284, 326
Hero, 227
History of the Stage, 330
Holinshed, 147, 274
Holywell, 41
Horatio, 78, 163, 215, 270, 316, 317
Hotspur (probably Henry IV.), 83
Hudson, W. H., Prof., 334

IAGO, 169, 178, 220, 221, 223, 229, 269, 270
Ibsen, Henrik, 11, 153, 158, 174, 177, 178, 189, 202
Imogen, 279, 284, 326
Impersonal Aspect of Shakespeare's Art, The, 335

JAMES I., 79, 80
Jaquenetta, 165
Jaques, 76, 261, 321, 325, 326
Jessica, 113, 114, 115, 116
John, Duke, 258
John Gabriel Borkman, 202
John, King, 240

342 SHAKESPEARE

Johnson, Samuel, 13, 15, 16, 17, 68
Jonson, Ben, 12, 60, 68, 77, 81, 85, 122, 130, 141, 142, 143, 144, 145, 146, 148, 149, 150, 151, 184, 192, 212, 286, 292, 293, 294, 311, 333
Jordan, 40
Judith, 35, 84
Juliet, 6, 107, 212, 226, 241, 255, 332
Julius Cæsar, 76, 81, 83, 100, 143, 168, 231, 264, 268

KATHARINE, 224
Kempe, Will, 45, 58, 70, 80, 126, 129, 130
Kent, 140, 270
King John, 73, 166, 225, 239, 241, 242, 308
King Lear, 11, 13, 60, 81, 107, 123, 130, 132, 133, 139, 144, 145, 157, 235, 249, 255, 256, 271, 277, 303, 309, 312, 313, 316, 333
Kyd, 37, 43, 47, 50, 60

LAMB, CHARLES, 310
Lady from the Sea, The, 158, 159
Laertes, 163, 317
Lafeu, 197
Lambert Edmund, 31
Launce, 197
Laurence, Friar, 251, 256
Law, Ernest, 331
League of Youth, The, 202
Lear, King, 3, 14, 17, 140, 203, 212, 229, 233, 270, 271, 272, 277, 278, 284, 292, 294, 295, 326
Lee, Sir Sidney, 329, 330, 335, 336
Leicester, Earl of, 38, 39
Lennox, 195
Leonardo, 113
Leontes, 278, 279
Levison, William, 71
Ligarius. 104
Little Eyolf, 175, 202
Lodge, 43, 47
Lodovico, 170, 270
London, 38, 129
Longaville, 224
Lorenzo, 114, 115, 116, 118
Love's Kingdom, 330

Love's Labour's Lost, 44, 50, 58, 73, 133, 155, 165, 224, 247, 248, 286, 314, 325, 326, 337
Love's Labour's Won, 73
Luciana, 225
Lucius, 101, 102, 104, 106
Lucy, Sir Thomas, 35, 38, 297, 311
Lysander, 252

MACBETH, 124, 125, 147, 187, 188, 192, 193, 194, 212, 230, 240, 256, 273, 274, 275, 276, 277, 278
Macbeth, 46, 60, 81, 124, 132, 144, 157, 164, 232, 273, 277, 334
Macbeth, Lady, 188, 192, 274, 275
Macduff, 167, 195, 275
Maiden Lane, 72
Maldon M.S., 329
Malone, 39
Malvolio, 76, 197, 226, 261
Manæchmi, 155
Man Shakespeare, The, 337
Margaret, Queen, 237, 238, 240, 241
Maria, 224
Marlowe, 37, 43, 46, 47, 49, 50, 132, 308
Marston, John, 77
Massey, 336
Master Builder, 202
Master Builder, The, 174, 202
Measure for Measure, 76, 81, 169, 227, 264, 265
Memoirs of Edward Alleyn, 330
Merchant of Venice, 73, 74, 98, 107, 111, 133, 167, 168, 256, 257, 323
Mercutio, 107, 108, 110, 179, 199, 250, 316
Meres, Francis, 50, 73, 337
Mermaid Tavern, 12, 68, 144, 149
Merry Wives of Windsor, 15, 198, 211, 298
Metellus, 143
Middleton, 276
Midsummer Night's Dream, 15, 73, 97, 147, 155, 166, 225, 248, 249, 252, 255, 257, 266, 303
Milton, 183, 209
Miranda, 82, 171, 279, 285, 314, 326
Modern Philology, 332

INDEX OF NAMES 343

Molière, 199
Montague, 250, 251, 255, 266
Morocco, 113, 116
Mountjoy-Bellott lawsuit, 311
Mountjoy, Christopher, 66, 149
Much Ado About Nothing, 15, 76, 83, 168, 227, 257, 258, 260, 261, 262, 263
Mugwell Street, 66

Nash, 46, 236
Nerissa, 112, 117, 119, 120
Newington Butts, 47, 52
New Place, 54, 63, 64, 66, 67, 83, 302
Nietzsche, 334
Nora, 177, 178
Norwich, 129
Nym, 197

Octavia, 175
Œdipus, 158
Oliver, 262
Olivia, 226
Ophelia, 161, 167, 196, 292, 294, 317
Origin of Tragedy, 335
Orlando, 226, 262, 295
Orsino, 226
Osric, 234
Oswald, 139
Othello, 7, 9, 99, 133, 168, 170, 179, 193, 219, 220, 221, 222, 223, 229, 233, 267, 269, 277, 278, 284, 295, 296, 326
Othello, 81, 83, 130, 132 144, 147, 154, 168, 169, 178, 222, 303, 309, 316
Oxford, 125
Oxford, Earl of, 337

Palladis Tamia, 73
Paradise Lost, 183
Paris (*Romeo and Juliet*), 251
Parolles, 179, 200
Peele, 46, 47
Peer Gynt, 202
Perdita, 149, 176, 279, 284, 326
Perkes, Clement, of the Hill, 61
Phillips, Augustine, 70, 80, 129
"Pierce Pennilesse," 46
Pisanio, 278, 279

Pistol, 197, 200
Plautus, 155
Plutarch, 147, 151
Pointz, 197
Polixenes, 149
Polonius, 160, 161, 162, 217, 232, 317, 319, 320
Pope, Thomas, 43, 70
Portia, 104, 106, 112, 113, 114, 116, 117, 119, 120, 133
Posthumus, 295
Prospero, 82, 171, 295, 314, 319, 320, 321
Publius, 105
Puck, 252

Quiney, Richard, 64
Quiney, Thomas, 84

Ragozine, 169
Rape of Lucrece, The, 48, 54, 58, 73
Rat-Wife, 175
Red Bull Theatre, 79
Regan, 140, 205, 229, 271, 272
Return from Parnassus, 293
Reynolds, G. F., 332
Richard II., 237
Richard II., 75, 78, 166, 201, 225, 239, 240, 241, 308
Richard III., 238, 240
Richard III., 58, 73, 225, 237, 238, 241, 246, 308
Richardson, John, 32, 33
Rideway, Prof., 334
Robinson, Crabb, 19
Rogers, Henry, 61
Rogers, Philip, 75
Rome, 100, 296
Romeo, 6, 19, 107, 108, 110, 212, 226, 250, 251, 256, 295, 316, 317, 320, 324, 332
Romeo and Juliet, 73, 107, 132, 133, 147, 155, 166, 167, 225, 230, 231, 241, 248, 249, 250, 253, 255, 256, 257, 259, 263, 266, 308
Rosalind, 226
Rosaline, 224, 337
Rose Theatre, 36, 43, 47, 50, 55, 68, 72, 129, 236, 256, 311
Rosencrantz, 161, 232, 317
Rosmersholm, 175

Ross, 124
Rowe, Nicholas, 39, 40, 81, 82, 297

SAINTSBURY, Prof., 334
Salanio, 111, 114, 117
Salarino, 111, 114
Salerio, 118
Sandells, Fulk, 32, 33
Savage, Thomas, 71
Saxony, 38
Scotland, 79
Scott, Walter, 301, 303
Sebastian, 226, 323
Seven Daily Sins, 46
Shakespeare as a Groom of the Chamber, 331
Shakespeare: His Mind and Art, 336
Shakespeare, John, 30, 31, 35, 63
Shakesperian Stage, The, 332
Shallow, Justice, 298
Shallow, Master, 298
Shelley, 283
Short Treatise of the English Stage, 330
Shottery, 33, 64
Shylock, 112, 113, 115, 117, 118, 135, 259
Silver Street, 66, 68
Sir John Falstaff (probably " *Merry Wives of Windsor*"), 83
Sly, Cristopher, 31
Some Principles of Elizabethan Staging, 332
Somerset House, 80
Sophocles, 158, 182, 210, 212, 303
Southampton, Earl of, 45, 48, 49, 50, 54, 78, 80
Southwark, 36, 40, 43, 72, 129, 236
Spanish Ambassador Extraordinary, 80
Spanish Tragedy, 132
St Helens, 41, 45, 68
St Marye Overyes, 72
St Paul's Cross, 57
Stanley, Ferdinando; Lord Strange, 39
Staple of News, 68
Stopes, C. C., 332
Strange, Lord, 41, 45, 51

Stratford, 30, 32, 34, 36, 38, 61, 62, 63, 64, 65, 72, 75, 81, 297, 298, 301, 302, 311, 329
Street, Peter, 71
Sturley, Abraham, 64
Sufflaminandus erat, 142
Surrey, 45
Sussex, 45
Swan Playhouse, 331
Swinburne, 20

TALBOT, 46
Tambourlaine, 132
Taming of the Shrew, 31, 60, 61
Tarleton, 43
Tempest, The, 82, 83, 128, 147, 205, 228, 231, 286, 303
Temple Grafton, 32
Tewkesbury, Battle of, 238
Theater, The, 8, 41, 42, 49, 52, 53, 55, 56, 58, 61, 62, 65, 68, 69, 70, 72, 73, 74, 256, 286, 308, 311, 329
Thersites, 130
Timber, or Discoveries, 12, 142, 333
Timon, 295, 303
Timon of Athens, 81, 132, 191, 335
Times, The, 336
Titus Andronicus, 50, 51, 58, 73
Touchstone, 130, 197
Torvald, 177, 178
Tragic Drama in Æschylus, Sophocles, and Shakespeare, 334
Trees on the Stage of Shakespeare, 332
Troilus, 191
Troilus and Cressida, 76, 81, 130
Twelfth Night, 34, 76, 130, 168, 261, 323
Two Gentlemen of Verona, 50, 58, 155, 166, 167, 248, 308
Tybalt, 107, 250
Tyler, Thomas, 336

VENICE, 170
Venus and Adonis, 23, 48, 58
Verges, 197, 258
Verona, 255
Viola, 226
Visor, William, of Wincot, 61
Volpone, 81

INDEX OF NAMES

WALKLEY, A. B., 332
Wallace, C. W., 330, 336
"War of the Theatres," 76, 292
Warwickshire, 61, 297
West, Rebecca, 153
Whately, Anne, 32, 33
When We Dead Awaken, 202
Whittington, Thomas, 62
Wilmcote, 30
Windsor, 199

Winter's Tale, A, 15, 82, 83, 145, 176, 228, 231, 278, 279
Wittenburg, 78
Woodward, Joan, 43
Worcester, 33
Worcester, Bishop of, 32, 33
Worcester, Consistory Court of, 33
Worcester, Earl of, 39
Wyndham, George, 336

PRINTED BY
TURNBULL AND SPEARS,
EDINBURGH

www.ingramcontent.com/pod-product-compliance
Lightning Source LLC
Chambersburg PA
CBHW021912180426
43198CB00034B/165